Hart Crane and the Homosexual Text

Hart Crane and the Homosexual Text

New Thresholds, New Anatomies

▼

Thomas E. Yingling

The University of Chicago Press

Chicago and London

The University of Chicago Press, Chicago 60637
The University of Chicago Press, Ltd., London

Printed in the United States of America
99 98 97 96 95 94 93 92 91 90 5 4 3 2 1

Library of Congress Cataloging in Publication Data

Yingling, Thomas E.
Hart Crane and the homosexual text : new thresholds, new anatomies / Thomas E. Yingling.
p. cm.
Originally presented as the author's thesis.
Includes bibliographical references.
1. Crane, Hart, 1899–1932—Criticism and interpretation.
2. Homosexuality, Male, in literature. 3. Gay men in literature.
I. Title.
PS3505.R272Z93 1990 89-48053
811'.52—dc20 CIP
ISBN 0-226-95634-2 (alk. paper)
ISBN 0-226-95635-0 (pbk.; alk. paper)

∞ The paper used in this publication meets
the minimum requirements of the
American National Standard for Information Sciences—
Permanence of Paper for Printed Library Materials,
ANSI Z39.48-1984.

Thomas E. Yingling is assistant professor of English at Syracuse University.

what of Hart Crane
—FRANK O'HARA

Contents

Acknowledgments

▼

"Go little book," ETC.

When I began this project a few years ago, gay studies had limited visibility and virtually no cachet in the academy. There were, of course, canonical writers by the score whom one could point to as "of the persuasion," but the onus of persuasion was always with the critic: was one sure? what difference did it make? who cared? There were also, of course, dozens of prominent gay critics and scholars—all of them silent or oblique in their address to the question of sexuality and its relation to literature. The few books and articles that had appeared hadn't the cumulative complexity and authority that gay male writing and culture seemed to me to offer and demand. Homosexuality, regardless of its historical importance to the genesis of any given text, remained marginal to literary and cultural analysis, a question seldom seriously entertained as of the first importance for critical thought.

Since that time, much has changed: the protocols of literary analysis now virtually require attention to cultural differences such as homosexuality. A number of important studies have appeared that promise—finally—to refocus homosexuality as central rather than marginal to the ways in which we understand our culture. This text, which began in relative isolation as an exercise in critical experimentation (what might a critical and theoretical inquiry into the textuality of homosexual writing and subjectivity have to take into account? what might it offer of value?) thus finds itself part of a more collective endeavor. I hope it may find some cohesive affection among that order—and elsewhere.

It is impossible, of course, to fully know, much less repay, the burden of one's deeper debts, but on the list of those I owe appear the names of the following friends and colleagues: Michael Awkward, Jim Baker, Pat Day, Chris Flint, Steve Goldsmith, Elizabeth Kerwin, Celeste Langan, Diane Lichtenstein, Art McMahon, Pidge Molyneaux, Keith Mooney, Dan Nemer, and Athena Vrettos. Each contributed to the possibility of this project, making both me and it more than we otherwise would have been. I found among them a generosity and intelligence that remain to this day fixed points of reference. Wendy Steiner and Stuart Curran (who offered endless advice, comment, and encouragement during early stages in this process) must stand in here for a longer list of faculty at the University of Pennsylvania who brought me to some understanding of my own stake in the critical act. May they accept this book as, in some measure, a return in kind.

Michael Moon and Donald Pease read and generously commented on earlier drafts of the manuscript, as did Robyn Wiegman, who offered her friendship, criticism, and help at crucial points in its revision. The faculty of the English Department at Syracuse University—in their dialogue about theory, politics, and history—have contributed much to the shape of certain arguments here, and I would like to thank Jean Howard, John Crowley, and Steven Cohan in particular for their interest in my work. I wish to acknowledge, as well, the financial support of the Frederick L. Emerson Foundation of Auburn, N.Y., which funded my work on a three-year post-doctoral fellowship in the English Department at Syracuse University.

Finally, I wish to express my deepest gratitude to my family, who, although they have not always understood the paths my life has taken, have always cared to understand.

Except where otherwise noted, passages from Crane's poetry and prose are taken from *The Complete Poems and Selected Letters and Prose of Hart Crane*, ed. Brom Weber (New York: Liveright, 1966), and passages from Crane's letters from *The Letter of Hart Crane, 1916–1932*, ed. Brom Weber (Berkeley: University of California Press, 1965).

1
Critical Indifference; or, Tradition and the Homosexual Talent in American Poetry

▼

If human beings were not divided into two biological sexes, there would probably be no need for literature.

BARBARA JOHNSON
The Critical Difference

THIS STUDY arises out of a concern to understand and correct the absence of male homosexuality as a central topic of investigation in American literary criticism, particularly in criticism of American poetry. In a tradition that claims Walt Whitman as one of its central figures, and that lists among its important names Hart Crane, Frank O'Hara, John Ashbery, James Merrill, Robert Duncan, and others, this absence seems not merely politically suspect but intellectually dishonest. Nor is there any longer theoretical justification for ignoring the issue. At one point, a reading of Whitman which suggested that his homosexuality was of central importance to his work would have seemed critically invalid if not disrespectful, tainted by biographical questions that had no place in literary study. However, the strictures against this kind of thinking have long since been superseded by an understanding that any textual production, readerly or writerly, is an effect of the material conditions of history, conditions that are not of secondary importance to some superior, disembodied aesthetic experience.[1] Nevertheless, if Houston Baker is correct in suggesting that "reconceptualizations of historical discourse have led to the laying bare, the surfacing and recognition, of myriad unofficial American histories" (*Blues, Ideology*, 61), including ethnic histories and the histories of women and workers, male homosexuality has remained, until quite recently, a relatively unexamined subject within the discourse of American letters.

In an attempt to correct the almost axiomatic absence of the homosexual from the discourse of American poetry—despite the presence of many canonical gay male poets—this study undertakes an analysis of the work of Hart Crane, a figure who has always been problematic for American criticism, partly because of the inability of critics to address his life and work on its most troubled and crucial level: the personal. Borrowing the following quoted phrases from "The Wine Menagerie," I set forth my premise here that Crane's work is evidence of a "new threshold" of gay subjectivity in modern Western culture, one that questions the received conventions for its interpretation and representation; my subsequent purpose is to project a "new anatomy" or structural vocabulary within which to investigate the homosexual as a minority discourse.

That task is made easier by the recent appearance of a number of strong theoretical and historical inquiries into the construction of sexual minority. This work, which collectively owes much to Foucault and much to feminism, makes it possible to write about homosexuality not as an identity or essence but as a process of cultural differentiation, as part of the history (and historicity) of modernity. It is Eve Kosofsky Sedgwick's work which has perhaps had the most profound impact on the restructuring of this field. Her writing is powerful and far-reaching in its historical and theoretical sweep, and has succeeded in shifting the discourse on homosexuality away from essentialist assertions of oppression and liberation toward questions of cultural power and knowledge—toward an understanding of how the discursive construction of homosexuality must be "placed appropriately in the context of various specific institutions and forms by which gender and class power are transmitted" (*Between Men*, 215). Her work is not primarily concerned with the history of homosexual writing in this century; rather, it is situated as an investigation of the homosocial continuum (including how homophobia insistently informs that structure) before the "appearance" or "invention" of the homosexual. My own project differs only superficially from hers (although the manner in which I phrase that difference here is completely in debt to her): this project is directed more toward an understanding of how homosexuality is articulated once the homosexual is indeed separated off as the abject of the homosocial continuum—once he "appears" in culture, and once he begins to understand himself as a being of a certain (stigmatized) social order. My concern, especially in this first chapter, is less with the production of an archaeological understanding of the sexual dynamics among and between men than with the question of disciplinarity, with the placement of subjects in discourse. In that sense, this is not a book about the structures and practices of a homosexual past but a book about the politics and practices of reading.

This first essay examines the process that has depoliticized and normalized our reading of American poetry, making any homosexual interest in its texts seem perverse. Before we can begin to establish a more committed analysis of homosexuality that is not content to stop with having established the homosexual content of this or that text or writer but sees homosexuality as the beginning and not the end of a certain literary question, a number of obstacles in our historical practices of reading American poetry must be removed. First, we must acknowledge that a materialist reading practice will be necessary to the delineation of those issues raised by a nonhomophobic literary criticism: a naive formalist strategy of interpretation will not address the issues that are important; secondly, we must rid ourselves of the notion that "America" as a critical term is natural rather than ideological in its origins and effects, and realize that its force silences issues such as homosexuality while validating others within a very powerful rhetorical scene of persuasion (not all American poetry, that is, demonstrates or is obsessed with characteristics that can be assigned to "American" traditions). Finally, we must see how the work of American myth criticism and formalist readings of American poetry came together to make the ahistorical and antimaterialist biases of America's New Critics naturalized examples of the Americanism the myth critics sought. New Critical readings were good, American readings in which democracy was imagined as a liberating condition that made universal and transcendent qualities in texts into "American" qualities.[2]

Terry Eagleton's *Criticism and Ideology* provides a ready example of how recent poststructuralist Marxism has addressed issues crucial to the reconsideration of canons and to the understanding of traditions as material, political practices that shape and discipline their material rather than provide transparent descriptions of an empirical literary reality. He suggests that the very act of identifying and investigating a tradition creates a set of literary objects without context and a literary criticism without the contextual or historicist base that would seem essential to any analysis of homosexuality as a minority discourse. In commenting on recent theoretical challenges to the discipline of literary study, Eagleton provides a useful working definition of literary traditions and the dialectic of their formation:

> What is finally at stake is not literary texts but Literature—the ideological significance of that process whereby certain historical texts are severed from their social formations, defined as 'literary', bound and ranked together to constitute a series of 'literary traditions' and interrogated to yield a set of ideologically presupposed responses. (57)

Therefore, Eagleton suggests, every text placed in such a position evinces for the critic those qualities and concerns he or she considers characteristic of the literary within that tradition, and questions of social formation—which homosexuality is for this study—are considered antithetical to the very process of literary study itself. If any text fails to evince these characteristics, it is either ignored or categorized as "failed art," as Crane's has been time and again. If it might evince other qualities or concerns for other readers or in other contexts, these are suppressed in favor of what are considered its primary and definitive features: those that mark it as literary within that tradition. Thus, even when it claims to investigate homosexuality, the heterosexist bias of Americanist criticism ensures that the homosexual text, writer, and reader will be positioned as abnormal, marginal, and exceptional. Each of them is marked as spectacle rather than meaning.

More typically, the problem for the homosexual[3] within American Studies has been homosexuality's invisibility, its nonstatus in a tradition conceived as addressing more "universal" cultural and social patterns or issues. American Studies has disciplined itself to an investigation of commonality, to an interest in the collective experience of American history and literature, and only recently has the representative nature of that supposed collectivity begun to be questioned by critics aware of the erasure of certain experiences from it. When Harold Beaver's essay in memory of Roland Barthes ("Homosexual Signs") appeared in *Critical Inquiry* in 1981, it began with a paragraph of mock objections to the need for "yet another" essay on homosexuality: "How crass! The subject is fascinating, all agree, but crass" (99). Beaver's essay demonstrates quite eloquently that his is not merely "another essay on homosexuality" but an attempt to establish homosexuality as a cultural and semiotically distinct mode of behavior within a different and dominant but not more important culture of institutionalized heterosexuality. The editors of *Critical Inquiry* unwittingly displayed another reason for the importance of an essay such as Beaver's, however, by placing it directly after an article on Whitman that took no significant note of Whitman's sexuality, Roy Harvey Pearce's "Whitman Justified: The Poet in 1855." It is ironic that Pearce chose as an epigraph for this essay a line from Adrienne Rich, for she has rejected as a false ideal the supposedly ungendered humanism to which Pearce appeals. Unlike his, her text is conscious of the political and sexual dimensions of literary codes, and she would never produce the reading of Whitman that Pearce offers in his article. At one point, he even quotes a particularly homoerotic passage from "The Sleepers," calls it evidence of "an altogether sexual sense" in Whitman, but still ends his discussion by suggesting that Whitman's later suppression of this passage was due to the fact that "he would appear to have been terrified . . . by his explorations into the relationship between what it would still be well to call personalism and historicism" (95).

Such euphemisms (the phrase "it would still be well to call" reveals itself as prototypical repression) still occur in discussions about Whitman despite important scholarly work by Robert Martin, Michael Moon, and others that challenges the intellectual squeamishness and political agenda behind their use. Martin is especially pointed in his critique of the "'liberated' version of Whitman's poetry" that universalizes the erotic energy of the text; he was among the first to offer instead a fully homoerotic reading of Whitman. He also identified one of the critical strategies employed in normalizing Whitman, in the following case analyzing that which was used by James E. Miller in his influential reading of "Song of Myself" as an "inverted" mystical experience:

> By seeing patterns of mystic symbolism (which is identical to erotic imagery, except that it does not mean what it purports to mean, but only uses sex to talk about God), at crucial points in [his reading of "Song of Myself"], Miller diverts the reader's attention from the poetry's frankly and directly sexual nature. ("Whitman's *Song of Myself*," 82)

Michael Moon's more recent work on Whitman goes further toward understanding how the homosexual discourses in Whitman's work in fact are not at all ancillary to its other interests but are "at all points interactive with other politics or economies . . . for the most part not specifically or obviously erotic." He suggests that we think of Whitman as the producer of a counterdiscourse that insists "on the fundamentally political and representational character of sexualities within a historical situation in which predominant forces were tending more and more powerfully to repress the relation of sexualities to a wide array of other social relations" ("Disseminating Whitman," 251). It is not, that is, that sexuality in Whitman is not intertextual with other discursive concerns (such as democratic and mystical cosmic unions); it is precisely the case that sexuality in Whitman *is* intertextual with (and thus not simply a screen for) these other concerns.

I refer to Whitman here because his poetry is "frankly and directly sexual" in a way that Crane's more often is not, and therefore the historical critical silence on it is that much more obvious. Whitman's text also highlights the problem of invisibility that surrounds homosexuality in American poetry (in a way that Crane's cannot) by virtue of his place at the origin of a tradition of "traditions" that erase the homosexual while praising his text. If Emerson is usually offered as the father of American poetry, his fathering is usually claimed—as he himself suggested—to consist less in his poetry than in his prose, and this makes Whitman the first public American poet one need not apologize for *if* one constructs one's discourse to admit stylistic eccentricities and prohibit sexual ones in the name of a mythic Americanism.[4] Whitman is one of the key figures to investigate on the question of critical silence about the homosexual because his text fits so well into archetypal schemes of American literature, because its canonical status has never been questioned by Americanists, and because his own thinking about the question of unity and tradition moved from the initial and staunch claims of *Calamus* that homosexual or "adhesive" affections would bind together the utopian communities he envisioned in North America to the more culturally conservative claims of *Democratic Vistas* that only democracy, religion, and literature would keep America a single and culturally coherent nation. That trajectory traces exactly the erasure of the homosexual that occurs in criticism and in later gay poets such as Crane, where the national displaces the homosexual, and may well be Whitman's response to having become more public, more central, himself a "fathering" presence whose opinions needed to be more in keeping with dominant ideology.

Myth criticism enshrined Whitman as the national bard, but it insisted that his homosexuality remain either invisible or extraneous to the supposedly more important nationalist concerns the discipline took as its central agenda. In a strictly Americanist reading of Whitman's *Children of Adam*, the text is interpreted within a convention most clearly delineated by R. W. B. Lewis[5]—the "Adamic" *topos* of American literature. Lewis suggests that *Children of Adam* offers "the most explicit evidence of [Whitman's] ambition to reach behind tradition to find and assert nature untroubled by art, to re-establish the natural unfallen man in the living hour" (*American Adam*, 43), and yet he cannot resist coding "the natural unfallen man" in Whitman through a heterosexual paradigm:

> We can round out our picture of Whitman as Adam—both Adam as innocent and Adam as namer—if we distinguish his own brand of mysticism from the traditional mysticisim. . . . We must cope with the remarkable blend in the man, whereby this Adam, who had already grown to the stature of his own maker, was not less and at the same time his own Eve, breeding the human race out of his love affair with himself. (51)

While Lewis's may be a defensible reading of Whitman's text, it ignores and (in its consonance with the naturalized authority of myth criticism) outlaws as *un*natural any interpretation that chose to investigate the chief object named by Whitman in this text: the homoerotic body. *This* Adam's body is new, and he offers his catalog of bodily names, knowledges, and parts in "I Sing the Body Electric" as if no one had ever named these objects before. Indeed, in poetry, they had not. Thus, Whitman says, "The love of the body of man or woman balks account, the body / Itself balks account" (*Leaves of Grass*, 94). A reading that sought to understand *Children of Adam* and its concern with language and literary production would have to ask questions about the nature of homoerotic configurations and could escape neither the question of Whitman's homosexuality nor the fact that *Calamus*, the section of *Leaves of Grass* Whitman called the "companion" to *Children of Adam*, agonizes over the literally unnamed feelings and behaviors clustered under the sign of calamus and named by Whitman "adhesiveness"—what we recognize as homosexuality.[6] If this is an *ab*normal reading of the Adamic in Whitman, Lewis's normal*ized* reading erases the homoerotic potential in the text, for he fails to note what most gay readers of Whitman latch onto almost immediately—that Whitman's most significant love affairs occur not within his neatly polarized and androgynous self (he is not his own Eve after all) but between and among men.

The power to claim a proper textual strategy, of course, always highlights cultural values and taboos, and the way in which Whitman's corpus has been divided and aligned into a canon that emphasizes his American qualities and de-emphasizes his erotic and homoerotic ones speaks to the manner in which critical evaluations may mirror cultural values while masking themselves as transparent to the text, as natural rather than produced. In "*Moby Dick* and the Cold War," Donald Pease has examined how approaches to texts of American literature are structured and controlled by the ideology of larger cultural scenes and contexts. In commenting on his inability to reconcile his "reading" of *Moby Dick* with the official one that reigned in the fifties (that the novel rehearsed the "universal" problem of totalitarian versus individualistic values), Pease writes,

> What is at issue here, however, is not my ability to convert this failure [to be convinced of the "proper" reading] into the power to prove the superiority of one reading over another, but the power of a cultural context to designate, in what I am calling a scene of persuasion, the terms in which a text *must be read* in order to maintain cultural power. (114)

This is important to a reevaluation of the approaches to and assessments of Crane's work, for his poetry has maintained its cultural power within a strange scene of persuasion: his work is almost universally deemed short-sighted, failed, or unreadable, and yet he remains a canonical presence. As such, Crane's work has been evaluated quite differently from that of H.D., whose poetry was not so much condemned as it was unread until recent feminist writers began to call attention to its value as a serious woman's text constructed at the margins of patriarchal high modernism (a task initiated by Susan Friedman, Rachel Blau DuPlessis, and Robert Duncan). This process in Crane's case is different as well from the writers of the Harlem Renaissance, whose entire milieu, until quite recently, was considered a scene of "failure" (On the scene of persuasion that frames this, see Houston Baker's *Modernism and the Harlem Renaissance*) and whose poetry was considered "minor" verse. As is true for almost no other figure in American poetry, Crane's status within the canon seems to be in spite of himself—he is the very sign of excess for American letters, and this was his original function for New Critics. Exhibiting all the faults and excesses of personal and cultural Romanticism, his work nonetheless was always accorded a certain seriousness of intention and deemed canonical (despite its "flaws") in large measure because he was a white male. Those excesses might now also take another name that they have hidden: the homosexual. Only within an intensely patriarchal tradition (one where, not long ago, only the figures of white, heterosexist, male-identified writers were accorded true value) would there be this insistent need to reproduce the "lesson" of homosexuality's failure; only within a tradition that needed to defend the manhood of its exemplary figures could this become a naturalized practice.[7]

While it may be obvious that monolithic consideration of American literature has led to certain excesses (for instance to relatively empty debate over how American Henry James or T. S. Eliot is), it may not be so obvious that the search for a single theme or pattern under which to organize studies of "the American" is itself a venerable tradition. Maurice Gounnod begins an essay for the English Institute's session on Emerson by suggesting a link between this critical drive for national literary unity and one of Alexis de Tocqueville's observations about Americans:

> Among the sweeping though perceptive judgments scattered about Tocqueville's *Democracy in America* is the notion that the Americans, like the French but unlike the English, are given to intellectual generalizations. They need to discover common rules in all things, Tocqueville claims, and to explain a broad constellation of facts by reference to one cause. Recent literary criticism in America must be very American indeed, if one considers the wealth of studies which purport to subsume a wide array of works, writers, or attitudes under common descriptions. ("Emerson and the Imperial Self," 107)

Such a drive toward cultural consensus is one of the active principles behind Whitman's *Democratic Vistas* as well, and our late nationalist criticism has shared certain premises with the Whitman of 1871: "The central point in any nation, and that whence it is itself really sway'd the most, and whence it sways others, is its national literature, especially its archetypal poems. Above all previous lands, a great original literature is surely to become the justification and reliance, (in some respects the sole reliance), of American democracy" (5). That American literature is a "great original literature" is now again in question, of course, because each of these terms is so contested. But for the generation of scholars that Nina Baym identifies in "Melodramas of Beset Manhood" as having codified the central concerns of American myth criticism, statements about national archetypes became the staple of literary criticism.

Still, each of these tendencies to generalization—that recorded by Tocqueville, Whitman's, and the American scholars'—ought to be seen as indicative of something more than sloppy or overzealous thinking. Each must be read as an assertion that seeks to hide and fill an absence or abyss. For the Americans Tocqueville observed, the absence is that most famous of all American absences registered from Crevecoeur to Henry James, the void of institutionless America, in which all things—including gender roles and language, according to Tocqueville—are subject to a massive instability. For Whitman, this swerve from the "adhesive" to the nationalistic occurs in part because the unthinkable has happened: the Civil War proved that America may not be a unified nation after all—"the fear of conflicting and irreconcilable interiors, and the lack of a common skeleton, knitting all close, continually haunts me" (*Democratic Vistas*, 8). And for the American scholars of the fifties and sixties, the attempt to bring together all of American literature under the homogeneous and disciplinary interests of academia was a response not only to increased nationalistic rhetoric in the wake of World War II but also to that literature's new institutional presence. This latter circumstance coincided, of course, with an increased academic population: more Americans than ever attended colleges and universities in the fifties and sixties, and curricular and scholastic patterns reflected this, making record numbers of American men and women culturally literate. Even the attempt to place Emerson at the Orphic center of poetic tradition in America is understandable in these terms, for we can certainly see his text as itself based in such a dialectic of absence and assertion. No figure of the nineteenth century agonized more insistently over the absence of a national culture or sought more vigorously to provide the ground for one in his own writing; therefore, a certain symmetry not without its own aesthetic appeal followed from making Emerson the center of American traditions.[8]

But "America," as Sacvan Bercovitch has dedicated his career to showing, is hardly an ideologically neutral sign; *as a sign* it is itself the most powerful and purely ideological marker in the cultural discourses America has produced. According to Bercovitch, "America" has signified for Americans not only a geopolitical reality but also (and more powerfully) a unifying and transcendent ideal under which all manner of personal differences are erased. In "America" the impact of cultural self-definition:

> bespeaks an ideological consensus—in moral, religious, economic, social, and intellectual matters—unmatched in any other modern culture. . . . Only in the United States has nationalism carried with it the Christian meaning of the sacred. . . . Of all the symbols of identity, only *America* has united nationality and universality, civic and spiritual selfhood, secular and redemptive history, the country's past and paradise to be, in a single synthetic ideal. (*American Jeremiad*, 176)

It is wholly in keeping with this seemingly natural circle of national literary identity that critics from D. H. Lawrence to Harold Bloom have attempted to center literary production in America under a series of national mythic terms such as the frontier, the self, the Edenic or Adamic—and it is clear from Bercovitch's work that each of these terms presumes some religious authority for itself as well, investing nationalist literature with theological connotations and imperatives. But criticism that engages the question of homosexuality as a cultural semiotic must position itself outside such naturalized discourse as a matter of course.

Two critiques suggest themselves here: one, a reading of the structural necessity of the separation of the homosexual and the national; the other a reading of desire. For the first, one need turn only to current practice in the American military, which sees a distinct conflict of interest between the profession of homosexual desire and the profession of defending one's country.[9] Perhaps the most interesting text in this light, however, is Genesis, where Jacob—after wrestling with the angel and refusing to allow him freedom without a blessing—is renamed Israel. In this text, the nation is born to its name, in its patriarchal certainty, and the relationship between two men in the culture defined as competitive rather than loving: when the man touches Jacob's thigh, the bone is displaced. In Genesis it is the displacement of homoerotic desire that signifies the institution of the nation, and homosexuality is conflated with impotence, sin, and national catastrophe. There are other texts to consult here as well, particularly Louis Crompton's *Byron and Greek Love*, which details homosexuality as structurally related to xenophobia and Francophobia in Regency England. One might also consult Victorian responses to Oscar Wilde, Walter Pater, and Aestheticism (all are homosexual as well), where part of the anxiety induced by these figures or their movement is the fear of cultural depletion, of the sapping of the empire's strength. Thus, Gilbert and Sullivan end *Patience* by having a squad of properly masculine dragoons win the love of Patience and the other maidens after the Wildean Bunthorne is proven inept and undesirable. Robert Hichens's *The Green Carnation*, which is a pastiche of Wildean conversations and bons mots, uses a similar marriage plot to oppose pederastic, Wildean decadence to proper imperial value (the heterosexual love interest centers in a widow whose husband was a colonel in India). In America, the most recent vigorous examples of the marriage between homophobia and nationalism are, of course, Senator Jesse Helms and evangelical ministers such as Jerry Falwell.[10]

On the other hand, we might entertain a psychoanalytic reading of this traditionary reading, and see in the American critic's quest for certainty and American-ism the desire for knowledge that a Lacanian analysis would interrogate as a potent but problematic desire centered almost exclusively on the Name-of-the-Father, in this case, "America." But to this reading we must add as well recent feminist inquiry into the nature of that continental object of desire; Annette Kolodny's *Lay of the Land* details the practice whereby male writers have figured the landscape as a female body and then figuratively raped it. Thus, although the critic who dreams this unity and presence of America receives authority in the name of the father, the object of his desire is a feminine (yet phallic) other, in Lacan's discourse, an *objet petit a* where the "*a*" now signifies "america" as well as "*autre*." And if we read a comment on psychoanalysis in Lacan's *Fundamental Concepts* as analogous to critical practice, we find an interesting Orphic parallel: "We have, in Eurydice twice lost, the most potent image we can find of the relation between Orpheus the analyst and the unconscious" (25). It would seem that Lacan means in this that the unconscious is recalled in analysis only to be lost again (if indeed one even grants the usefulness of the spatial metaphors and considers the unconscious "there"—or somewhere from which it can be (re)-called—before being hailed in the process of analysis). But we have here a conjunction of metaphors that suggests something like the following: the American critic (male and heterosexual) seeks to possess the female unconscious of the text (that which identifies it as American *beyond its conscious knowledge*), seeks this with a fervency of Orphic recovery, and thus finds in the tradition of Orphic utterance a figure of almost uncanny richness, a figure in which is predicted his own inability fully to recover that presence the text has itself failed completely to articulate (both "meaning" and "America" as the Beautiful, the Unparaphrasable). Within such a scene of desire and language, the homosexual is by necessity repressed and short-circuited, the national becomes the heterosexual (or Oedipally and Orphically resolved), and the female is "immasculated."[11]

If Whitman's text has been made *the* poetic text of American democracy primarily through diverting attention away from its homoerotic elements, the assessment of Crane as a homosexual writer has likewise suffered because his work is interpreted professionally only within an academy that identifies American Studies as a legitimate curricular field but has not yet recognized gay studies as more than of minor interest. Certainly Crane's choice of "America" as one of his terms of value and contest in *The Bridge* has granted critical transparency to this practice of reading him as in search of America, but this choice was determined by factors such as the cultural invisibility of homosexuality and the ideological power of the literary to determine the content and manner of representation. What I wish to do is to produce a new and alternative reading of Crane's work, placing it within a sexual-cultural matrix that highlights the problem of sexual identity and practice rather than allowing it to be glossed in a national-cultural matrix in which the issue disappears. By reading Crane's text in this way, I would claim, we can begin to see the cultural, aesthetic, and hermeneutic articulations that determined the act of writing for him.

Tony Bennett, in "Texts in History: The Determinations of Readings and their Texts," suggests that the purpose of a poststructuralist Marxist criticism would be "to detach texts from socially dominant reading formations and to install them in new ones" (8). By reading the history of readings of a text, and by historicizing that process of reception, as well as by installing that text in a different practice of reading, the critic may engage the political nature of literature without naively attempting to recover something the text helplessly holds in embryonic form.[12] As Bennett had stated in *Formalism and Marxism:*

> The task which faces Marxist criticism is not that of reflecting or bringing to light the politics which is already there, as a latent presence within the text which has but to be made manifest. It is that of *actively politicizing* the text, of *making its politics for it*, by producing a new position for it within the field of cultural relations and, thereby, new forms of use and effectivity within the broader social process. (167–68)

In advancing a homosexually centered reading of Hart Crane and in politicizing his text in a way that Crane himself might not recognize or perhaps appreciate, one produces for it a new position within the field of cultural relations and new forms of use and effectivity within a broader range of homosexual awareness than Crane would find familiar. But making the politics of a homosexual text means moving beyond a merely biographical, intentionalist centering of the homosexual question. For too long, criticism has produced a Freudian critique that is content to see the homosexual as the exposed secret of the author's psyche, the psychiatric appearance of which reinforces the vocabulary and process of repression. Such criticism actually has little to say about homosexuality as a material site in culture. An articulation of that materiality, and its relation to the materiality of literary production and reception, is what is now required of criticism if we are to move beyond the equally disabling economies of a repressive, psychiatrically defined homosexuality and a repressively desublimated, liberationist homosexuality that becomes visible only within the patriarchal language that represses it.

Lack of adequate attention to the materiality and historicity of homosexual practices and cultures vitiates much of the early Americanist work on the question of homosexuality. Leslie Fiedler's *Love and Death in the American Novel*, for instance, argues that, unlike the heterosexual interests of British fiction, American fictions tend to evince a homorather than hetero-centric imagination: "We continue to dream the female dead, and ourselves in the arms of our dusky male lovers" (29n). For Fiedler, "the dark vision of the American"[13] (28) expresses itself in an adolescent masculine fantasy of "avoid[ing] the facts of wooing, marriage, and child-bearing" (25). But in the very act of making homosexual libido attachments visible (and after Fiedler, who has been able to read Queequeg/Ishmael or Bumppo/Chingachgook as if the base of their relation were anything else), Fiedler erases actual homosexual practices. The inter-male relations that structure the texts he finds most significant in American cultural history are precisely what Eve Sedgwick would define as "homosocial" rather than "homosexual":

> "Homosocial" is a word occasionally used in history and the social sciences, where it describes social bonds between persons of the same sex; it is a neologism, obviously formed by analogy with "homosexual," and just as obviously meant to be distinguished from "homo-

> sexual." In fact, it is applied to such activities as "male bonding," which may, as in our society, be characterized by intense homophobia, fear and hatred of homosexuality. (*Between Men*, 1)

To see Cooper, Faulkner, and Mailer as significant exemplars of his thesis is to see *not* homosexual but homosocial desire at the center of American psychic life. But even to have said that is to realize that, as a myth critic, Fiedler begs the question of what constitutes American psychic life, who the "we" is that he speaks for (in the above citation, the "we" who dream the female dead are clearly not the "we" now spoken for and of by a number of feminist scholars whose work began with a dismantling of myth criticism's heterosexual male biases: Judith Fetterley, Nina Baym, Annette Kolodny). In writing of *Uncle Tom's Cabin*, Fiedler suggests that "there are two contrasting studies of marriage" in the book, ignoring Tom's and Chloe's, among others. And he imagines himself in privileged relation to what "America has chosen to preserve" in its cultural memory, but that memory is founded in a male- and white-identified gaze: "Only Uncle Tom and Topsy and Little Eva have archetypal stature; only the loves of the black man for the little white girl, of the white girl for the black, of the white boy [*sic*] for the slave live the lives of myths" (264–65).

In its drive to discover the archetypes of American culture (a move premised on the erasure of historical specificity), and in placing Fiedler himself inside rather than outside the culture he interrogates, Fiedler's text reads as dated thirty years later. But the act of formulating any tradition will by definition make choices and judgments about what is or is not central to that tradition, and any traditionary scheme will be a disciplining one, producing a set of discourses that control individual texts by making them speak to one another within a discipline and by disciplining those texts that somehow threaten to deviate from the norm of that tradition. Thus, the impulse toward identifying a tradition always involves legislation on the critic's part—even when the tradition in question is itself a deviant or "law"-less one. Robert K. Martin's *The Homosexual Tradition in American Poetry*, for instance—the first study of its kind—admits to two conscious exclusions that might seem questionable: W. H. Auden and Frank O'Hara. Auden is excluded from Martin's study because "he insisted so often that his poems must not be seen as homosexual, that they were universal"; O'Hara is excluded because "he does not seem . . . to use his homosexuality as an element of self-definition" (xix). *The Homosexual Tradition* is an early and important book for the study of gay texts, but Martin's notion of rectifying an exclusionary tradition has fallen victim to the same strategy of exclusion at its outset and its founding exclusions need to be questioned. It would seem relatively impossible to read any poet so conscious of the self as a construct as is Frank O'Hara and not see that homosexuality was central to his investigation of subjectivity. O'Hara seems especially unable to falsify or obscure the fact that his "personism" obtains among gay men or among one gay man (him) and various friends of various sexual persuasions. To read O'Hara as a "straight" poet is to devalue the historical significance of his work and requires that one bring a flat ear to his text, missing almost all of the nuance, humor, and insight of it. It also means missing—if this is possible—some of its most direct references. In any case, if a gay poet seems not to write about homosexuality, one might investigate why not, what is substituted in its stead, and how the homosexual appears surreptitiously despite its apparent absence. Certainly Auden's claim to universality should be investigated: from what vantage point is the universal constructed, why did Auden find it the "proper" one for poetry, what subjects did it make illegitimate? The critic, as poststructuralist theorists such as Macherey, Jameson, and Eagleton have argued, needs to be aware of what a text is necessarily silent about, how it negotiates ideology through absences that signify (if they do not represent) what the text cannot say within its own scene of persuasion and still maintain its cultural authority.

If we look briefly at certain other critical texts that have offered schemes for the definitive evaluation of American poetry, not only can we find examples of the disciplining of particular works and figures but we may also see the ahistorical bias which grounds the traditionary act.[14] For instance, a pattern of transhistorical comparison emerges from Hyatt Waggoner's *American Poets from the Puritans to the Present*, where Emerson is cast as the central hero and Waggoner interprets every figure in American poetry since Edward Taylor in terms he essentializes as Emerson's. Taylor, he claims, is "the initiator of a great tradition" (22), although the work that initiated this tradition was unknown until 1937 and must be wrenched far from its Puritan context in order to make it consonant with later, more consciously Emersonian texts. This is achieved by focusing on questions of form and style, what Waggoner calls the "purely poetic aspect of [Taylor's] poetry": "If his doctrines are Puritan, his attitude toward language and forms of verse might just as well be called Transcendental" (16). We see in this last statement especially how language and poetry are supposedly free from Puritan ideology and therefore by extension from all material or historical burdens. Such concentration upon a single figure, linguistic pattern, or form may lead to transparently absurd studies such as that of Edwin Fussell, who claims that the diction of American poetry defines it as American and dismisses Wallace Stevens as having "whored after the Roman vernaculars" (*Lucifer in Harness*, 109),[15] but this centralizing may also produce subtler, more pernicious effects when anything remotely connected to morality enters the critic's field of view. Waggoner, for instance, is able to dismiss Poe from his canon not merely because Poe was a "bad" poet but also because he was perhaps a pathological one: "Even in the handful of his best poems, both ideas and emotions are generally so simple that no great maturity . . . is required to appreciate them. . . . His psychic development ended at a very early age" (*American Poets*, 146). A multitude of assumptions about the writer, the audience, the use and effect of poetry stand rigorously against Poe in this formulation, and this attitude may seem of little consequence (Poe does, after all, usually seem to get his due) until we realize that homosexuality as well has been read as a condition of stunted psychic development where perversity and immaturity produce a subject who is emotionally and ideationally incomplete. It is the confluence of injunctions against poetic immaturity and homosexuality that was in part responsible for a generation's reading of Crane as morally, psychologically, and intellectually truncated. R. P. Blackmur ends his essay on Crane in *Language as Gesture* with this damning praise:

> It is said that Crane's inchoate heart and distorted intellect only witness the disease of his generation; but I have cited two poets [Yeats and Stevens], if not of his generation still his contemporaries, who escaped the contagion. It is the stigma of the first order of poets . . . that they master so much of life as they represent. In Crane the poet succumbed with the man. . . . And there is about him . . . the distraught but exciting splendour of a great failure. (316)

Blackmur's assessment, of course, places Crane in a context designed to find him lacking, and naively considers all modernists to have the same historical burden of subjectivity simply by virtue of their contiguity in time; he locates Crane in a rhetorical scene of persuasion that guarantees a reading of him as homosexual (although this word does not appear), and implies that both he and his "condition" are distorted and pathological.

Blackmur's canon of acceptable modern literature, as was that of Winters, Tate, and most other early critics of Crane (including more academic critics such as Pearce and Waggoner), was largely shaped by T. S. Eliot, the single most influential critical figure in Anglo-American letters during the first half of this century, and the modernist figure Crane considered himself most rigorously against.[16] Eliot's notions of the value of literature influence all the men mentioned above, and the terms he develops in "Tradition and the Individual Talent" stand directly behind most of the assessments offered here, particularly the insistence upon a poet's learning and maturity, on an organically "present" and self-continuous tradition, and on the paradox that poetry escapes the whim of personality but not its demands. When he dismisses Philip Freneau as of little importance to American poetry, Waggoner uses Eliot's terms in a way that suggests they need not be questioned:

> If Freneau accomplished little that compels our interest, he anticipated not only Emerson but also Bryant and Poe—in theme and subject, and even, occasionally, in style. Whether he was born at the wrong time, culturally speaking, to write greater poetry, or whether, instead, we should say he lacked the "individual talent" to make his own creative and original—and expressive—contribution to the "tradition" of late eighteenth-century British poetry is a question I suspect must remain unanswered. (*American Poets*, 32)

What the dismissal of Freneau (like the dismissal of Poe) highlights is how Anglican were those traditions proposed for the study of American poetry in the sixties, and that *talent* (like sexuality, housed in the psyche of the writer) *had to be* disciplined, brought in line with *tradition*, made normative. We have now enough distance from that generation's reverence for Eliot to examine his historical role in producing a traditional and traditionary reading of American poetry and a damning assessment of Crane's place in such a tradition.

For its day (1919), Eliot's "Tradition and the Individual Talent" seems to be a step forward in the demystification of literary history. Eliot begins the essay by insisting upon the importance of a historical sense for the writer and critic, and he makes the important statement that "art never improves, but . . . the material of art is never quite the same" (39), and this is the essay in which he makes the famous claim for the impersonality of poetry, a claim that could (but didn't) ground a more interrogative and less reverential attitude toward textual production: "What happens [to the artist in writing] is a continual surrender of himself as he is at the moment to something which is more valuable. The progress of an artist is a continual self-sacrifice, a continual extinction of personality" (40). The problem, of course, is precisely what Eliot means here by terms such as "more valuable" and "self-sacrifice," for we cannot but read these surrenders as repressions, and we must ask what repressions or sublimations on the part of the poet are to be desired and what potential liberations rejected. When he writes that "it is in this depersonalization that art may be said to approach the condition of science" (40), Eliot is interested in science only as it may be employed metaphorically in a reinscription of the mysteries of artistic production. In making an analogy between the poet writing and the "action which takes place when a bit of finely filiated platinum is introduced into a chamber containing oxygen and sulphur dioxide" (40), Eliot insists upon the writer's separation from his own experience, from his own body: "The more perfect the artist, the more completely separate in him will be the man who suffers and the mind which creates" (41), for the mind of the poet is platinum, a precious metal unchanged by the forces around it. This claim for the poet's transcendence of history and the image of the poet's psyche as an uncontaminated space in which exist simultaneously all the equally uncontaminated (i.e., nonideologically produced) "monuments" of his culture is not, of course, unique to Eliot or even to modernism. But it represents an aesthetics completely counter to Crane's theory of poetry as experiential. In "General Aims and Theories" Crane writes that the poet will "define" the modern period not by remaining above it and transmuting the past into the present but "by reacting honestly and to the full extent of his sensibilities to the states of passion, experience and rumination that fate forces on him, first hand" (*Poems*, 218). While Crane qualifies this by claiming the poet must still obtain some "universal" perspective to insure that his reactions are not simply idiosyncratic, it is clear that he posited a more somatic relation between text and writer than did Eliot (and through him a generation of reader-critics).[17] It is as if Crane and Eliot were themselves avatars of two quite different French Symbolists: Eliot taking from Mallarmé mostly the rejection of the body and the trope of impotence; Crane from Rimbaud mostly the opacity of the flesh and the trope of intoxication.

In the end, Eliot's essay not only mystifies the writing process in ways that are antithetical to those that inform Crane's text, but his very notion of tradition, of its orderliness and "impersonality," is limiting as well, for he admits no agency in the formation of canons: "The existing monuments form an ideal order among themselves"—the existing monuments, of course, are "the whole of the literature of Europe from Homer" and "the whole of the literature of [the writer's] own country" (38). And yet we know from his own canonical revisions how Eliot parsed these supposedly seamless wholes, how important it was to him to discriminate among texts, and how unfavorably he viewed those writers that Crane particularly privileged as important precursors: Melville, Whitman, Blake. And where Eliot and Crane agreed on a canonical figure—Donne, for instance—we feel they were reading two different texts: Crane reading the discourse of religion in Donne erotically, Eliot reading the erotic in him religiously. We are confronted here not only with a narrow vision of canonicity (the attack on "canon" is now so successful that one no longer feels any authority in statements such as Eliot's), but also with a reminder of how restricted were the notions of the literary that surrounded Crane's discourse. These restrictions meant that in addition to the question of his homosexuality and his lack of "maturity," Crane faced charges of being unlearned and unschooled in classical languages and in the "whole of literature of Europe from Homer" (Eliot, "Tradition," 38). There can be no doubt that Crane found this a burden to his career and that critics (old and new) have found it a defect in his work.

Eliot is central here not only because he has traditionally served as Hart Crane's literary other but also because his work seems to stand provocatively behind that of the most recent critic to advance a revisionist theory of traditions: Harold Bloom. Bloom's theories of influence and misreading have generated much debate and have made it possible, as Cary Nelson suggests, for criticism to discuss issues it could not before. As such, they have provided an indispensible service to criticism. But while Bloom's theories may correct naive assumptions about literary indebtedness and the problem of authority, they consistently reaffirm the most mystifying of humanist values; his assumptions—and often his vocabulary—are surprisingly consistent with those of Eliot. In "The Internalization of Quest Romance," for instance, Bloom claims, "There is no better way to explore the Real Man, the Imagination, than to study his *monuments* [italics added]" (15): the terms for Bloom are borrowed from Blake rather than Dante, but the value of literature in such statements is not unlike what Eliot supposed. Both Bloom and Eliot adhere to a notion of literature's unquestioned and unequaled ability to produce a transhistorical understanding of the human condition. Despite his introduction of a Freudian paradigm, Bloom's discourse merely refigures and does not challenge former notions of tradition, for it is concerned only with the relation of the individual talent to a self-sufficient, "whole" tradition. Like Waggoner, Bloom still evaluates poets according to their "maturity," and despite his work's apparent interest in questions of history, it is marked by all the indices of immanent criticism—his vocabulary is Orphic, incarnational, and supremely transhistorical. Bloom's central, useful insight into literary production is that the writer enters a system of discourse in which s/he is a trope rather than a presence, in which s/he is already written in a discourse not her own. But rather than producing a materialist or historicist inquiry into literary production, the rhetoric of textual Oedipal resolution functions to allow Bloom to ignore all history except literary history and to reduce that to the question of the poet's transcendence of materiality. His work sanctifies poetic identity to such a point that he can claim in *Poetry and Repression* that "the aim of self-presentation is not defeated" (246) in American poetry. As Eric Cheyfitz has noted in a more extended critique of Bloom's theory of revision, "Bloom . . . does not want to talk about poets as historic personages . . . , but rather as 'authentic forces' that appear in the figures of competing poems" (*The Trans-parent*, 84).

Bloom has done a great deal to reevaluate the canon of American poetry formed by Pearce, Waggoner, and others in the wake of Eliot's career. He was among the first, after Northrop Frye, to understand Stevens as more than ironic poseur, and he has always understood Crane as a serious, "Orphic" poet rather than as a mere enthusiast seriously lacking in discipline. But Bloom has achieved this valuation of American poetry by claiming Emerson as the "natural" center of a tradition of American self-expression, and the terms that follow as consequences to that claim do not provide the surest manner for reading Crane's text as a homosexual one. It is not necessary to state that Crane can be read through an Emersonian vocabulary; his transcendentalism may have developed historically from his reading of Whitman and from his acquaintance with Waldo Frank more than from any knowledge or close study of Emerson, but his texts are often congruent with what Bloom and others would identify as the central concerns of Emersonian poetry. But, as the fifth chapter of this study will explain, the vocabulary of American transcendentalism is overwhelmingly heterosexual, and the practice of naming Emerson the father of American poetry (in Bloom's work and elsewhere) is only an extension of the tropes of patriarchy present almost as first principles in the history of American transcendentalism. Just as one must read in Dickinson a dissenting voice in the transcendental discourse as well as a female voice whose refiguration of the transcendental was determined by the position it assigned her gender, it is necessary to read Crane's refiguring of Emersonian discourse according to the position it allowed his homosexuality. And Bloom's wholesale acceptance of the Oedipal paradigm, of a movement into patriarchal authority that reads homosexuality always as an intermediate rather than final destination,[18] will always—through the power of allegory—be inhospitable to homosexual writers.[19]

The final word on the tradition of American literature and its suppression of the homosexual must belong to the premier critic of American Studies, the man who most significantly focused the discipline, who brought it (dramatically) into respectable existence—a man who (like Crane) was also homosexual and who (like Crane) was also a suicide. The irony of the fact that his death occurred immediately before he was to appear before the House UnAmerican Activities Committee—a committee charged with ridding American institutions of gays as well as Communists—ought to remind us that the erasure of the homosexual from the discourse of American literature and from American society is not an inconsequential act. The figure I refer to here is F. O. Matthiessen, whose *The American Renaissance* was and perhaps remains the single most influential text in the history of American Studies. Jonathan Arac's essay in *The American Renaissance Reconsidered*, "F. O. Matthiessen: Authorizing an American Renaissance," argues that Matthiessen's text achieves its authority partly through making "America" a term of unity and reconciliation after the fractious debates of the thirties when self-styled leftist and reactionary critics battled for rights to the term.[20] Arac suggests that Matthiessen creates a "canonical moment in history" by "harmonizing, centralizing, normalizing, and identifying . . . [by] tucking in elbows" (107). This last figure, which Arac takes from a letter Matthiessen wrote to his lover, Russell Cheney, becomes a recurrent motif in Arac's essay and signifies the sexual and political repressions of Matthiessen's text. In the letter, Matthiessen notes the erotic thrill[21] of a "Whitmanesque" encounter with a workman in England, how he allowed his elbow to graze the man's torso as they parted. What Arac points out is the difference between Matthiessen's use of Whitman in this letter and his "official" response to Whitman in his master text. What Arac suggests about that difference is the lesson of all disciplinary maneuvers performed on the homosexual text: "To create the centrally authoritative critical identity of [the] American Renaissance, much had to be displaced or scattered or disavowed. Loose elbows had to be tucked in" (92). What we need now is a reassembled homosexual text, a text with its elbows attached at their appropriate, cruisey angles, not merely for the sake of understanding Crane or Matthiessen or Whitman but for the sake of understanding the cultural production of signs that surround and identify sites such as the homosexual from within and without. Shortly after beginning their affair, on 21 September 1924 in a letter to Cheney, Matthiessen wrote, "I carried Whitman in my pocket. That's another thing you've started me doing, reading Whitman. Not solely because it gives me an intellectual kick the way it did last year, but because I'm living it" (*Rat and the Devil*, 26). It is time to acknowledge this use of gay texts for gay readers and to investigate the function of writers such as Whitman, Crane, and Matthiessen to the production of a homosexual culture within an American culture. What we are engaged in is a battle for the scene of persuasion in which the text of homosexuality will be interpreted.

2
Homosexuality and the Matter of Style

▼

Act so that there is no use in a centre.

GERTRUDE STEIN
Tender Buttons

RECENT critical theory has been successful in challenging the narrow criteria for interpretation and evaluation that the previous chapter suggested were inappropriate to gay studies in American literature. Projects for the rewriting of literary history and for reimagining the relation between literature and other cultural discourses have received institutional sanction, and questions of gender, race, class, and state now receive serious attention from scholars in virtually all historical and national fields. Minority discourses and previously invisible or marginalized communities now compel this institutional interest in part because the history of their marginality highlights with precision the fact that literary discourse is an ideological construction rather than an innocent, aesthetic one. Feminists, for instance, have recentered the question of textual discourse in sexual difference and have employed theories of object-relations, psychoanalysis, linguistics, and sociology in advancing what is perhaps the richest field of current literary study; Afro-American critics have likewise furthered the field of literary theory in producing exactly the effect Derrida envisioned as the project for deconstruction: the pressuring or shaking of "white" mythologies. My interest is similar in that it would rearticulate the dynamics that have forced homosexuality to the margins of the literary despite the centrality of many homosexual figures in literary history—especially in the history of modern and postmodern literature and theory. The question I would pose in this chapter is perhaps deceptively simple: What would constitute the study of homosexuality as a textual system in the current climate of theoretical concerns?[1] How may homosexuality be organized as a system of inquiry that moves beyond the question of thematics to the problem of representation?

To a considerable degree, merely to pose this question is to redirect critical attention away from traditional approaches, and although my ultimate aim is to move beyond them, gay studies need not eschew more traditional methods of anaylsis. Thematic approaches such as Louis Crompton's *Byron and Greek Love* locate heretofore invisible moments in the history of homosexual experience, its representation and reception; such work is invaluable for the way in which it demonstrates the strength of institutional and national repressions and intolerances. A more archaeological historiography such as that of Michael Lynch or Eve Sedgwick is likewise needed—not only for the way it may inform our reading of historical texts but also for the ways it may inform our understanding of homosexuality as one point in a cultural system of oppressions and controls. Gay studies might profitably ally itself with biography at times—in order, for instance, to read the homosexual Henry James[2]—or it might forego the literary altogether and situate itself with respect to sociological and psychoanalytic researches such as those of Jeffrey Weeks or Guy Hocquenghem. Like its sororal and fraternal disciplines of women's studies and Afro-American studies, gay studies clearly offers a challenge to the taxonomy of liberal arts upon which institutions of higher learning have been founded, and that challenge represents the value lesbian and gay studies can have for the academy at this time.[3]

My interest here is in the problem of textual production as a system of culturally determined codes that gay men have historically had access to by virtue of their biological identities yet have been unable to employ as they might because those codes denied validity to their experience as homosexuals. Thus, gay writers seem often to have found literature less a matter of self-expression and more a matter of coding: from Byron through John Ashbery, the consistent locus of parody in gay texts suggests a self-consciousness about what texts may and may not do. As such, the silence imposed on gay male writers is different from the literary silence imposed on women in previous eras because of their lack of access to education and publishing. And although it is important to note those themes that appear most important to the practice of homosexual writing (be they present or absent in it), it is perhaps more important to see that homosexuality is not merely a theme but comes to define a style, both as a lifestyle and as a mode of semiotic expression.[4] It should not surprise us, therefore, that Oscar Wilde made the paradox his literary stock-in-trade, for it is the stylistic analogue to his position as a literary subject: empowered to speak, but unable to say, he elaborated a new form of literary discourse, the conversation that was all high style and irrelevance. In Wildean discourse it is repetition rather than content that signifies value—the circulation of *bons mots* and the coining of quotable phrases mark the literary subject as sophisticated, modern, and (dare we say it?) homosexual. Language becomes, in Wildean discourse, a truly floating signifier without reference to anything except the context of its own utterance and the style or lack thereof of those who employ it. The true value of language occurs for Wilde in the being memorable rather than in the being profound. Thus, Wilde's final conceptual paradox: while words are never the property of their speaker, nothing demonstrates the boredom generated by the proper and the deliciousness of the improper (including the homosexual) better than words.

From within this contradiction of being empowered to speak but unable to say, gay writers have historically hidden, erased, universalized, or otherwise invalidated not only their homosexual desire but also the shape (or mis-shape) their lives have taken as a result of the social taboos against it. Until Genet and Barthes, and until a vocal and political homosexual community began to demand more positive self-representations, overtly homosexual autobiography, for instance, seems to have been profoundly limited to confessional texts of guilt such as Wilde's *De Profundis*. I disagree here with Foucault, who claims that it is in the discursive practices of the nineteenth century that the homosexual "begins to speak on its own behalf"—or would at least insist that we see the "half" speech buried in those discourses, for that voice became audible only at a much, much later date. Gay historians have most often identified the years around World War II as a more meaningful date for such watershed events as homosexual self-articulation in its more contemporary (American) sense. Until quite recently, that is, the homosexual has been almost literally unable to speak of itself coherently except in a vocabulary of remorse—and remorse, if we trace its post-Enlightenment heritage back to Coleridge, has traditionally been seen as that which results from breaches in male conduct, from seriously mis-taking one's responsibility within the systems of male bonding that Eve Sedgwick has defined as the homosocial contract. Indeed, this is the rhetoric in which *De Profundis* is written: *not* I have transgressed social and religious values but *we* have betrayed one another's manhood and respectability through this dirty business.[5]

Crane himself faced a number of serious injunctions (both private and public) against homosexuality. Although his straight literary friends knew of his homosexuality, most warned him about the debilitating effects of it and of the alcoholic binging that seemed to accompany it for him. It is not clear that his father ever knew of his sexual inclinations, and it is quite clear that the knowledge of it—when transmitted to his mother—caused a rift between mother and son that lasted until Crane's death. As a good, grandstanding son of the American Midwest who paraded even minor achievements before his parents in an attempt to justify his life and career, Crane could not write openly of his homosexuality without facing the possible censure of his family. It is also clear that the ideology of literary and cultural authority under which Crane wrote would have made homosexuality an inadmissible center from which to write about American life. Thus, homosexuality appears under a number of screens and covers in his text: in the allegiance to Whitman, for instance, where it is important for us to see that the screen in this case was facilitated by an unchallenged reading of Whitman not as a sexual or homosexual but as a national, cultural, and/or philosophical spokesman.[6] Finally, Crane was impelled to produce a poetry whose authenticity was grounded in its style—a style without a content, critics complained, a style not unlike Art Deco: florid and overproduced yet streamlined and wishing to appear simple.

In order to see how Crane's homosexuality invests itself not merely as a thematic but as a style, it will be necessary to turn to the question of semiotics. But I would like to begin here with a few words about thematics—indicating some of those themes that inform the problem of gay male stylistics. In an essay in which he coined the term "homotextuality," Jacob Stockinger identified a number of important textual features as classic *topoi* in homosexual literary expression. For Stockinger "the most frequent type of homotextual space is the closed and withdrawn place that is transformed from stigmatizing into redeeming space," its "archetypal examples" the rooms in Proust, cells in Genet, and the cell of *De Profundis* ("Homotextuality," 144). He extends this preoccupation with space to other "open" spaces such as "the open country side, which is privileged space for the homosexual because it marks both his ostracism and the chance to recuperate his 'unnatural' love in nature," and this interest in open space leads him to speculate on the importance of travel and voyaging in homosexual texts, that "external itinerary that corresponds to an internal journey of self-discovery" (144). Certainly homosexuals have no monopoly on journeying as a motif in their fictions or on self-discovery as a narrative quest, but Stockinger's point deserves attention precisely because homosexual quests and selves ought to become visible as taking reference within a specific historical and cultural materiality and not be erased under the sign of the universal. As do many of his poems, Frank O'Hara's "Meditations in an Emergency" circles around the question of emergent identity, and figures the solution to its identity crisis in a movement from a closed to an open space. Having fended off depression and its two causes, the failure of homosexual romance and the possibility that heterosexuality will, in this disappointment, displace any future homosexual romance ("Heterosexuality! you are inexorably approaching. (How discourage her?)" [*Complete Poems*, 197]), O'Hara's speaker nonetheless chooses to step into the cruisey street (itself a site for self-determination with specific gay references). And it is a sign of his "victory" over this crisis that he enters it dressed according to the codes of a certain class and style of homosexual nonchalance: "I choose a piece of shawl and my dirtiest suntans. I'll be back, I'll re-emerge, defeated" (197). Evidently, heterosexuality has been discouraged. Although the point needs to be expanded beyond the question of open and closed space, it is clear that one cannot understand the pointed reversals and political affirmations in O'Hara's text unless one first grants its specific homosexual referents: a universalized "quest for self" will not do as a paradigm for its reading.

More provocative than this problem of enclosure and wandering, however, is the discussion Stockinger begins on what the quest for a homosexual self might encounter and detail. Although he does not use this terminology, his essay suggests that homosexual identities, both as social facts and literary representations, foreground the problem of the subject. "By need and nature," Stockinger writes,

> the psycho-dynamic of the homosexual is fluid and could be called transformational in the sense that it is comparable to transformational grammar: out of an underlying "deep structure" (the homosexual identity) emerge many variations of "surface structure" (either an affirmed or assumed heterosexual identity, or, at the very least, modified and repressed forms of a homosexual identity). (139)

One needs less to question the naiveté of Stockinger's binary conception of identity than to take up his perception of the instability or decentered quality of being. Certainly nonhomosexual identities also exhibit a dynamic of masking and loss through "deep" and "surface" structures,[7] but the instance of homosexuality makes this apparent in different cultural registers and sites. Stockinger alludes to Sartre's fascination with homosexuality as a paradigm for authentic identity in *Being and Nothingness* (Sartre is concerned with the intersubjectivity, alterity, and displacement of self in Other that constitutes the existential ego). For Stockinger, the hallmark image of this theme is the mirror (Stockinger's text was written in a time when theme and image were the interests of the literary critic; what is most interesting about his work is that it discusses in relatively outmoded terms issues for which poststructuralism has developed a better vocabulary).[8]

What this notion of self-displacement most clearly calls to mind, of course, is the Lacanian notion of "lack" or absence as constitutive of identity (and of desire). And in the case of an identity defined almost exclusively in terms of its sexual desire (as homosexual identity has classically been defined), the Lacanian "lesson" of the uncanny becomes an inescapable "lesson" in subjectivity as that encounter with the uncanniness and sexuality of any "self." But we must insist that male homosexual articulations of desire are materially different from other sexual articulations. For the homosexually defined subject, the following comments from John Rajchman strike a cultural and historically specific chord beyond their intention: "Lacan holds that there is a basic incompatibility between love and sexuality. Sexuality is traumatic as such; it is a matter not of happiness and pleasure but of the uncanniness or otherness of desire. It refers us not to our common existence but to our constitutive 'lack' of one" ("Lacan," 45). The homosexual encounters his sexuality as a division from himself in a manner which does not usually have to be read through the displacements of his unconscious. His rejection of culturally central, bourgeois institutions of sexual pleasure and his participation instead in relatively *un*sanctioned, decentered (although perhaps, finally, equally bourgeois) experiences and rituals of desire foregrounds for him the lack of commonality in social existence and (as ideology allows only heterosexual desire to appear as "love") the difference between sexual desire and love. Homosexuality, as it is constructed in twentieth-century Western cultures, has most typically resisted the domestication and naturalization that make heterosexuality seem the only adult sexuality compatible with love, and it can remain (as it seems to have done for Crane) an almost permanently radical experience of alterity and liminality. In the work of Genet in France or John Rechy in America, the homosexual is theorized as a privileged site outside cultural convention from which it is possible to critique the patriarchal structures of bourgeois desire: in both Genet and Rechy, the homosexual's place in culture is explicitly linked to the proletariat's—it is represented as marginalized and potentially revolutionary. I do not wish here to reiterate an old interpretation of homosexual desire—that it is by definition incompatible with love. Nor do I wish to imply that heterosexual desire is any less disruptive or discontinuous in its psychological impurity than is homosexual desire. But I would stress that Western patriarchal culture has overwhelmingly solicited heterosexual rather than homosexual desire as the key to sanctioned social and legal identities. It is important to note that homosexuality was constructed for Crane in such a way that its congruence with more bourgeois, affective modes of bonding was virtually impossible.[9] For Crane, homosexuality initiated what Rajchman calls the peculiar ethics of modernism (modernism defined as a "literature of 'sexuality' that is not love, happiness, or duty but trauma, otherness, and unspeakable truth"): "Sexuality becomes the ruination of harmonious, 'centered' love. It turns the conjugal or familial forms into structures of Law and repression. . . . Sexuality comes to lie at the heart of a writer's relation to his culture. In modernism, one writes out of a sort of sexual necessity" ("Lacan," 53). Crane's homosexuality is not, therefore, merely a biographical curiosity or an index of critical over-reading; psychoanalysis would see it as the central issue of his text—even when his texts are not "about" homosexuality, they are instances of homosexual writing.

Seeing homosexuality as fundamentally disruptive rather than harmonious, Crane defiantly wrote in 1926, "Let my lusts be my ruin, then, since all else is a fake and mockery" (*Letters*, 250). Written during the period when he wrote most of *The Bridge*, on the Isle of Pines off Cuba, the letter from which this is taken details the pains and pleasures of homosexual experience in urgent detail, but no one has before noticed how greatly its sentiment undermines and complicates the reading of Crane and his epic poem as monuments intended to produce or evoke something like "harmony."[10] The intense alienation from self and society registered in this letter bespeaks the impossible position from which Crane wrote: a quite consciously "ruined" and displaced figure who nevertheless followed the critical dicta of his day and conceived of literature as that cultural form of expression best suited to provide a center for the examination and exchange of civilized values.

Harold Beaver's "Homosexual Signs: (*In Memory of Roland Barthes*)" opens the question of semiotics and its relevance to the study of homosexuality. Beaver's essay takes up the quite difficult question of how homosexuals more than others seem consumed by (insatiable consumers and producers of) signs:

> The homosexual is beset by signs, by the urge to interpret whatever transpires, or fails to transpire, between himself and every chance acquaintance. He is a prodigious consumer of signs—of hidden meanings, hidden systems, hidden potentiality. Exclusion from the common code impels the frenzied quest: in the momentary glimpse, the scrambled figure, the sporadic gesture, the chance encounter, the reverse image, the sudden slippage, the lowered guard. In a flash meanings may be disclosed, mysteries wrenched out and betrayed. (104)

This catalogue of "signs" is itself an example of the very order of signification it details; it is not enough for Beaver to note the phenomenon without himself producing a long list of signs in support of his observation. In the opening chapter of *Cities of the Plain*, Proust offers a similarly abundant catalog of signs in explaining the furtive but fertile production of homosexual recognitions; for Proust, the "freemasonry" of homosexuals:

> rests upon an identity of tastes, needs, habits, dangers, apprenticeship, knowledge, traffic, glossary, and ones in which the members themselves, who intend not to know one another, recognise one another immediately by natural or conventional, involuntary or deliberate signs which indicate one of his congeners to the beggar in the street, in the great nobleman whose carriage door he is shutting, to the father in the suitor for his daughter's hand, to him who has sought healing, absolution, defence, in the doctor, the priest, the barrister to whom he has had recourse; all of them obliged to protect their own secret but having their part in a secret shared with the others, which the rest of humanity does not suspect. (14–15)

Beaver's essay uses semiotics (what we might, following O'Hara, call a "semiotics of emergency," a semiotics emergently produced in and producing crisis) to explain particular phenomena and images within gay subcultures. For instance, he finds "the multiplication of signs . . . in a constant play of double entendres and innuendoes," the vapid, campy chatter of certain gay moments, "predatory, intent on invalidating specific gestures, specific meanings" ("Homosexual Signs," 105). He does not ignore the queen (the effeminate, bitchy man who might be rejected as a false stereotype rather than analyzed as a type) but situates him/her in a textuality of gay behaviors:

> A young fellow flouncing back to the bar to retrieve his duffle coat calls out, "I forgot my mink!" The remark is addressed to no one; nothing in particular is validated; the sign is empty. . . . Queens need not necessarily be amusing nor even charming as long as their signs generate signs in constant mimicry from a circle of admirers. . . . Though obviously referring to the duffle coat, "my mink" does not denote the duffle coat. The duffle coat is displaced; it is replaced by the *sign* of the mink.
>
> No wonder such chit-chat tends to seem disappointing, vacuous, even cruel—in a word, "bitchy"—to out-siders: all coherent discourse is betrayed. ("Homosexual Signs," 105)[11]

The "typicality" of the person identified in this example requires a brief comment; "queens," of course, are no more or less representative of homosexuality—in number or style—than other types that might be offered for investigation, and there is certainly reason, given the stereotyping of gays as effeminate men, to resist using such a figure to establish a central point about gay semiotics. In fact, the iconography of homosexual self-representation has almost aggressively swerved from this "type" in the past two decades in urban America, as writers such as Dennis Altman and Charles Bronski have commented upon. But the figure of the queen (and the style that accompanies it in language and manner) is one of the inescapable legacies of gay culture in the West, and part of the recent rejection of it by that culture would seem to be a reiteration of dominant ideologies. Surely effeminacy is not in any sense the natural condition or expression of homosexuality, nor vacuous conversation its only verbal quality, but the presence and importance of such phenomena within gay culture historically and at present should not be denied in the pressure to normalize its visibility. Male-female gender drag (cowboys and queens) informs the gay culture depicted in John Rechy's *City of Night* (1960), where men are defined inflexibly by roles that mirror and perhaps parody the social constructions of masculinity and feminity in the culture at large. More historically relevant for reading Crane is the writing of Quentin Crisp, who offers detailed accounts and incisive analyses of gay life in London since World War I. Crisp quite clearly equates his own homosexuality with the femininity described above and is not terribly sanguine about more recent claims of self-justification from the homosexual community; and he has been rejected by some as an ideologically insupportable spokesperson for gay men. But Crisp comments quite pointedly on his verbal behavior in terms quite like those Beaver suggests for identifying gay chatter: "In middle age I found that I had gone beyond my original aim of purging my speech of the dross of sincerity. I had robbed it of all meaning whatsoever" (157).

The notion that queeny chatter is incoherent or meaningless is apparent, of course, only from a position outside of it; as Beaver suggests, the semiotics of gay ritual have their own codes of coherence, one of which is the master code of coherence in modern Western cultures and, according to Susan Sontag, the master code of Camp: "art." Beaver posits a link between a particular articulation of homosexuality and a particular fascination with the signs of "Culture," whether that be found in Proust, James Merrill, or, in one of Sontag's examples, "a woman walking around in a dress made of three million feathers" (*Against Interpretation and Other Essays*, 293):

> Deprived of their own distinctive codes, homosexuals make art itself into their distinctive code. Aesthetic absorption is all. For Wilde (and his successors, Cocteau and Auden), it was no longer homosexuality that was duplicitous but its paradigm, art. That is the revelation which all the paradoxes from Wilde to Barthes pursue. Art and sex are analogous activities since both are projections of fantasy. (Beaver, "Homosexual Signs," 106)

But the manner in which modern art is analogous to homosexuality goes further than this. Order and disorder become the dynamic of the Wildean and Barthesian paradox, for instance, precisely because homosexuality is the "disorder" whose articulation as such allows other orders to appear natural, and once homosexuality is fully pathologized as a mental and not merely a moral disorder, the project of decadence (Rimbaud's disordering of all the senses) becomes of paramount importance for certain homosexual artists. Similarly, if gay men often seem overly enamored of the very culture that stigmatizes them (the collector or connoisseur who gives proof of his possession and appreciation of "class" and his refined values of exchange in his every acquisition and act—the stereotype Liberace played on; the gay bureaucrat who, like the title character in *The Dresser,* serves his master patiently and in suffering love; Oscar Wilde via Dorian Grey): we must see beneath this the paradox that such men actually exist without a culture, without reference outside themselves. The culture they discover or produce upon coming out—gay subculture—has no relevance to their natal culture; be that upper or lower class, of whatever ethnic extraction or blend, their natal culture is still heterosexual in its institutions and values—in fact, heterosexuality is its chief institution.[12] This lack of outside reference may be one of the reasons for modern art's intrigue with what we call non- or self-referentiality and for homosexuality's constitution as one of the modern arts (in this case an art where "self"-referential and "non"-referential gloss similar meanings). In either of these explanations, whether one sees art or homosexuality as the initiating gesture of this modernist relationship, both exist in their most self-affirming form without reference to an outside world and serve as paradigms for one another.

The gay absorption into signs, meanings, interpretation, and art is related to the fact that for the homosexual the "problem of homosexuality" is in fact the problem of signs. This is not just another version of the lesson all minority peoples learn about power and language—that they are already inscribed within a language not their own and in a position incongruent with their experience of and aspirations for themselves. Nor should this appear merely another version of poststructuralist notions of the construction of subjectivity. The contentions here draw on Althusserian and Lacanian notions of the subject—both of which suggest that subjectivity is constructed (ideologically and erotically) through loss, displacement, and oppression. But I wish to preserve a distinction between this "everyman" reading of the subject's oppression and what seems to me a particular formation built upon the repression of homosexuality. The problem of signs for the homosexual is inescapable. One is taught young, for instance, that homosexuality is a semiotic, that there are *signs* of it, and that one ought not to produce those signs. Even as children (perhaps especially as children), gays are taught to hide their own signs and substitute those of the dominant culture: boys who are sissies internalize quite early that the signs of their sissihood are (absurdly, for they seem self-produced and contiguous with identity) their enemy. They may in fact recognize that those who object to these signs are also enemies, but the outcome is more often than not the repression of the signs of sissihood (assuming here that children have not yet the code words "gay" or "homosexual"). One false (and therefore true) sign is enough to bring on danger in certain situations, literal exposure to persecution. So the problematic of the sign is forced upon the homosexual at an early age—and in a manner that differs experientially from that detailed, for instance, in Afro-American texts, for there the sign of difference (blackness) is not considered to be within one's control.[13] The sign of homosexuality, however, is a behavior, an attitude, is (if one follows Beaver on this) the very production of signs itself; it is assumed therefore that this sign is within one's control and is something one has chosen to produce. The ascription of choice or agency is what makes homosexuality not merely a pathological or pitiable condition according to the ideology of Western cultures but a "perverse" one as well.

For such reasons, homosexuality comes to the homosexual early as a denaturalized sign, intruded into his life *as a sign*, turned by others from a "natural expression" into a sign that can henceforth be significant only of his own alienation from his body and from the social fabric woven by the power of others. Even in his privacy, his self-consciousness, the homosexual knows himself by the sign he must deny—or, alternatively, the sign he must affirm. In a remarkable passage from *The Naked Civil Servant*, Quentin Crisp comments upon the experience I have been describing here. He locates the source of his liberation in that moment when he took control of his own signs, when he decided to exploit the appearance of homosexuality in makeup and dress:

> I was from birth an object of mild ridicule because of my movements—especially the perpetual flutter of my hands—and my voice. Like the voices of a number of homosexuals, this is an insinuating blend of eagerness and caution in which even such words as "hello" and "goodbye" seem not so much uttered as divulged. But these natural outward and visible signs of inward and spiritual disgrace were not enough. People could say that I was ignorant of them or was trying without success to hide them. I wanted it to be known that I was not ashamed and therefore had to display symptoms that could not be thought to be accidental. (28).

Whether a self-denying or -affirming gay man (and Crisp is—especially for his generation—singularly brave in his ability to flaunt signs and thereby flout conventions), the self a homosexual constructs must resist multiple pressures of erasure, most of which he is conscious of; and even when it is recuperated into political conservatism, the homosexual's subjectivity is always already poststructural, a personal narrative experienced as absence and denial.

The thicket of issues surrounding homosexuality's relation to narcissism will be taken up in more detail below, but it is important here to suggest that homosexual writers so consistently take as their text the construction of the self that one is tempted to claim there is only one genre of homosexual writing: the autobiographical. If, as the conclusion to Quentin Crisp's *The Naked Civil Servant* suggests, the homosexual knows nothing, the nothing with which he is most intimately acquainted is his self, and the homosexual may well be so absorbed in the status of his self because that self has had only negative definitions in culture—religious, legal, and (more recently) pathological ones, all of which have found homosexuality to be a lack of positive virtue, civic responsibility, and mental health. Guy Hocquenghem's claim that "homosexuality is first of all a criminal category" (*Homosexual Desire*, 53) still has relevance.[14] If he is only an after-image of others, an example of style rather than the possessor of an achieved, whole identity, the only question for the homosexual is "Who am I?" or, in its bitchier versions, "How do I look?" This is the disturbingly true force of the humor in Frank O'Hara's "Poem (The eager note on my door said 'Call me)." In that poem, the speaker arrives home, finds what he takes to be an invitation on his door, and stops briefly to "straighten" his "eyelids and shoulders" before racing off to what he expects will be a sexual rendezvous. When he arrives at his destination, the "host" (whom he knows "only casually") is dead, "flat on a sheet of blood that / ran down the stairs," presumably a suicide. The speaker responds to this spectacle in a manner that chills us because of his inability to respond emotionally to the death of another: he says only, "I did appreciate it. There are few / hosts who so thoroughly prepare to greet a guest" (14). Perhaps most chilling in this is the implication that the scene is a display with the casual viewer rather than the corpse at its emotional center. All that O'Hara's speaker can say is "What has this to do with me? How do *I* look?" That such self-absorption is not true of all homosexuals in all times and places needs, of course, to be stated; but as with most of O'Hara's work, this particular text reads fully only when one recognizes the semiotics of gay culture it exploits—in this case, self-absorption.

The issues identified here as homosexual are essential to a more informed study of Hart Crane. For instance, Crane's ubiquitous metaphors of voyaging and bridging quite obviously admit of the kind of analysis Stockinger provides, and his trope of poetry as a bridge where the local may become the transcendental likewise echoes Stockinger's theme of transformed space. The notion of identity and ego formation is more complex in Crane than in Stockinger's paradigm of deep/surface structure, but certainly Crane employs the iconography of narcissism or mirror-transformation that Stockinger finds important to the theme of homosexual identity (the reading of "Recitative" that closes this chapter focuses on one instance of this image in Crane's text). The thematics and semiotics of identity in Crane are not easily glossed, but one may briefly say that the self is for him a fragmented series or sequence of events that has no continuous, coherent narrative behind it, no transcendental signified. In "Passage," which alludes to the quests in Whitman's "Passage to India" and "Out of the Cradle Endlessly Rocking," the speaking subject in the poem fails to achieve the integrated personhood that provided Whitman with a tropic triumph over death. In "Passage," the journey of one's life becomes the book of one's life, leading to the death that is experienced as writing. One's "too well-known biography" eventuates only in the knowledge that "Memory, committed to the page, had broke"—an odd and ungrammatical participial that suggests both the brokenness of the syntax of memory and the incomplete, bankrupt quality of biography: this is a far cry from the transcendent ego of Whitman (*Poems*, 21, 22). There are, of course, less complex figurations of identity in Crane, but subjectivity is most often for him indeterminate in precisely the way that Marjorie Perloff has suggested Symbolist poetics from Rimbaud to Cage are indeterminate; it is decentered, syntactically skewed, glimpsed rather than known. For Crane there are only signs of self-knowledge—signs behind signs behind signs. Leo Bersani, in *Baudelaire and Freud*, has suggested that "literature has always celebrated marginal or partial selves, . . . a disseminated, scattered self which resists all efforts to make a unifying structure of fragmented desire" that is different from "both the socially defined self and the transcendent (or free or universal) self" (3). But

Crane's is not simply a universalized "scattered self," either; his much-bemoaned linguistic density might best be seen as congruent with the notion that homosexuals are "beset by signs."[15]

In discussing *Roland Barthes sur Roland Barthes* and its desire for multiple meanings, sexualities, and desires beyond any taxonomy, Harold Beaver writes that "a plurality of signs constitutes Sodom; or rather, Sodom becomes wholly a matter of the plurality of signs" ("Homosexual Signs," 199). The latter half of this statement deserves our attention, for while Crane may not see homosexuality as precisely symmetrical to semiotic plurality, as "*wholly* [my emphasis] a matter of the plurality of signs," his work does posit a relation between plural semiosis and homosexual experience. This may be due in part to the fact that homosexuality for Crane lacked a fixed meaning and could only be interpreted and represented in a variety of discourses each of which assigned it a position of meaning but none of which defined it. In "Voyages," the sequence of poems that began in celebration of his affair with Emil Opffer, one of the poem's stated purposes is to show how the "tendered theme" or expression of love for another man "bears" "Infinite consanguinity" (*Poems*, 37) to any number of other themes or discourses. While critics have attempted to restrict "Voyages" to universalist readings—claiming that an insistence upon its reference to homosexuality would reduce its consanguineous or intertextual life—this seems to me the very opposite of the poem's significance: in it Crane insists that homosexuality be seen as infinitely consanguineous. But if one moves from the question of theme to the question of signs (the homosexual question), "Voyages" becomes an even more pointed example of the homosexual text. Just as the sequence may not celebrate marriage but finds it necessary to displace that honored image of closure, so the marriage of signifiers and signifieds is deferred throughout the text. Words move horizontally among the poems of the sequence or break into morphemes that find momentary couplings with other morphemes, none of which "means" with the finality and hierarchy associated with phallocratic readings that pursue the single, virgin Word. For instance, the penultimate stanza to "Voyages IV" reads:

> In signature of the incarnate word
> The harbor shoulders to resign in mingling
> Mutual blood, transpiring as foreknown
> And widening noon within your breast for gathering

All bright insinuations that my years have caught
For islands where must lead inviolably
Blue latitudes and levels of your eyes,—
(*Poems*, 38)

On the poem's most external, referential level, this stanza depicts the lover's physical return to the harbor, once again enabling that mingling of the "mutual blood" of passion and the miracle of communication in love where the "bright insinuations" of one seem gathered in the "Blue latitudes and levels" of the other's eyes. This "widening noon" within the breast, this love gathers an "incarnate word" full of meanings where the body and its languages are coterminous.

But Crane's text is extraordinarily complex; this brief gloss can only be the initiatory gesture of an analysis. For instance, it would at first seem that the "bright insinuations" are the poet's words become islands where the blue eyes of his beloved may read "inviolably," the poem on the page no longer susceptible to mutability. But on further consideration, we see that this reading is wrong; it is not the poet whose words lead the lover's eyes inviolably on the page but the blue latitudes and levels of the lover's eyes that do the leading—inviolably. Thus, Crane inverts agency and action here, refusing the categories of grammatical subject and object just as homosexuality refuses the easy sexual categories of activity and passivity, the possessor and "his" possessed. Our own eyes, violated by this, suddenly read backward in search of the "key" to this verbal clue, as if some antecedent will settle this dilemma. They are led back to "islands" and to the floating preposition "for," but this preposition is attached not so much to what the years have caught in insinuations as to the parallel constructions "for gathering" and "foreknown" (and in this context "for gathering" becomes "foregathering"). Surely this construction strains at meaning, and we are forced to compound the problem by asking how it is exactly that one leads "inviolably." One leads inevitably, perhaps, but not "inviolably." Here Crane breaks the semantic plane of the poem while seeming to remain true to the paradigmatic choices provided by syntactical drives. On first reading this passage, then, we read the line "wrong," and on further reading have decided that the only way to read it "properly" is to say that the poet has used the wrong word. But in fact, it is exactly the right word, for to lead "inviolably" would be to lead toward some specific goal but a goal kept secret and sacred—just as meaning is in this text.

The trick in reading Crane, and what amounts to his investment in the problem of language, is that none of these meanings (and one hesitates to use such a teleologically tainted word) is final, better, or even "right." As in this brief passage, Crane forces his reader into the problematic conjunction of language and authority throughout his work. Well beyond the strict determination which grounds irony in most modernist writing, meaning, such as it occurs in Crane, is a process of indeterminacy, is constituted precisely in the abrupt disfigurements and dislocations, in the sudden clarities and semantic possibilities of writing. Meaning in Crane is always structural and relational, and, finally, even the morphemes "trans" and "sign" in the passage above locate themselves as meaningful only in their relation to other passages of the text. This play with language even on the level of the morphemic is not a leitmotif but the radical impossibility of simultaneity: it is Crane's practice of what deconstructionists term dissemination.

Although he does not pursue this analogy, Guy Hocquenghem's comments on homo*sexual* promiscuity are relevant to this homo*textual* promiscuity. He writes, "It is generally assumed that what we may call homosexual "scattering" . . . expresses the fundamental instability of the homosexual condition. . . . But instead of translating this scattering of love-energy as the inability to find a centre, we could see it as a system in action, the system in which polyvocal desire is plugged in on a universal basis" (117). As is clear from one's first encounter with the above passage, as with any of Crane's more difficult texts, "Voyages" is a virtual orgy of meanings—every linguistic position is tried, every coupling imaginable exploited. We can see this as well in the poem's moment of self-referentiality, that point at which Crane names the process of composition the "silken skilled transmemberment of song" (*Poems*, 37). As in the above example, meaning in this phrase depends upon a process that is at once both strictly determined and strangely indeterminate; it is easier, for instance, to say what the word "transmemberment" points toward as shadow meanings than it is to say what it means in a positive, referential sense. It is not "transformation," for instance, where one thing becomes another, more privileged thing. Nor is it "dismemberment" or some naively whole "rememberment"; it is a term whose axes of reference and meaning reach in all of these directions at once, suggesting in its very constitution that a rhetoric of metonymic desire and misrecognition, of catachresis or misnaming, is relevant to the figuring of homosexual relation in a way that a more conventional poetics of metaphor, memory, and transcendental transformation would not be.[16] If the final "meaning" of "transmemberment" is unsettled and unspecific, if it remains a term without positive reference definable only in its differential relation to all these other terms it is not, it is nonetheless neither more nor less but exactly the sum of its parts. What makes Crane's text difficult, and where the "plurality of signs" takes its deepest root, is on this level of syntax and semantics: his words know no limit to the orbit of their "meanings."

Allen Grossman, who is perhaps the best reader of Crane among those who have attempted a systematic evaluation of his work, links this style to desire in writing about the "trope peculiar to" Crane, the trope of condensation:

> This crowding of the frame (Crane's "verbal *bricolage*") came to constitute a trope peculiar to himself—not the modernist "ambiguity" which hierarchizes, or ironically totalizes a plurality of meanings—but a singularly naive rhetoric of shadowed wholeness (the impossible simultaneity of all the implications of desire) that struggles merely to include all meanings in the one space of appearance. ("Hart Crane and Poetry," 229)

John Irwin also writes of Crane's dense, obscure style:

> The characteristic surface form of many of his short, highly compact poems is simply a linked series of complex vehicles for a suppressed tenor. And the dynamics of these poems hinge on the reader's discovery, through his knowledge of connotations, of the one tenor to which all the vehicles can possibly refer. ("Hart Crane's 'Logic of Metaphor,'" 212)

The poems Irwin has in mind here are those of "Voyages," poems whose suppressed tenor is homosexual love.[17] It should not be surprising that this subject results in a poetics of "inferential mention" (Crane's phrase echoed by Irwin), in a simultaneous multiplication of signs and obfuscation of meanings. By refusing "natural" language and employing in its stead a language full to the very limit of meaning, Crane invites his reader into a process equivalent to the transformative space Stockinger calls homotextual. The reader enters what appears to be a narrow linguistic cell in which the text appears overdetermined, suffocated in the density of its own semiotics; but once there, if s/he accepts the full gambit of that text, s/he participates in the production of an elaborate and powerful transformation from overdetermined but opaque signs into indeterminate pluralities of meaning. Whitman's *Calamus* provides an interesting gloss on this triangulation of homoerotic desire, linguistic displacement, and readerly identification in terms that suggest the relation "inferential mention" might have to the secret nature of homosexual desire: "Ah lover and perfect equal, / I meant that you should discover me so by faint indirections" (*Leaves of Grass*, 135). Gertrude Stein's *Tender Buttons* offers a lesbian equivalent to this based on the principle that the difference of writing is "not unordered in not resembling" and provides, therefore, "an arrangement in a system to pointing" (9).

Given the closeted nature of homosexuality in Crane's era, it is not surprising that we find the more literal figure of an enclosed space as homosexual refuge in a number of his poems. More interestingly, Crane's text often gestures quite dramatically toward a utopian site of order, meaning, and significance. Other places become the locus of a union and meaning unattainable in this "broken world" (*Poems*, 193): Atlantis, Belle Isle (in "Voyages VI"), the internalized tower that is "healed, original now, and pure" in "The Broken Tower." These are the sites on which interpretation will no longer be the human problematic. This may seem quite obviously a version of Romantic quest, or of what Julia Kristeva has called "an adult (male and female) fantasy of a lost continent . . . , an idealization of primary narcissism" that is at base consecration and longing for the maternal ("Stabat Mater," 99). But although this site becomes desirable for Crane as an escape from the historical oppression of homosexual desire, his is not finally a homosexual utopia as in *Calamus* or as in the nostalgic revolution championed by Allen Ginsberg. The utopian space in Crane is a transformation of historical space, often a homosexual and limited space, but it usually marks an escape from rather than a fulfillment of homosexual desire. Thus, although it is often approached through love or quite explicitly through orgasm, the utopian in Crane signifies a desire to escape history and becomes a site on which homosexuality—as a historical, material condition of modernity—is annihilated. The desiring homosexual body remains in his text, like the Brooklyn Bridge in the "Proem" to *The Bridge*, "obscure as that heaven of the Jews," only the "Terrific threshold of the prophet's pledge, / Prayer of pariah, and the lover's cry" (*Poems*, 46).

But this annihilation can itself become the site of a certain textual jouissance: the final orgasm that does not merely release but destroys desire. This sexual utopian fantasy is often figured in Crane either as death or as ecstatic dismemberment. It is one of the paradoxes of homosexuality's ideological construction that it finds meaning both in liberation and in guilt, and this is the paradox expressed in Crane's trope of erotic suffering, seen in the figure of "This cleaving and this burning" in "Legend." Guy Hocquenghem writes that, under the clinical norms of heterosexuality, homosexuality:

> is experienced only at the price of castration; to be homosexual is to have been castrated by the father. The homosexual receives his meaning from the sex-dispensing phallus. Castration/sacrifice: the expiatory gift of masculinity. . . . Schreber [in Freud's famous account] experiences homosexuality as a heterosexual would imagine it to be experienced. In a way, Sartre's Genet (for Genet belongs to Sartre as surely as Schreber belongs to Freud) also affirms the sacrificial role of passive homosexuality. . . . Homosexuality is redeemed by the absolute gift—the total sacrifice, where pleasure is what is prohibited. (*Homosexual Desire*, 70)

Thus, castration or dismemberment becomes in Crane the moment of controlled desire and meaning, of entry into and submission before the Symbolic law of the father—not so much the prohibition of pleasure as one of its only "legitimate" (i.e., sublimated) sites.[18] This, too, performs its ideological work; as Leo Bersani suggests, "Perhaps the principal strategy for stabilizing the self, both for individuals and for entire cultures, is to plot the immobilization of desire" (*Baudelaire and Freud*, 61). Harold Beaver also suggests one of the ways in which orgasm and death are structurally related:

> Erotic arousal, much as verbal arousal, is not capable of functioning as unmediated or uncontrived expression. Neither verbal nor genital play is ever self-sufficient in this sense. Other objects are needed as signifiers in thought or deed for our fantasies of self-projection. The crisis of discharge, moreover, far from being transparent, cuts us off from even the least glimpse of ourselves since consciousness notoriously blanks out at the point of communication, in consummation or orgasm. Such climax is literally ecstatic, a jubilant dislocation or short-circuit of the self. ("Homosexual Signs," 116)

For the homosexual, less rapidly interpellated into the mediating structures of social relation, law, and order, such ecstatic blackouts are all the more pursued as the true, ecstatic end of sexual bliss—and of personal, social organization. In its location of meaning in orgasmic annihilation, Crane's text is congruent with erotic tropes in Mishima or with the terms Roland Barthes develops in one of his homosexual texts, *The Pleasure of the Text*. In its trope of loss as sublime, Crane's is what Barthes would call a text of bliss rather than a text of pleasure:

> Text of pleasure: the text that contents, fills, grants euphoria, the text that comes from culture and does not break with it, is linked to a *comfortable* reading. Text of bliss: the text that imposes a state of loss, the text that discomforts (perhaps to the point of a certain boredom), unsettles the reader's historical, cultural, psychological assumptions, the consistency of his tastes, values, memories, brings to a crisis his relation with language. (14)

Crane's text indeed "brings to a crisis his [reader's] relation with language" in a manner few texts of other modernist poets in America do. In their insistence upon linguistic deviations, and in their castration of socially comfortable reading, Crane's texts unsettle the reader's "historical, cultural, psychological assumptions."

Each of the motifs of homotextuality glossed here is not evident in all of Crane's poems, of course, and there are some poems to which these concerns seem completely irrelevant. But the emphasis in that phrase should fall on "seem," for if the question of homosexuality has been unexamined in responses to Crane's work, a fuller understanding of its thematic and semiotic parameters can help illuminate the problem of Crane's textual impenetrability and make something of texts that have remained largely impenetrable to straight criticism. R. W. B. Lewis is perhaps the most normative and "American" of Crane's major critics, the one least likely to admit analysis of homosexuality into his criticism, and I would like to turn to a poem that clearly baffles Lewis, "Recitative," to show how treating it as a homosexual text can explain some of its obscurities. "Recitative" is a poem concerned with dualities of many kinds, but especially with the interweaving of self and Other identified above as a crucial homotextual site; it places a particular (if at first mysterious) premium upon the power of the sign *as sign*. In attempting to analyze the poem—which he calls a minor effort to be read in an "exemplary rather than exhaustive" fashion (*The Poetry of Hart Crane*, 132)[19]—Lewis cites a letter Crane wrote to Allen Tate that describes "the poet, say, on a platform speaking" the poem (*Letters*, 176). Crane admits that the poem is "complex, exceedingly," and he offers this avenue into it:

> The audience is one half of Humanity, Man (in the sense of Blake) and the poet the other. ALSO, the poet sees himself in the audience as in a mirror. ALSO, the audience sees itself, in part, in the poet. Against this paradoxical DUALITY is posed the UNITY, or the conception of it (as you got it) in the last verse. (*Letters*, 176)

Lewis is correct to suggest that this gloss is at once a "helpful and a baffling explanation," for while it does permit us to recognize the mirror images in the poem (a "plate of vibrant mercury," a "glass") it baffles by leaving much unsaid, and it has the predictable effect of limiting Lewis's reading to a Blakean paradigm. Lewis claims that the letter alerts one to the universal concerns of the poem, that it "intimates the three kinds of actual division and potential unity the poem is concerned with: the relation between the poet and his audience, or mankind; the relation between mankind and itself (the divided world); the relation between the poet and his own self" (*The Poetry of Hart Crane*, 128–29).[20] Lewis adds this last possibility because Crane added it later in his letter: "In another sense, the poet is *talking to himself* all the way through the poem." The strength of the italics suggests that this may have been one of the poem's central concerns. What is more interesting, however, is what Lewis ignores from the letter. Crane links "Recitative" to "Possessions," a poem clearly concerned with the metaphysics of homosexual desire;[21] he wrote the two poems at the same time, sent them together to Tate, and refers to them both in the letter cited here as examples of his work's movement toward what he calls "a more perfect lucidity." He claims, rather disingenuously it would seem, that neither was intended as "wilfully obscure or esoteric."[22] But Crane disallows some of the meanings of "Recitative" in the very letter in which he explicates others, and this denial should draw our attention. After writing that the poem perhaps represents the poet's conversation with himself, he goes on to add that he ought not to go too deeply into the matter, implying that some breach of decorum might be made: "There are, as too often in my poems, other reflexes and symbolisms in the poem, also, which it would be silly to write here—at least for the present" (*Letters*, 176). Certainly, this last sentence may merely indicate artistic modesty, or Crane's weariness with explaining texts often considered overwrought and *too* meaning-full. But then Crane was not a particularly modest writer, and modesty itself covers with silence a number of otherwise inappropriate subjects. As the third chapter of this study suggests, Crane felt compelled in his correspondence with figures like Tate, as in his poetry, to elide the specific details of his homosexuality. As early as 1923, less than one year before this letter to Tate, he had written to Gorham Munson, "I discover that I have been all-too-easy all along in letting out announcements of my sexual predilections" (*Letters*, 138). And in sending a copy of "Recitative" in manuscript to Munson in December 1923, Crane alluded to an earlier version of the poem that was written in his "somewhat flamboyant period" of New York (the homosexual nature of which period is also examined in chapter 3), adding that he felt this tighter version better than the "original confession." The poem remains confessional in its finished version, and one of the "silly reflexes" that Crane feels he cannot divulge in the letter to Tate might include (among other "symbolisms") the poem's homosexual iconography and referents.

"Recitative" opens in a swirl of virtually unreadable images, asking the reader in its first phrase to "Regard the capture here" of something not yet perceptible, a thing that remains obscure even after the poem has been read. In this, it is identical in strategy to "Possessions," which opens, "Witness now this trust!" The difficulty of these texts Robert Combs rightly ascribes to the fact that they "[delay] interpretational clues which serve gradually to orient the reader," and their images seem therefore "elements in a mysterious allegory" (*Vision of the Voyage*, 65). The initiating dislocation of both these poems is, I would claim, a homosexual gesture, and their intrigue with secrecy an allegory of homosexual experience. Lewis sees the poem as an investigation of Crane's anguish over how lust disrupts the poet's vision and suggests that the poem rejects a "lust-centered" vision of creativity for a more centralizing notion of community. But he never asks why or how lust had become a question of urgency for Crane. In fact, among Crane's serious critics only Robert Martin is able to do so, and it is only Martin among those critics who reads the trope of divided consciousness in "Recitative" as a problem of homosexual identity, as referring to the paradox of discovering oneself whole in the double known as the lover. Martin takes the poem as a discourse between lovers, as I do below, and his summary of the poem's movement fits quite neatly into the paradigm of transfigured or bridged space in which the homosexual discovers himself no longer alienated. Although I have severe disagreements with some of Martin's tenets, his comments on "Recitative" are worth noting:

> He [the poet] appears to identify his quest for sexual union with the Platonic theme of the quest for reunion of the divided self, so that the meeting of two men as lovers becomes a restoration of lost twinship. Only the discovery of this other "half" can restore the speaker's lost unity. . . . Thus the speaker in "Recitative" calls upon his "shadow" to accept the love which is proffered him and to respond by crossing the bridge. . . . The single stride of the last stanza . . . is a triumphant coming together, in which what was once separate is now perceived to be whole. The "darkness" of lust "falls away," and the lovers can now "walk through time with equal pride." (*The Homosexual Tradition*, 129)

Clearly Martin is correct. Although one may deconstruct the familiarizations Martin valorizes here, the poem still reads as a lover's plea to a "brother," it investigates the marginalization of homosexuality and the privatization of desire, it offers a conclusion in the union of two men—formerly defeated rebels, now self-possessed and whole.[23]

The opening stanzas of the poem present the problem of mimesis and subjectivity in terms of a binary opposition—that duality both Crane and his critics have identified in the text. Reader and writer are "brother[s] in the half," and the text is that field in which, as in a mirror, they recognize one another and themselves through one another. Crane signifies the split consciousness implied in this binary formulation as "Janus-faced," suggesting in the colloquial idiom of the "two-faced" a hint of romantic betrayal between the men. Reading this seme as a figure for mimesis, it suggests that art's ability to mirror reality is not to be naively trusted, that there is something duplicitous, "twisted" rather than transparent and innocent, in the rhetoric of art. Crane uses two other binary oppositions ("Such eyes at *search or rest* you cannot see; / Reciting *pain or glee* how can you bear!" [my emphases]) to invoke a classic claim about the value of intersubjectivity in art and in sexual relation: that one cannot really "know" oneself or the truth of one's emotional states without some objectifying and mirroring Other whose presence makes the self real. The poem begins:

> Regard the capture here, O Janus-faced,
> As double as the hands that twist this glass.
> Such eyes at search or rest you cannot see;
> Reciting pain or glee, how can you bear!

Twin shadowed halves: the breaking second holds
In each the skin alone, and so it is
I crust a plate of vibrant mercury
Borne cleft to you, and brother in the half.
(*Poems*, 25)

The play of identity and difference that obtains in the moment of mirroring for subjects who share the same sexual identity makes Crane's description of his beloved's eyes in the second stanza ("Twin shadowed halves") more than a tropological appropriation of the lover's body. The trope of the mirror suggests not only an old figure for identity and mimesis but is also that enclosed safe space precious to the homosexual text. In this space the two may define their relation to one another without reference to an outside heterosexual world that cannot see them in differential relation to one another (and hence defined by one another) but only as different from itself. But as in all moments in Crane's dense texts, there is certainly more: if we think of each of these eyes as affected by this shadowed halving, that would suggest some duality embodied in each lover himself. His "condition" is one of alienation from himself ("Reciting pain or glee, how can you bear!"), and some space will always intervene between the two lovers despite the mirror's promise of union: "the breaking second holds / In each the skin alone." Finally, it is not so much the flat plane of the mirror itself as the act of presenting it to another ("I crust a plate of vibrant mercury / Borne cleft to you") that represents the bridge over that gap. In *Roland Barthes*, Roland Barthes comments on the desire to see oneself whole and on the lack of self-knowledge such desire announces: "You are the only one who can never see yourself except as an image; you never see your eyes unless they are dulled by the gaze they rest upon the mirror or the lens (I am interested in seeing my eyes only when they look at you): even and especially for your own body, you are condemned to the repertoire of its images" (39). Crane would have his poem, like the mirror which is its initiating trope, become that field in which the gaze is not dulled, become the site rather where one might see one's own eyes as they appear when they take their pleasure—when they look at "I" in "you."

The narcissistic imagery in this has been a conventional sign for homosexuality at least since Oscar Wilde; at least since that time homosexuality has been coded as a gaze in the mirror, and through that image both its sexual symmetry and its purported limitations have been stressed. Guy Hocquenghem has argued that under the regime of Oedipalized desire, the narcissism of homosexuality has indeed been enforced: "Just as neurosis becomes homosexuality's mode of existence, so too does narcissism become the theme of its operation" (*Homosexual Desire*, 67). It is the latter of these that has been used to censure homosexuality by charging it with everything from immaturity to moral and political failure.[24] Under the Oedipal repression of pleasure, as Hocquenghem sees it, homosexuality is defined as a lack (in this case by its inability to identify a proper sexual object in women), and since woman is the phallus homosexuality may never possess except in internalized parodies that lack can never be overcome.[25] Freud's 1910 edition of *Three Essays on the Theory of Sexuality* provides the classic formulation that homosexual men "proceed from a narcissistic basis, and look for a young man who resembles themselves and whom *they* may love as their mother loved *them*" (11n), and it is very possible (if not certain) that Crane was familiar with this theory of homosexuality as arrested development; it may in fact be the referent for "the legend of their youth" in the homosexual text of "Legend." Although particular texts are not mentioned in his published correspondence, he seems to have read on the subject, and Unterecker's biography even suggests that he passed some texts and theories on to his mother when he came out to her in 1927 (*Voyager*, 534–35).

If by the poem's close Crane has constructed a way out of the imprisoning conditions of homosexuality for himself and his Other/lover (the injunction to "leave the tower" may be seen as a call to come out, as an image of abandoning the closet), this transformational strategy is already in place in the poem in Crane's transformation of the trope of narcissism in the poem's opening stanzas. Rejecting the familiar charge of solipsism as the constitutive effect of narcissism, Crane "twists this glass" of limited self-interest into the possibility for doubling. The relation established between writer and reader is one of initiator to initiand, and the existentially authentic homosexual self, developed in the dynamic between two men, is no longer adequately identifiable as a stable, narcissistic icon in the mirror. It must instead be seen as inhering in the act of mirroring and doubling itself, as a process that refuses the very notion of subject and object. Rather than being evidence of the inability to adequately imagine an Other, narcissism (finding the likeness of self in the other as mirror) becomes for the homosexual the only productive way in which to imagine an Other. And as the poem develops, we see a dynamic of sympathy, seduction, and instruction that is made possible only by the speaker and the lover sharing the same position in culture: the ritual enactment in the poem brings its initiand into a state of being and knowledge already inhabited by the speaker.[26]

The third stanza of the poem presents three imperatives meant to guide the naive brother through the duplicities of homoerotic attachment and it begins Crane's examination of the way in which obstacles to homosexual affirmation may be overcome. This section of the poem seems to ask, "Once one has been freed from the prison of self-oppression through identification with an other, what is it that one may experience or claim to know emotionally? What is the ego's store of pleasure and pain?" The answer Crane offers suggests that the ego has only signs through which to construct the meanings of affective states, that "love" or intimate connection of the type exemplified when the self is "born/e" to and in another is a matter of interpretation, of choosing among multiple signifiers:

> Inquire this much-exacting fragment smile,
> Its drums and darkest blowing leaves ignore,—
> Defer though, revocation of the tears
> That yield attendance to one crucial sign.
>
> (*Poems*, 25)

The latter half of the stanza is obscure, but the advice offered in the first half seems actually rather mundane: attend, the speaker seems to suggest, the bright rather than the stormy aspects of relation; emphasize the joy that is possible in relation (the "smile") even if that joy is always fragmented by virtue of the intractable nature of desire—in this case a homosexual desire that refuses social centering. This may argue for repression, for forgetting altogether the "drums and darkest blowing leaves" of desire (one hears here Stevens's "Passions of rain, or moods in falling snow; / . . . gusty / Emotions on wet roads on autumn nights" [*Collected Poems*, 67]). But even if Crane is arguing here for a platonic rather than a sexual relation (the smile is often read in Crane criticism as a maternal and therefore supposedly asexual writing of desire), we must see that as part of the constitutive paradox of homosexuality for his generation. As Robert Martin and others have pointed out, the homosexual was allowed a positive self-image if he or she had no homo*sexual* desire or experience, and we see in the Matthiessen-Cheney letters that the sexual *and* emotionally fulfilling nature of their relationship seemed to make little sense to them because they had been taught never to expect to find these two qualities in the same relationship. Hence, Crane's concern for the dual structure of identity is part of a discourse that constructed homosexuality as itself a set of dualities and contradictions, and we can see that the platonic was one half of the homosexual problematic rather than an escape from it. In directing the emotional vocabulary of homosexuality away from its stereotypical tragic style, Crane does not simply counsel the substitution of "happiness," as might at first be expected; the poem is not simply an argument for disco. "Defer . . . revocation of the tears," it says, and while it is not immediately clear what those tears signify (although they are perhaps themselves the "crucial sign")[27] it is essential to see that Crane does not discount them. They are merely deferred. For Crane, suffering is constitutive of identity—of homosexual identity.

The next stanza suggests as well that the darker side of homosexuality, its "lust," cannot be ignored, and it seems to imply that pain and dislocation can be transformed:

> Look steadily—how the wind feasts and spins
> The brain's disk shivered against lust. Then watch
> While darkness, like an ape's face, falls away,
> And gradually white buildings answer day.
> (*Poems*, 25)

It is difficult not to read this as a series of binary oppositions that imply and substitute for one another in a cycle as "natural" as dawn's displacement of night. Apollonian and Dionysian orders compete for control in the figures of the brain and lust, and the "ape's face" of darkness gives way to purity cast across a huge cultural space: the entire city now a structure not of discontent but of purpose and oneness, an "answer" or solution. But what we find here is not so much a balance achieved as an irreconcilability exposed—the mutually exclusive categories of homosexual desire and civic order. If the wind alludes to Shelley's inspiriting Other, it does not supersede or solve the problem of sexuality in the modern world, for "lust" remains fixed in Crane's formulation. It is, rather, repressive rationality ("the brain's disk") which is "shivered" by the force of this wind: sensual, feasting inspiration destroys rationality by shattering it against eros, and eros gives way to a dawn in which "white buildings" write the phallic as a pure civic space. If the enclosed space is a privileged site for the homosexual, so too is darkness a cover and the realm of romantic possibility a cruisey street (in *The Bridge*, Crane writes: "Under thy shadow by the piers I waited"; "—As I have trod the rumorous midnights, too"). But the darkness in this stanza is certainly threatening as well, perhaps an index of the way in which homosexuality is interpreted or a symbol of its inability to signify and articulate itself. Sexuality figured as an ape's face implies not just the bestial quality of lust but also the uncanniness of sexual desire, for the ape's face mimics in a false mirroring that threatens always to become a mockery. As such it is the cultural Otherness of homosexual desire, its uncanny ape face, rather than desire itself that the text claims here must and will pass. Once one acknowledges the legitimacy of that desire, the repressions of the brain's disk are shivered, and homosexuality no longer seems a darkness. At that point, one may even read the phallic mirrors of production that define culture, "white buildings," as positive transformations of desire. Thus, the ape's face figures a theory of evolution as well, Crane's dream of cultural melioration in which the homosexual would no longer be the "shadowed half" of himself.

But this desublimated homosexuality does not resolve the issue of duality for the homosexual; the gulf between desire and civic order still remains, and Crane's next two stanzas historicize this gap as a problem produced within contemporary culture by patriarchal repression. The homosexual is figured here within an Oedipal script, as Absalom, and the phallic buildings of the previous stanza are exposed as girders of steel whose promise of wholeness is an illusion. Some irremediable division, a "nameless gulf," is still the constitutive element of identity:

> Let the same nameless gulf beleaguer us—
> Alike suspend us from atrocious sums
> Built floor by floor on shafts of steel that grant
> The plummet heart, like Absalom, no stream.
>
> The highest tower,—let her ribs palisade
> Wrenched gold of Nineveh;—yet leave the tower.
> The bridge swings over salvage, beyond wharves;
> A wind abides the ensign of your will . . .
>
> (*Poems*, 25)

The poem heretofore has sought symbolic terms and structures through which to produce some hope of synchronic unity from the fragmentations it glosses. What Crane emphasizes about the poem by taking its phrase "white buildings" as the title for his volume is a Symbolist notion that poems themselves may be read as "white buildings," as the structures Grossman calls "orphic machines" of "shadowed wholeness." But the individual text in this case, "Recitative," will not allow this desire for synchronic perfection to obscure what is problematic about the image. These two stanzas examine the image of the white building in terms that manifest its status as a construct ("built floor by floor on shafts of steel"); they deconstruct it as a pure presence and expose its understructure as allied to a system of patriarchal acquisition and repression "that grant / The plummet heart, like Absalom, no stream," a system in which the homosexual will always be punished and alien.

These stanzas suggest, finally, that the phallic cannot be the locus of a liberated homosexuality, that masculinity is too compromised in its current cultural construction to provide any answer to the problem of identification that the homosexual finds himself forced to enact. As Jeffrey Weeks writes in his preface to Hocquenghem's *Homosexual Desire*, "As money is the fetish, the true universal reference-point for capitalism, so the Phallus is the reference-point for heterosexism" (24). Thus, one must "leave the tower" of civic order to find one's liberation. The feminine pronoun describing the "highest tower" may be Crane's coy refusal of gender categories but seems more probably to point to the fact that in capitalist culture the "female" is the highest tower, the highest fetish, sign and seal of male accomplishment, with no value except in her ability to reflect male worth. The female may at first seem a refuge for the homosexual, either providing sisterly or maternal protection for him or offering a model of identification. But such a hope is complicated by the fact that the feminine is itself a category of the patriarchy, is itself trapped in the tower of narcissistic lack. It is not clear that Crane had himself worked out a theory of gender as a system of differences within capitalist culture, but it is clear that the difference of gender is encoded in this text at the same moment that capitalism enters. We can only conclude that heterosexuality—as an institutional practice—is implied here as the highest tower or reification of desire just as gold is the fetish of labor, and that the homosexual must reject both if he is to have access to any sense of self-definition and empowerment.

Certainly there is here some biographical trauma; the poem should not be read without at least some acknowledgment of Crane's financial estrangement from American culture, an estrangement that in his (as in other gay men's lives) might be interpreted within the Oedipal paradigm of the family romance. Certainly we can read his rejection of a career in his father's business and his almost willful inability to find and keep gainful employment throughout his adult life as instances of Oedipal rebellion. But the Oedipal is exactly what "Recitative" attempts to overturn; "far from being a product of the Oedipus complex, as some Freudians imply," Jeffrey Weeks writes, male homosexuality "constitutes a totally different mode of social relationships, no longer vertical, but horizontal" (*Homosexual Desire*, 23). In rejecting the tower (the constructed phallus of law and order), Crane rejects the vertical arrangement of culture that includes the Oedipalized control of homosexual desires; the bridge, an image of horizontal organization, is what Crane privileges instead. For the homosexual, to do battle within the Oedipal family is always to lose his homosexual desire—either to the "triumph" of heterosexuality or to repression: he will always be Absalom suspended from the verticality he sought to challenge.

The wind that "abides the ensign of your will" in this other space is the wind from the fourth stanza become transparent to a homosexual libido free to pursue its own desires. The crucial sign of homosexuality is no longer an external one of difference but has become incorporated as an "en-sign" into the will of the individual—a word whose suggestion of immanence makes homosexuality the same to itself rather than different from some other. This wind is the signature of homosexual identity, recalling Whitman's claim at the close of "Song of Myself"—"I depart as air" (*Leaves of Grass*, 89), and Crane claims that the coherence and transparency of this en-signature is analogous to the illusion of many bells seeming one:

> In alternating bells have you not heard
> All hours clapped dense into a single stride?
> Forgive me for an echo of these things,
> And let us walk through time with equal pride.
> (*Poems*, 26)

The poem seems at this point to have found its final image of triumph over duality, an eternal moment ("All hours clapped dense into a single stride") that will resist the narrative intrusions of a homosexual life. But the poem undercuts itself: the last two lines suggest a continued split rather than a union. The poet is no longer Narcissus but that other figure of reflection, the nymph Echo, only a partial presence, able only to call to mind half-truths, half-speech—authored by others rather than by himself (and Echo is, of course, a female rather than a male figure, allowing the notion of difference to intrude even in the mention of a "single stride"). And, if the poem begins with the problem of making homosexuality visible to itself, it ends in making it *in*visible: no one sees Echo; she is voice alone. This does not "solve" the problem of homosexual desire but merely gets rid of the body as its site. Yet these reversals help us see that the poem's conclusion is more tentative than critics have suggested: it acknowledges that words and signs are written, read, spoken, and heard but that they may not be authentic, that they are perhaps illusory and unsatisfactory instead, echoes rather than presences and hence requiring apology. Nevertheless, it is only through access to such unifying myths of desire as are recorded on the surface of the text that the homosexual and his "brother in the half" may acquire the authority to pass meaningfully through history: the equality sought in the final line surely refers to the existential *in*equality homosexuals more usually face.

Crane places "Recitative" at a crucial point in *White Buildings;* he makes it the culmination of a series of increasingly conceptual and difficult poems that include some of the most demanding in the modernist canon: "Passage," "Lachrymae Christi," "The Wine Menagerie." It is the final short lyric before the first of the volume's two major pieces, "For the Marriage of Faustus and Helen," and as such is itself a bridge from the earlier, private meditations of the volume to Crane's first attempt at larger, more culturally inclusive forms. A recitative in opera is also a bridge, of course, a bridge between arias, and "Recitative" is for *White Buildings* the bridge from personal insight to cultural prophecy, from homosexuality treated as a problem of individual difference to homosexuality understood as a cultural issue of some magnitude and intertextuality. It is very possible that Crane's use of the word "recitative" points back to Whitman's "Thou Mother with Thy Equal Brood"—not perhaps one of the bard's more felicitously titled poems, but one in which we find the following:

> A strong bird on pinions free,
> Joyous, the amplest spaces heavenward cleaving,
> Such be the thought I'd think of thee America,
> Such be the recitative I'd bring for thee.
>
> (*Leaves of Grass*, 456)

For Crane, the recitative he brings to America takes on a dimension that Whitman had abandoned by the point in his career that he wrote this stanza (1872, for the Dartmouth commencement, by which time he had rejected the utopian dimension of his own homosexual text). The poem Crane made in 1925 is more like the early, iconoclastic Whitman and takes homosexual relations seriously (if obscurely) as the center of a cultural articulation. It ignores America and seeks instead to make of the homosexual "A strong bird on pinions free, / Joyous, the amplest spaces heavenward cleaving," thereby offering a critique of American culture as powerful as anything his straight contemporaries or his homosexual predecessors had offered.

3
Homosexuality and the Subject of Literature

▼

I saw that I was capable
of pleasure: I supposed myself incapable,
strictly speaking, of desire.

ANDRÉ GIDE
Corydon

"RECITATIVE" is a telling example of how we might better understand Crane's investment in style as generated within a structure or economy of homosexual desire. But it is only in light of recent theories of the dialectical relation between language and subjectivity that we can begin to articulate that, to paraphrase Emile Benveniste, the basis of homosexuality is in the exercise of language.[1] Earlier critical responses to Crane's work most often found his language bafflingly obscure and his poetry inarticulate if intense. For instance, his first volume of poetry, *White Buildings*, appeared to ambivalent if not hostile reviews in 1926. While both text and author were granted seriousness of intention, and while the volume was reviewed by significant critics as a work of literary importance, there is in even the praiseworthy reviews a hint of suspicion and perplexity, a doubt or confusion that had already become something like a standard evaluation of Crane's work by that point. Allen Tate, persuaded to write an introduction to *White Buildings* after Eugene O'Neill was either unable or unwilling to fulfill his promise of one, addresses the complaint of Crane's obscurity as a distinct flaw: "If the energy of Crane's vision never quite reaches a sustained maximum, it is because he has not found a suitable theme" (19). And Edmund Wilson, who reviewed Crane's work as one of only "two [poetic] events which emerge as of the first interest" in 1926 ("The Muses Out of Work," 197), offers praise that is all the more damning because the tone of his essay becomes sarcastic just at the point where accolades seem about to appear: "Mr. Crane has a most remarkable style, a style that is strikingly original—almost something like a great style, if there could be such a thing as a great style which was, not merely not applied to a great subject, but not, so far as one can see, applied to any subject at all" (200). In returning "Passage" to Crane earlier in his career, Marianne Moore had struck a similar note of baffled admiration, registering some ambivalence about her rejection of the poem. She nevertheless writes as an assured editorial "we" in rejecting it: "We could not but be moved, as you must know, by the rich imagination and the sensibility of your poem, Passage. Its multiform content accounts I suppose, for what seems to us a lack of simplicity and cumulative force. We are sorry to return it" (*Letters*, 215).

What each of these criticisms registers is the degree to which Crane's work differed from that of his contemporaries in its idea and execution—and especially in its style. What Crane lacked, according to each of these assessments, was precisely what Eliot and the Imagist poets had demanded as necessary for the successful modernist poem: an objective correlative or object, a "suitable theme" or "great subject," what Stevens called an "external referent."[2] Tate recognized that Crane's verse perhaps required a different mode of evaluation than that applied to other texts of modernism, that it was difficult and intertextual in a way that broke the boundaries of the discrete poetic object:[3] "A series of Imagistic poems is a series of worlds. The poems of Hart Crane are facets of a single vision; they refer to a central imagination, a single evaluating power" (Intro., *White Buildings*, 19); he even saw that Crane's is an intertext with Blake, Shelley, and Rimbaud, but he could not sanction its "vision." Wilson also implied that Crane's appeal was to a different order of vision, and claimed that Imagism in comparison afforded "an entirely inadequate ideal of what poetry ought to be," that "persons of reading and taste" in the twenties were "tone-deaf" to the fuller poetic rhetoric in Milton and Wordsworth ("The Muses Out of Work," 198, 199). But he could not find criteria congenial to an analysis of Crane's text. Lee Edelman has recently identified the cause of this inability, and of the misrecognition of Crane's work: "Considered within a rhetorical tradition that favors tropes of integration (such as synecdoche) or analogy (such as metaphor) these unusual figures [Crane's characteristic tropes of anacoluthon, chiasmus, and catachresis] often have been overlooked completely or else misunderstood" (*"Transmemberment of Song*, 58). We will speak later of the role homopobia has played in the misunderstanding of Crane's work.

That Crane's poetry has generally been judged to be misguided in one aspect or another is beyond debate. Even as recently as 1985, Edward Brunner found such critical rhetoric inescapable, and his award-winning study of *The Bridge* is titled *Splendid Failure*. But the problem of how to evaluate Crane was exacerbated in the twenties by the incompatibility of what we might call synecdochic modernism (exemplified, albeit differently, in Moore, H. D., Eliot, Pound, and Williams) with the discourses of Romanticism that Crane took as central to his cultural project. That generation of critics who first encountered and codified the interpretation of his work almost universally excoriated Romanticism. In a particularly scathing review of *The Bridge*, for instance, Yvor Winters completely rejects the work of his former friend and claims that Crane has "demonstrated one thing": "the impossibility of getting anywhere with the Whitmanian inspiration. No writer of comparable ability has struggled with it before, and, with Mr. Crane's wreckage in view, it seems highly unlikely that any writer of comparable genius will struggle with it again" ("The Progress of Hart Crane," 108).

R. P. Blackmur offers what is perhaps one of the most succinct formulations of those assessments that have found Crane's work lacking. He closes his 1935 essay on Crane (reprinted in *Language as Gesture*) with an indictment that negates his earlier praise of specific passages and invokes the specter of biographical failure as the cause of poetic incoherence:

> It is said that Crane's inchoate heart and distorted intellect only witness the disease of his generation; but I have cited two poets [Yeats and Stevens], if not of his generation still his contemporaries, who escaped the contagion. It is the stigma of the first order of poets (a class which includes many minor names and deletes some of the best known) that they master so much of life as they represent. In Crane the poet succumbed with the man. . . . And there is about him . . . the distraught but exciting splendor of a great failure. (316)

Blackmur's interest is exclusively evaluative, canonical, and morally judgmental, and his terms "inchoate heart and distorted intellect" are precise if not necessarily intentional codes for the supposed limitations of homosexuality. But Blackmur does not dismiss Crane from the canon of modernist texts; rather, he uses him to mark one of the boundaries of the literary. Winters does this as well: "The flaws in Mr. Crane's genius are, I believe, so great as to partake . . . of the nature of a public catastrophe" ("The Progress of Hart Crane," 105).[4] As Blackmur's terms suggest, as is implied in Winters's criticism, and as can be seen even in Tate's introduction to *White Buildings*, those critics we now consider exemplary of New Criticism in America found it virtually impossible truly to separate the literary work from its author. The questions of literary merit and personal character informed one another for them, and, at least in Crane's case, fear, confusion, and misunderstanding of homosexuality accounted for some of the moral and psychological sanction placed on his work. It is only an index of the power of homophobia that the word "homosexuality" had never to be spoken or written in these contexts for injunctions against it to remain powerfully in place. Winters is surely the most extraordinary in this regard: conceiving the task of criticism "an act of moral judgment" (370) wherein the critic settles which poems are better than others according to ethics rather than aesthetics, his collection of essays, *In Defense of Reason*, ends with an indictment of Crane unsurpassed in its censure of him and his work. There is for Winters virtually nothing redeemable in Crane as poet or man, so given to a dangerous, "Emersonian" doctrine of impulse is he, and Winters's dismissal of him ends on an almost hysterical note about the dangers of demonic possession. Winters insists that critics must be on guard against possession by minds such as Emerson's, Whitman's, or Crane's, each a demon, and demons being "one of the most dangerous forces in the universe" (601). Winters's stated objection to Crane is not his homosexuality, but the vocabulary of moral imperative that surrounds both the critical and the literary acts for Winters makes Crane's appearance as a homosexual writer already a scandal.

If, despite their inability to say it, notions about the "contagion" of homosexuality affected the reception and evaluation of literary texts for members of Crane's generation, the disease this vocabulary notes was also part of the production of literary texts on homosexuality and/or by homosexuals in that era. As the next two chapters will suggest, homosexuality was the central experience of Crane's life, and it became—over and over again—one of the central issues in his work. That it is often absent from that work is both the result of ideological injunctions against its appearance and the inevitable result of its instability as a discourse or cultural system that might be taken up and employed in literary texts. Ultimately, Crane could only understand or imagine his homosexual experience and its meanings through the words he had to name it. As Paul De Man has suggested, "If there is to be consciousness (or experience, mind, subject, discourse, or face) it has to be susceptible of phenomenalization. But since the phenomenality of experience cannot be established a priori, it can only occur by a process of signification" ("Lyrical Voice in Contemporary Theory," 62). This chapter will be interested in the phenomenality of Crane's experience of the object he called his homosexuality and in the linguistic mediations of his body and its homosexual experience and desires. This is offered not simply as one more example of the long history of homosexual oppression and enforced self-misrecognition but also as an avenue into understanding how the literary subject fashions and frames what he takes to be homosexuality's self-evident or unmediated moments—those episodes of love and desire that he imagines as transcending the negativity of culture.

A severe moral vocabulary, of which there are many traces in Crane's letters and poems, surrounded the experience of homosexuality for Crane's generation, and perhaps there is no more eloquent plea for an end to its authority than the manifesto for "inverts" that was banned as pornographic (read "subversive") during the years of Crane's final work on *The Bridge*. Radclyffe Hall's *The Well of Loneliness* has been criticized for its tragic ending, and for its patriarchally tainted acceptance of "deviance" and lesbian sexuality, but it is also a radical protest against the persecution of lesbians and gay men. It argues cogently for the naturalness of same-sex affection and strongly against the injustice of society. We can see in an article by Allen Tate printed twenty years after Crane's death how debilitating to his critical reputation (as to his life) has been this continuing legacy of moralistic control and punishment of homosexuality's cultural visibility. Tate implies that homosexuality is equivalent to "intellectual deterioration" and finds that because Crane was "confirmed in his homosexuality" he was "cut off from any relationship . . . in which the security necessary to mutual love was possible." He considers Crane an "extreme example of the *unwilling* homosexual," and it is little wonder he has this opinion since he sees all homosexuals as victims, men "convinced that they cannot be loved" and therefore "incapable of loving" (*The Man of Letters in the Modern World*, 296). We can only imagine how hegemonic and disempowering this cultural interpretation of homosexuality was for Crane during his life, especially since Tate was the main person to whom he turned for literary advice and personal support during his most productive period, the mid-twenties. And it was perhaps even more politically and existentially oppressive to Crane that Tate and other straight friends considered him an exception to the general horror and depravity of stereotypical homosexuality; they virtually assured that he consider himself from a heterosexual point of view, naturalizing as a perfectly understandable personal response any alienation he might have felt from other homosexuals or from his own homosexual desire. Tate seems quite proud of Crane in the following passages, but the sentiment suggests again how heterosexually identified Crane probably was at least while among his literary associates and how alienated from his own homosexual life his literary identification left him:

> His deepest friendships were not with homosexuals; they were with Malcolm Cowley, Slater Brown, Kenneth Burke, Gorham Munson, Waldo Frank, and myself; it was with these men that he lived the life of the mind and the imagination. He could not pretend that the alienated society of the committed homosexual was complete; for this unhappy person—for his epicene manners and for his irresponsibility—he felt compassion and contempt. (*The Man of Letters in the Modern World*, 298)

It is not unnatural that Crane sought identification with "the life of the mind," of course, but in this case it certainly meant that the life of his body would remain intellectually obscure to him, and we can see how such admonitory tones toward homosexuality would have allowed Crane no authority from which to produce culturally significant texts, how they would have forced him into silence on the very issue about which he now seems perhaps to have had much to say to us. In this, his case is quite different from that of Willa Cather, for instance, who, exhibiting all of the conflicted and contradictory impulses of "unnatural love" for other women, nonetheless found in Sarah Orne Jewett a mentor who (according to Sharon O'Brien) "encourag[ed] her to find her own material and to speak in her own voice" (*Willa Cather*, 335).

A letter Crane wrote to Yvor Winters in the summer of 1927 provides Crane's most radical articulation and defense of homosexuality and its relation to the production of culturally significant texts, but it also demonstrates how deeply alienated from the literary profession as a profession he was. Unlike Pound, Moore, and Eliot, whose literary professionalism was beyond question, Crane's theories, poems, and presence held little force or authority during his own lifetime. Certainly he was a figure of some importance, but he was nothing like a professional writer, and he lacked the academic and journalistic credentials of Winters, Wilson, Tate, and other critics he felt had betrayed him toward the end of his life. Among other things, this alienation turns on the issue of education, for Crane had not been a Harvard, Penn, or Bryn Mawr student as had Pound, Eliot, Stevens, Moore, and Williams. It would seem that the culture expected poets to obtain a degree of higher education, and that this expectation helped Crane in 1924 to produce for his family the fiction that he was staying in New York in order to study at Columbia University when in fact it was a love affair with Emil Opffer that kept him there. But his perceived inability to command a tradition of texts that defined literary competence in the vogue of Eliot, Pound, and Joyce sentenced Crane to a lifetime of reputed literary inferiority and to his generation's suspicion about his worth as a poet, about his ability to engage himself fully in significant literary questions. What Crane's early critics failed to realize was that his refusal of the standard modernist canon and his allegiance to an alternative, Romantic, and homosexual set of writers in Whitman, Melville, and Rimbaud assumed a different set of literary questions and a different relation between poetry and culture than the one found, for instance, in Eliot's work.

The 1927 letter to Winters is a truly extraordinary critique of the institution of literature from the perspective of a homosexual positioned on its margin; it is a response which implies that Winters found homosexuality culturally dangerous to writers because it undermined their moral authority and kept them from producing anything but fragmented, flawed work (amazingly enough, Winters seems to have pointed to da Vinci for corroboration of this).[5] Crane's letter begins by attacking Winters's demand for ethical responsibility on the part of the poet: "You need a good drubbing for all your recent easy talk about 'the complete man,' the poet and his ethical place in society," and he continues by lambasting Edmund Wilson for the class interest of his critical position:

> It is so damned easy for such as he, born into easy means, graduated from a fashionable university into a critical chair overlooking Washington Square, etc., to sit tight and hatch little squibs of advice to poets not to be so 'professional' as he claims they are, as though all the names he has just mentioned [in his review] had been as suavely

> nourished as he—as though 4 out of 5 of them hadn't been damned well forced the major part of their lives to grub at *any* work they could manage by hook or crook and the fear of hell to secure! (*Letters*, 298)

Crane then moves back to the question of ethics, asserting that he does indeed have an ethics, although it is uncodified (i.e., it is codified according to principles at odds with the ethics of others); his rhetoric circles in preparation for the heart of his address—the pressing question of whether or not homosexuals may contribute to Western civilization:

> I cannot flatter myself into quite as definite recipes for [moral] efficiency as you seem to, one reason being, I suppose, that I'm not so ardent an aspirant toward the rather classical characteristics that you cite as desirable. This is not to say that I don't "envy" the man who attains them, but rather that I have long since abandoned *that* field—and I doubt if I was born to achieve (with the particular vision) those richer syntheses of consciousness which we both agree in classing as supreme. . . . I have a certain code of ethics. I have not as yet attempted to reduce it to any exact formula. . . .
>
> You put me in altogether too good company . . . I think I am quite unworthy of such associates as Marlowe or Valery—except in some degree, perhaps, "by kind." If I can avoid the pearly gates long enough I may do better. Your fumigation of the Leonardo legend is a healthy enough reaction, but I don't think your reasons for doubting his intelligence and scope very potent. I've never closely studied the man's attainments or biography, but your argument is certainly weakly enough sustained on the sole prop of his sex—or lack of such. One doesn't have to turn to homosexuals to find instances of missing sensibilities. Of course I'm sick of all this talk about balls and cunts in criticism. It's obvious that balls are needed, and that Leonardo had 'em—at least the records of the Florentine prisons, I'm told, say so. . . . [The] whole topic is something of a myth anyway, and is consequently modified in the characteristics of the image by each age in each civilization. Tom Jones, a character for whom I have the utmost affection, represented the model in 18th Century England, at least so far as the stated requirements in your letter would suggest. (Parkinson, *Hart Crane and Yvor Winters*, 88–89)[6]

What we see here is that Winters's homophobia touched on a number of classic constructions: homosexuality is really castration, a lack of masculinity; it keeps one from fulfilling one's potential as an artist (supposedly the case with Marlowe and da Vinci); it wrecks one's "intellect and scope," creating "dissociated sensibilities"; homosexuals are promiscuous and their only sustaining interest sexual contact, as was the case with . . . *Tom Jones?!*

This last detail shows how uncowed Crane was by Winters; he points out the absurdity of Winters's position by showing that Tom Jones—the epitome of healthy masculine heterosexuality, according to one version of what that would be—exhibits the same qualities Winters attributed to homosexuals. We see a certain brash resistance as well in his challenge of Winters's denigration of da Vinci, the language of which gives us the wonderfully snide and subtly homosexual construction of Winters (and his argument) "sustained" on the "sole prop" of Leonardo's "sex." If Winters's attitude made Crane defensive enough to assert that artists need "balls," we cannot remove that statement from an ideology that insists on the masculinity of the artist-subject, but we might see that Crane's remark seems more intended as a counter to the charge of homosexual castration than as a serious declaration that art can only be produced by biological "men."[7] The most crucial thought in this paragraph, however, is Crane's exposure of homosexuality as a construction with ideological and historical rather than "essential" meanings—"You don't seem to realize that the whole topic is something of a myth anyway, and is consequently modified in the characteristics of the image by each age in each civilization." In this sentence, Crane simultaneously declares homosexuality universal through time and space and denies the validity of any "universal" reading of its qualities and implications. He wrests interpretive authority from Winters on this point, suggesting that the critic does not know what he is writing about when he condemns homosexuality.

Winters's homophobia would be irrelevant to Crane's career were it not for the fact that Winters is himself a spokesman of some literary authority for his generation; in fact, John Unterecker claims Crane respected Winters's opinion more than that of any other critic. Throughout his life Crane seems to have sought from literary acquaintances the personal validation he never consistently received from family or from any positive homosexual identification; time and again his letters beg friends for evaluations of his work. These letters suggest that he had little internalized authority and needed external corroborations of his (and his poetry's) value from figures such as Winters, Tate, Munson, and Frank. And for Crane as a poet, the most damaging aspect of critical homophobia was its intertextuality with the notion of poetic authority—with what appears in Crane's letter to Winters variously as "the complete man," "the poet and his ethical place in society," the whole moral and literary agenda layered in the phrase "dissociated sensibility." Crane seems to have resisted reactionary ethical injunctions as best he could throughout his lifetime, arguing in his response to Winters, for instance, that the homosexual *is* a "complete man" rather than a castrated one (although it is interesting that he does not deny that homosexuals have dissociated sensibilities so much as suggest that they are not alone in this). But such resistance could not have been easy and was ultimately overwhelmed by the benign homophobia of his best friends. Tate argued that the poet's first responsibility was "to define the limits of his personality and to objectify its moral implications in an appropriate symbolism" (*The Man of Letters in the Modern World*, 293), but the question for a writer like Crane was how to objectify the moral implications of a homosexual personality when they would by the definition of the time point to that personality as immoral. The end product of this ideology was that, as a homosexual poet, Crane led a transparently contradictory existence: to be a poet was to cease to participate in his own life as a homosexual; to be a homosexual was to cede all claims to poetic, cultural authority.

Denied personal validity as a homosexual, Crane seems to have located his only sustained and sustaining cultural worth in his definition of himself as a poet, but as a poet to have found no base from which to legitimate his claim to cultural worth. He could not define poetry according to theories of impersonality, and so could not separate his supposedly illicit or illegitimate life from it. His philosophy of composition required "passion, experience and rumination"—in roughly that order, it seems.[8] In "General Aims and Theories," he wrote, "A poet will accidentally define his time well enough simply by reacting honestly and to the full extent of his sensibilities to the states of passion, experience and rumination that fate forces on him, first hand. He must, of course, have a sufficiently universal basis of experience to make his imagination selective and valuable" (*Poems*, 218). But even with this theory as a rationale for his experiments in verse, Crane was faced with the problem of whether or not the passion and experience "fate force[d] on him, first hand," the passion and experience of homosexuality, "ha[d] a sufficiently universal basis . . . to make his imagination selective and valuable." Faced with this situation, Crane would seem to have had a limited number of choices: to challenge the notion of universality on which this poetic theory was grounded, to sublimate homosexual interests in the interest of universality, or to insist on the validity of homosexuality as a threshold to the universal. It seems that the first was virtually unthinkable for him: so essential for his day was the notion that literature traded in universals that it was practically impossible to think against it as an injunction.[9] To some extent Crane was able to insist on the last possibility mentioned above, that homosexuality was a valid ground from which to imagine the universal—as in "Possessions" or sections of "Voyages" and *The Bridge*. More often, however, he chose to sublimate homosexual experience in the name of so-called universal significance and, as homosexual writers had done before and have done since, chose heterosexual images for the depiction of that universality. Certainly we can read "For the Marriage of Faustus and Helen" and "Voyages VI" as heterosexualized versions of homosexual motifs, as places where the venerability of heterosexual desire naturalizes its images as substitutes for and (fore)closures of less acceptable homosexual figures. It is especially important to remember that Crane considered "Faustus and Helen" his masterpiece not only in the sense of proving the end of his apprenticeship but also as a definitive response to *The Waste Land*—its images calculated to oppose Eliot's vocabulary of embattled heterosexuality as a trope for depleted Western culture. Crane carried the manuscript of "Faustus and Helen" with him to New York as though it were a passport to artistic circles, and dominant literary ideology certainly would have asserted itself strongly in a work conceived under such autobiographical and cultural pressure. This is not in any way to claim that "Faustus and Helen" is somehow "about" homosexuality, but to claim that our understanding of it as a text in history must include our understanding of how and why it is *not* thematically "about" homosexuality.

Throughout his career Crane also wrote poems that were more explicitly concerned with homosexuality,[10] and just as the letter to Winters suggests that we should think of homosexuality within the general problematics of language and knowledge rather than as a moral issue, his homosexual poems search (often quite explicitly) for a vocabulary in which to register and examine the meanings of homoerotic experience. It would be well, before attempting to analyze those poems in more detail, however, to establish with a bit more precision how homosexuality was historically constructed for Crane, for we can best explain his work as produced through the contradictions of discourse and ideology if we first understand what homosexual experience meant to men and women of his time. Dennis Altman has pointed out that "while homosexual behavior is widespread across both time and place, according to all available historical and anthropological evidence, the concept of a homosexual identity is a recent and comparatively restricted one" (*The Homosexualization of America*, 47). Crane's generation stood precisely on that historical threshold when homosexuality began to be articulated as an identity through Western cultures, and Crane's is one of the first texts to provide literary representations grounded in that articulation. John D'Emilio and Estelle B. Freedman's *Intimate Matters* suggests that this era in American culture initiated "real changes in the social organization of same-sex eroticism," that:

> the spread of a capitalist economy and the growth of huge cities were allowing diffuse homosexual desires to congeal into a personal sexual identity. Labor for wages allowed more and more men, and some women, to detach themselves from a family-based economy and strike out on their own; the anonymous social relations of the metropolis gave them the freedom to pursue their sexual yearnings. Some men and women began to interpret their homosexual desires as a characteristic that distinguished them from the majority. Slowly they elaborated an underground sexual subculture. (226–27)

Whatever the dangers in attempting to synthesize a complicated and furtive social history in space as brief as this passage, D'Emilio and Freedman are correct in their analysis of the unprecedented formations of homosexual identities and cultures in early twentieth-century America. As Michel Foucault suggests in *The History of Sexuality*, "The nineteenth-century homosexual became a personage [whereas "sodomy" had been a forbidden act], a past, a case history, and a childhood, in addition to being a type of life, a life form, and a morphology, with an indiscreet anatomy and possibly a mysterious physiology. . . . The sodomite had been a temporary aberration; the homosexual was now a species" (43). And that "species" began, as he states elsewhere, to speak for itself, to articulate itself against those discourses (such as sexology) that threatened merely to contain it.

In trying to understand the material base for this "new" social articulation of sexual subjectivity, it is important to keep in mind that the crisis of modernity, as defined by someone such as Walter Benjamin, is a crisis of alienation—not only the classic alienation from labor that

Marx first critiqued but also an alienation from collectivity. Benjamin's essay on the Russian storyteller Leskov (*Illuminations*, 83–109) turns on a distinction between information (which he reads most powerfully in the differentiated but fragmentary text of the newspaper) and experience (which he reads most powerfully in the storytelling that connects Leskov to others through the processes of orality and collective wisdom). With that loss of collective experience, there is a concurrent increase in the culture of privatization quite distinct from what he calls "experience," an increase in what *cannot* be communicated: the information that becomes mere noise. Although this brief summary constructs it too simply, Benjamin's work is undeniably haunted by nostalgia; nevertheless, his insight into the alienations of urban, industrial culture is crucial to our understanding of the particular burdens of anomie that modernity placed upon its subjects, and it is quite necessary that we understand the changes in sexual identity that attract our attention here as part of this larger process of modernity's pressure of alienation.[11]

What is most interesting about this process with respect to the formation of new homosexual subcultures is how the temporary failure of collective regimes of power and knowledge produced in the seams of culture various sites on which marginal peoples began to construct and empower their own collectivities, their own access to "experience" understood *not* simply as the "experiential" (and therefore individual) but as their link to a meta-narrative (and collective) that might explain their being. There is, in fact, ample evidence that sexological definitions of homosexuality, while now appearing oppressive, actually served a positive function for certain people in the twenties. In *The Well of Loneliness*, for instance, Stephen Gordon's reading of a sexological text is part of her growth toward self-acceptance as a lesbian because it offers a name for what she is. Although Hall's politics appear to a later generation of readers to be seriously compromised by her final consignment of Stephen to a lifetime's isolation, the text seems nonetheless radical in its attempt to break the conspiracy of silence around lesbian desire and in its unwavering insistence on the naturalness of lesbian sexuality: "She fell quite simply and naturally in love, in accordance with the dictates of her nature. To her there seemed nothing strange or unholy in the love that she felt for Angela Crossby. To her it seemed an inevitable thing, as much a part of herself as her breathing; and yet it appeared transcendent of self, and she looked up and onward towards her love" (146).[12] Similarly, Sharon O'Brien claims that Willa Cather accepted the notion that same-sex friendship between women was "unnatural," yet used that as the category through which to legitimate her feelings for Louise Pound (see "Divine Femininity and Unnatural Love" in *Willa Cather*, 117–46). And F. O. Matthiessen comments on the value of reading "Ellis' volume on inversion" in his coming to acceptance of his homosexuality as an identity. "Then," Matthiessen writes, "for the first time it was completely brought home to me that I was what I was by *nature*" (*Rat and the Devil*, 47). Jeffrey Weeks summarizes the surprising use some gay people seem to have made of early sexological definitions: "Apparently what was objectionable . . . could be jettisoned while the kernel of apparent relevance was abstracted, bounced around and put into effective operation. . . . Against its intentions usually, countering its expectations often, sexology did contribute to the self-definition of those subjected to its power of definition" (*Sexuality and Its Discontents*, 95). This link to being—and the quest to understand homosexuality as constitutive of an identity—are two of the key elements in Crane's threshold experience of it.

In all that follows it is important to keep in mind the following assessment of gay life in the twenties from George Chauncey, Jr.:

> Even a brief look at New York in the Jazz Age reveals that many of the things in gay life we commonly think of as new—from bars and bathhouses to restaurants and public dances, gay neighborhoods and dress codes—were already flourishing 60 years ago. . . . [But] it would be wrong to conclude that gay life was easy in the 1920s. Many people were isolated from the gay world or alienated from its dominant forms, and—as the hundreds of convictions I have uncovered in the records of the municipal courts indicate—many suffered loss of liberty, jobs, family, and respect when they were caught in periodic crackdowns. Even many of those who participated most fully in "the life" felt it essential to keep that aspect of their lives hidden from straight co-workers and families. ("The Way We Were," 29, 34)

This understanding can help us see the urgency that surrounded lesbian and gay identifications at that time, for if that era saw an increasingly empowered homosexuality, it by no means lost the vocabulary that was its heritage from the nineteenth century.

Robert Martin's *Homosexual Tradition in American Poetry* establishes how very strong was the response of self-hatred to the "curse" of homosexuality for members of this historical moment:

> [S]elf-hatred was common in homosexuals of Crane's time, who could find no way of fulfilling their desires without violating the image of the ideal, spiritual relationship which had been constructed for homosexual love. This was the "trap" of Platonism. Homosexuality was "higher" than heterosexuality because more spiritual and less physical; the assertion of a homosexual identity was then at odds with the fulfillment of homosexual desire. . . . Crane's homosexuality was for him a "secret vice" even when he proclaimed it loudest. (122)[13]

We see this in a number of Crane's poems, particularly in late texts such as "Reply," where bliss is built in the silence of shame,[14] and we see it in Djuna Barnes's *Nightwood* (published a few years after Crane's death), where same-sex attraction is doomed to fail. And we can see it in Wallace Thurman's *The Blacker The Berry* (1928) as well. Set mainly in Harlem, and overtly concerned with the political issues of intraracial discrimination (in the case of Emma Lou, the novel's protagonist, this occurs because of her dark skin), the novel nonetheless duplicates a strict cultural script around the question of homosexuality (despite the fact that Thurman—himself gay—no doubt found that script oppressive). There are two incidents in the novel when homosexuality breaks through the placid surface of heterosexuality, and in both cases the homosexual is introduced as a scandal and/or threat. On the first occasion, Emma Lou is propositioned by the female proprietor of an apartment house she hopes to find a room in:

> She grew more familiar, placed her hand on Emma Lou's knee, then finally put her arm around her waist. Emma Lou felt uncomfortable. This sudden and unexpected intimacy disturbed her. The room was close and hot. Damask coverings seemed to be everywhere. Damask coverings and dull red draperies and mauve walls.
>
> "Don't worry any more, dearie, I'll take care of you from now on. . . . There are lots of nice girls living here. We call this the 'Old Maid's Home.' We have parties among ourselves, and just have a grand time." (135–36)

Emma Lou flees this "discomfort," but lesbianism (although figured as quite suffocating here) is not surrounded with the moral injunction that marks the appearance of male homosexuality at the novel's close. There, homosexuality is seen as part of a general breakdown of character suffered by Alva (the man Emma Lou has lived with but has decided to leave). His homosexuality is only the final step in a downward spiral of behavior that begins in womanizing and drinking and ends in virtual suicide. "She saw the usual and expected sight: Alva, face a death mask, sitting on the bed embracing an effeminate boy whom she knew as Bobbie" (261); "Then once more she saw Alva, not as he had been, but as he was now, a drunken, drooling libertine, struggling to keep the embarrassed Bobbie in a vile embrace" (262).[15]

This essay began by suggesting that Crane's verse has been criticized for its lack of appropriate objective correlatives, for the fact that his style seems a bewilderment of images in an uninterpretable swirl of syntax. I would now suggest that each of these qualities is also descriptive of homosexuality as it was discursively available to someone of Crane's culture. In some sense, it had no positive content but functioned mainly as an umbrella term under which were grouped a large number of sexually distinct practices whose only common factor was their alterity to heterosexuality. In addition, homosexual personalities were themselves read as unstable. The discourses that articulated homosexuality as culturally meaningful, whether they located it on a spectrum of pathology or on a spectrum of pleasure, were themselves not fully codified. We generally see in texts from this period a confusion and self-doubt arising from homosexuality's lack of historical and social visibility and from the absence of a vocabulary in which to express and interpret the contours of a homosexual life. Thus, Stein makes her title character in *Melanctha* "complex with desire . . . always full with mystery and subtle movement and denials and vague distrusts and complicated disillusions" (341–42) but unable finally to bring her desire through language into understanding. She remains trapped in a somatic realm only other women may understand; she dies, killed (it almost seems) by Jeff Campbell and his words. And F. O. Matthiessen, writing to Russell Cheney in 1925, makes the point that homosexual identity must invent its own language: "Of course this life of ours is entirely new—neither of us know of a parallel case. We stand in the middle of an uncharted, uninhabited country. That there have been other unions like ours is obvious, but we are unable to draw on their experience. We must create everything for ourselves. And creation is never easy" (*Rat and the Devil*, 71). This is understatement of the most extraordinary sort; in fact, that "creation" (as this entire study suggests) was particularly difficult when it encountered institutions and ideological apparatuses such as the literary. There were serious injunctions against homosexuality's appearance in literature (as the suppression of *The Well of Loneliness* made quite apparent). In fact (our notions of twenties bohemianism notwithstanding), within literary circles homosexuality was contained and defined by the strongest of prescriptive arguments, as the opinions of Tate and Winters above also suggest.[16]

Our current beliefs would have it that the twenties were a nonrepressive era of experimentation, a moment congenial to uncodified behaviors and identities, and as George Chauncey, Jr., has suggested, "the prominence of drag balls in New York's cultural life [in the twenties] should disabuse us of the notion that the gay world was a wholly secretive and invisible one before Stonewall" ("The Way We Were," 29). But Quentin Crisp suggests that "society was at that time much more rigid than it has ever been since."

> The short skirts, bobbed hair, and flat chests that were in fashion were in fact symbols of immaturity. No one ever drew attention to this, presumably out of politeness. The word "boyish" was used to describe the girls of that era. This epithet they accepted graciously. They knew that they looked nothing like boys. They also realized that it was meant to be a compliment. Manliness was all the rage. The men of the twenties searched themselves for vestiges of effeminacy as though for lice. (*The Naked Civil Servant*, 21)

And homosexual men and lesbians found themselves conveniently if oppressively defined between those two gender categories in the equally rigid but seemingly empty category of "the third sex."

But this is not the only rigidity of social convention the same-sex identified men and women of the twenties faced. Homosexual men such as Matthiessen and Crane often experienced their sexual desires as "lust" and noted over and over again the incompatibility of that "lust" with what they saw as more stable expressions of affection such as friendship or love. There is little or no sense of a continuum of experience between these two poles in the letters between Matthiessen and Cheney, for instance. They quite explicitly relegate certain kinds of sexual desire to a netherworld of immorality. Matthiessen, writing to Cheney, remarks on cruising: "I could have drunk in a lot of luscious slime through my eyes"; but he moralizes that this temptation needs to be fought: "That eye business is just a little dirt on an open wound. It doesn't seem like much but pretty soon it begins to fester, and you find that your whole body is full of its poison" (*Rat and the Devil*, 33). Cheney, writing to Matthiessen, compares cruising the street "between one and two" to being "a dead leaf blown before the wind" (28), a phrase that recurs almost verbatim in one of Crane's letters. The compartmentalization of experience registered in this, the marking of homosexual desire as dangerous or dessicating, and the appearance of these in a letter addressed to a homosexual lover, signals some of the deep contradictions Matthiessen and Cheney experienced as their homosexuality. And their need to distance themselves from the "luscious slime" they still quite obviously were tempted by may be explained in part by the fact that both men habitually indulged their "lust" with multiple partners before beginning their affair in 1924, and often not in the most genteel circumstances.

But if this rhetoric of homosexuality as "lust" can be found over and over again in texts from the twenties, so can the supposedly more stable affections of love and friendship characteristic of one of its other constitutive categories.[17] Robert Martin notes that if he inherited the notion that homosexuality was socially and morally less than heterosexuality, "Crane had [also] inherited a tradition which held that homosexuality offered a higher, purer form of love" (*The Homosexual Tradition*, 116). One can see in the Matthiessen/Cheney correspondence how they also use the notion of a higher love to protect them from the imputation of lust: "I haven't mentioned sex lately. . . . Occasionally faces attract me. Often I feel lust. . . . But right now my body and soul are too full of you to allow any environment to really disturb them" (46). They faithfully describe to one another how they overcome temptations to sexual activity with others, offering such details in the description that it seems the letters provide them a means to represent and indulge in now-forbidden desires without leaving the protective confines of their new-found stability in one another. At one point it seems Matthiessen may even have come upon Quentin Crisp in Hyde Park (Crisp's "trademark," his most outrageous sign, was his red hair):

> Yes, there they are. I can see them as I swing off the bus. Little crowds of them pretending to listen to the soap-box orators. . . . Hard faces. One, Red-hair. White flower in his button hole. Compelling eye. I look—the blood rushes hot to my face—and what then? I swing right past the whole damn bunch of them out into the broad sweep of the park where the grass is long, and there are some fallen leaves, and the kids are playing soccer in the twilight. (33)

One sees here how the pastoral and the detail of the children, which is at once suggestive of the progenitive and the innocent, serves to distance Matthiessen from his former activities. Evident in this passage as well is an internalized homophobia that expresses itself not only in his fear and censure of other homosexuals but also in the barely concealed nostalgia for a nonsexual existence, for a state of being where one is not torn by and subject to the differences of this particular desire.

Homosexuality was (for Matthiessen and for his generation as a whole) then, multiply self-contradictory, a "problem" for which Matthiessen (in words, at least) often desperately sought an "answer." In reading his letters one is often moved by the extraordinary experiential abyss from which he makes discoveries such as the following—that there is a "third alternative" to (a) a homosexual life of "lust", and (b) a homosexual life of self-denial:

> Two alternatives? I had never dreamed of the third. . . . Was it possible? I had known only lust. I prided myself that it had never touched the purity of my friendships. Was it possible for love and friendship to be blended into one? But before I had time to even ask the question it was answered. What is this wistful yearning I feel on these grey mornings? It's not the fog in my throat but an inchoate surge from my heart. What makes this new sensitive tingling in the tips of my fingers, and on my lips? It isn't the cold. It's love. (48)

What we realize from the Matthiessen/Cheney letters is that even if Crane's literary associates had not cautioned him against the dangers of his homosexuality (and if this occurred explicitly at times how heavily and often the implicit cautions must have come!), this confused vocabulary, this reticence and discursive silence, would have made it difficult to represent homosexuality in any strong and transparent fashion. It is perhaps for just this reason that one finds far more explicit reference to it in Crane's letters than in his poems, for there he is able to speculate in a fashion that literature's supposed textual wholeness militated against. I would like to turn now to Crane's letters before offering a reading of what is perhaps his most homosexually interested text, "Voyages."

The parallel between Crane's understanding of his homosexuality and that found in the above examples is striking: like Matthiessen and Cheney he wrote of homosexual union as the answer to a problem, as a miracle that changed his life. It is, alternately, a "golden halo," "God," "the Word made Flesh." Unlike them, he seems to have experienced this miraculous effect on a number of occasions and to have sought it rather obsessively toward the end of his life, long after having discovered that no relationship could long bear the burden of metaphysical meaning Crane longed to attach to it. As did others in his generation, Crane responded to the urban landscape as an arena in which his homosexuality found itself "at home," expressible without fear of censure. He wrote to his mother in June 1923, in terms that suggest quite clearly the freedom of expression a more provincial homosexual man might have found in New York City at that time, "I begin to see N.Y. very much more intimately since I've been working. It makes living here far more pleasant than ever before. Such color and style (on men, too) I've never seen before—no two alike. That's what is so interesting—the perfect freedom of wearing what you want to, walking the gait you like (I have a much less hurried gait than you're familiar with) and nobody bothering you" (*Letters*, 136). But this new environment was not always liberating; Crane, like Matthiessen, often depicts a strongly internalized homophobia at certain points in his life. Writing from the Isle of Pines in the summer of 1926, he seems to accept the definition of homosexuality as lust—implying that he accepts the homophobic construction of its meanings despite the tone of defiance registered in the letter. After bitterly accusing his literary acquaintances in New York of betraying his friendship, he praises the impossibility of betrayal in homosexual cruising:

> Immortally choice and funny and pathetic are some of my recollections [of brief homosexual connections]. I treasure them—I always can—against many disillusionments made bitter by the fact that faith was given and expected [of friends]—whereas, with the sailor no faith or such is properly *expected* and how jolly and cordial the tonsiling *is* sometimes, after all. Let my lusts be my ruin, then, since all else is a fake and mockery. (*Letters*, 264)

Part of what marks the cynicism of these remarks is an acceptance that his isolated condition was the "natural" outcome of homosexual behavior—that if he was alone, that was because he had been *only* a sexual being.

We see a cognate objection to homosexual community in Crane's late twenties California experience. Like Garcia Lorca in his well-known rejection of gay New York at about the same time (see the "Ode to Walt Whitman"), Crane found the atmosphere of homosexual abandon in California morally and personally threatening. If he participated in that abandon for a while, he finally rejected it in sarcastic, ridiculing terms that could not but be internalized as well. As Unterecker remarks, Crane "couldn't help but be amused by their extraordinary evenings and by the tight little world of gossip and vanity in which they lived" in California; it "threw Hart into a hedonistic orgy from which, panting, he would occasionally emerge" (*Voyager*, 520) and which he ultimately rejected. But the following passage from a letter to Slater Brown records a considerable fascination with the decadent life of the "pinkpoodle paradise" Crane elsewhere deplored (*Letters*, 324), and it shows that his understanding of homosexuality is at this point clearly one of consuming sensual experience and neither a political question of social restrictions nor a metaphysical one of identity transformation:

> My blessings—from the fairy God Mother in her native clime, here where the evenings are made lustful and odorous with the scent of lemon flowers and acacias on the sea-salt air!
>
> A paean from Venusberg! Oy-oy-oy! I have just had my ninth snifter of Scotch. . . . Try to imagine the streets constantly as they were during that famous aggregation last May in Manhattan . . . such a throng of pulchritude and friendliness as would make your "hair" stand on end.
>
> Besides which I have met the Circe of them all—a movie actor who has them dancing naked, twenty at a time, around the banquet table. O Andre Gide! no Paris ever yielded such as this—away with all your counterfeiters! Just walk down Hollywood Boulevard someday—if you must find something *out* of uniform. Here are little fairies who can quote Rimbaud before they are 18—and here are women who must have the tiniest fay to tickle them the one and only way. (quoted in Unterecker's *Voyager*, 523)

How tame Gide seems, indeed.

Crane's inability to think of this hedonism as political is not surprising given the time in which he lived, and his general refusal of political questions (writing from Mexico after the Revolution, he claims that "red" holds no interest for him). He tends to see sexuality in the modern world as contaminated by the pressures of commodification only when he can construct that sexuality as an innocent feminine one. But as Russell Jacoby has suggested, "Advanced capitalism requires a programmed hedonism as much as earlier capitalism needed Calvinism and sacrifice" ("Narcissism," 64), and we can see how this works itself out in the repressive tolerance of a community such as the one Crane encountered in California. By no means radical or politically thoughtful, it merely marks the epitome of one strain of bourgeois self-indulgence that could be found in America in the twenties. But Crane's inability by 1928 to understand the articulation of homosexuality within an ideology bent on controlling it is even more astonishing when we realize that physical violence against him and against gay men more generally was not uncommon. The letter quoted here refers to Bert Savoy—a Hollywood comic known for the expression "Oy-oy-oy"—and his loss of an eye, "the result of some midnight with a mariner." Crane's letters record violent attacks upon him and Emil when they had ceased being lovers in any conventional sense and cruised the waterfronts together. "We were held up and beaten by a gang in San Pedro . . . The story is complicated and lengthy"—"Both of us were robbed of everything, and E practically unconscious" (quoted in Unterecker's *Voyager*, 530–31). And what is particularly pernicious about the lack of understanding on Crane's part is the inability even decades later to address the issue of violence against gay men as a real political question. It is unmistakably clear, to name one such episode, that the event precipitating Crane's suicide was his beating by sailors whom he had solicited aboard the ship on which he was returning from Mexico to the United States. There are slight variations in the telling of that final episode, but Peggy Baird and Malcolm Cowley, who would seem to have been best situated to know about it, both suggest that violence was its most immediate cause.

Toward the end of his life, even "lust," however, became "a fake and a mockery" for Crane, and while the etiology of personality disintegration can never be laid to a single cause, the role of internalized homophobia in this cannot be overestimated.[18] In his characterization of this later phase of Crane's biography as a Jeckyll/Hyde existence, John Unterecker is perhaps less homophobic than at first appears, for Crane's life was at certain points a ritualized enactment of the self-hatred and homosexual self-punishment we find suggested in the following:

> But his real feelings on those nights when he pursued lust, not love—when he got drunk in order to free himself to search the sailor bars on Sands Street—those desperate feelings seemed, once they had passed, like fictions lived by an invented character rather than by the flesh-and-blood man who tried to calculate what precisely had driven him to the gestures he had made, the words he had said, the brute violence of sudden passion or the risk of the more brutal vio-

> lence that sometimes left him black and blue and penniless, an object dumped in an alley for the early-morning policeman to discover and haul off to the station house. (*Voyager*, 429)

Certainly Unterecker's prose is sensationalistic, and some of his assumptions need to be questioned. The behavior he describes here seems too neatly logical, for instance, as if homosexual cruising were inherently an act of desperation leading always to a fictionalized and therefore psychically violent account of one's life.[19] Unterecker seems, too, to imply that all "sudden passion" is an instance of "brute violence," and he depicts homosexuality here as almost a possession. But even after we filter through the language of this passage and the way it constructs homosexual behaviors (remembering, too, that not everyone must be inebriated to "free himself" for homosexual encounters), we must admit that the tragic tone of its vocabulary and the behavior it describes are rather appropriate to Crane. As Unterecker writes in another section of *Voyager*, Crane:

> was far too much a product of Cleveland and its moral code to turn against it lightly, and what he could not help but regard as his own moral transgression was to torture him until the day of his death. In later years, when companionable drinking would drift over the line into drunkenness, he would drag out for friends the details of his sins, sometimes bragging of them, sometimes defending them, always hounded by them. (81)

If we have seen this tragedy rehearsed too often as a natural telos of homosexual desire, if we now have alternative paradigms for thinking of homosexuality, neither of these facts should alter our perception that Crane's self-destruction was a lethal combination of alcoholism, homosexual self-hatred, and the personal failures that both obsessions induced. This is not to make him a martyr once again, or to reinscribe him within a pathological script. We must simply see that if his life became literally unlivable for him by 1932, part of the reason for that was that homosexuality was central to his life but was itself socially and psychically designed as an unlivable existence. Allen Tate is correct in asserting of Crane that "his world had no center, and [he was] thrust into sensation" (*The Man of Letters in the Modern World*, 293), but Crane's movement toward self-destruction can now be understood as an episode in ideology rather than as one in character.

Competing with this vocabulary of "lust" and ruination, however, is its structual opposite and complement: a vocabulary of transformation.[20] This reaches its height in Crane's attachment to Emil Opffer, what he calls in a letter written to Waldo Frank an experience of "the Word made Flesh." But a tone of fervency and almost religious intensity attaches to Crane's homosexual experiences from early in his life. His early letters show that homosexual attachment enlivened and punctuated what was otherwise a dull, Midwestern literary apprenticeship; it gave him some sense of being uniquely alive in an otherwise mundane world of work and social convention. We can see the power of this experience by comparing two letters, both written in December 1920. What is perhaps most remarkable in the comparison is that this transformation produces a completely different style of writing as well:

> I am filled with a kind of bleakness of mind and spirit lately, so that even this answer to your appreciated interest in my bland career is somehow an unsatisfactory effort. I should like to be able to see and talk to you,—the mere technical mechanics of writing have become so foreign to me from long neglect, that I feel awkward at best. . . . [T]here is a possibility of my being sent out on the road again as salesman. On the other hand, it seems to me that it will be about as much as I can endure to remain at my present work in the shipping dept. (*Letters*, 48)

> NEWS! News! NEWS!—the "golden halo" has widened,—descended upon me (or "us") and I've been blind with happiness and beauty for the last full week! Joking aside, I am too happy not to fear a great deal, but I believe in, or have found God again. . . . [I]t may please you, as it often might have helped me so, to know that something beautiful can be found or can "occur" once in awhile, and so unexpectedly. Not the brief and limited sensual thing alone, but something infinitely more thrilling and inclusive. I foolishly keep wondering,—"How can this be?—How did it occur?" How my life might be changed could this continue, but I scarcely dare to hope. I feel like weeping most of the time. . . . Of course it is the return of devotion which astounds me, so . . . it makes me feel very unworthy,—and yet what pleasure the emotion under such circumstances provides. I have so much now to reverence, discovering more and more beauty every day,—beauty of character, manner, and body, that I am for the time, completely changed.—But why aren't you here to talk with me about it! How I wish you were here. (*Letters*, 49–50)

The first of these is written to Munson, the second to Wilbur Underwood, a homosexual friend, government employee, and literary scribbler Crane had met in Washington, D.C., earlier in the year, and the difference in audience in part determines their difference in tone. But that difference depends more upon the content of the later letter (written December 22 whereas the first letter is dated December 5) and the presence of a sexual other in Crane's life at that later date. Even the "technical mechanics" of the second letter suggest Crane's exuberance: the dashes suggest the run-on emotion and connectedness of feeling; commas and periods are not the end points of thoughts; words appear in quotation marks as if they were voiced or intoned rather than written. It is a letter altogether—even typographically—overflowing with "capital" NEWS! But it is clear from the full context of his correspondence that the letters quoted here indicate two distinct discursive communities in each of which Crane held a position not congruent with his position in the other. While certain literary friends became confidants of his sexual or romantic life, he was never free when writing to them to express or meditate upon his homosexuality in the way he was when writing to homosexual friends. These two interests remained compartmentalized throughout his life, and one sees in Crane's letters unmistakable differences in style and vocabulary, in tone and persona, that speak to the differences between these two discursive communities.

These two letters reveal that *as a homosexual* Crane was led to mistrust his own affections and those of others ("It makes me feel very unworthy") so that reciprocity of affection astounds him even though he feels himself otherwise utterly transformed ("I am for the time completely changed"). The second letter also suggests that Crane experienced homosexual "news" as a surprise, as something that appeared with power but without specific agency in his life; therefore it seems beyond his rational understanding ("How can this be—How did it occur?"). So inexplicable and powerful is this surprise that "God" seems to be the only appropriate metaphor for what Crane has found. Clearly what sets this experience apart in kind from other articulations of his homosexuality—especially when read against the lament of isolation and dessication that precedes it by a few weeks—is the change in himself that he feels: a "golden halo" of being joins him to another and he is no longer a "me" but an "us." The word "inclusive" that appears here is used to signify homoerotic union and its transforming capacities in

"Possessions" as well, and this inclusiveness reaches beyond the paradigm of homosexuality as lust; it seems almost to figure for Crane what "adhesive" did for Whitman—a sexual and emotional base for relations among men that offered a rationale for ethics and politics. It is not this "brief and limited sensual thing alone" that moves Crane, for lust is by definition self-invested and self-interested, but the "pleasure" of "emotion" and the process of "discovering . . . beauty of character, manner, and body." We see in this letter that homosexual experience can be the surprisingly beautiful discovery of something other than lust, can be figured other than in the terms of its ideologically negative constructions. It is a transcendent moment that Crane, "blind with happiness," seeks to give personal and ideological continuity, both through its hoped-for continuance ("How my life might be changed could this continue") and through a clearer understanding that can be articulated only through dialogue and presumed commonality of experience with another homosexual man ("But why aren't you here to talk with me about it").

Writing to Munson almost exactly one year later (10 December 1921) Crane again describes homosexuality in a way that suggests how central it is to his personal happiness. But this letter suggests that it is tied to his ability to write as well, that it provides him no longer with "God" (as in 1920) but with something that compensates for the lack of money in providing an emotional currency:

> [A new job] has enabled me, though intensely occupied, to get free of the money complex that had . . . reduced me to ashes. This item added to a total lack of any sex life for a long period had left me so empty that I gave up insulting you with a mere heap of stones for a letter, and though I haven't more to offer you now, I have sufficient interest again in the activity of writing to make my meagreness seem less obvious. Erotic experience is stumbled upon occasionally by accident, and the other evening I was quite nicely entertained, in *my* usual way, of course. And thus the spell is broken! I can't help remarking that this "breaker of the spell" is one very familiar with your present haunts, "La Rotunde," etc., etc., only a few years back. You see, then, that one may enjoy a few Parisian sophistications even in Cleveland! (*Letters*, 72)

What is most striking here is the tone of worldly sophistication. How far from the brash innocence and excitement of the "golden halo" effect is this pose as a connoisseur of sexual "entertainment," but that pose is also the effect of the literary audience Crane addresses here. If the phrase "Erotic experience is stumbled upon occasionally by accident" is radically different from the earlier "it may please you, as it often might have helped me so, to know that something beautiful can be found or can 'occur' once in awhile, and so unexpectedly," this *may* be due in part to another year's erotic experience on Crane's part, but it is more likely that this change marks another year in Crane's literary apprenticeship, that this pose of worldly knowing is a literary construct rather than evidence of Crane's self-assurance within a personal homosexual identity (the next paragraph of the letter even begins, "The *Ulysses* situation is terrible to think on," underscoring Crane's position as one literarily "in the know"). If we deconstruct the suave pose, the discourse of homosexuality it covers is *not*, in fact, very different from that identified a year before: sex is still a matter of the unpredictable and may itself be here a "meagreness" made "less obvious."

Recognition of the fact that audience influenced Crane's discursive constructions of homosexuality helps us to realize that when he wrote to Waldo Frank in 1924 exclaiming about the sublime effects of his newfound love ("I have seen the Word made Flesh," "a purity of joy was reached that included tears," "sex was beaten out")—in a letter often used to suggest the sexual purity of the affair—he was consciously constructing for his reader a discourse of the sublime, "the ecstasy of walking hand in hand across the most beautiful bridge of the world" (*Letters*, 181). But at times Crane seems to have been able to fool even himself on this, sublimating into a "literary" interest what were clearly erotic episodes and interests. Writing two letters back-to-back to Waldo Frank from Havana and from the Isle of Pines (in September 1926), for instance, he ascribes an interest in learning Spanish to: (a) his interest in Hispanic men, and then, (b) his desire to write a major work about Mexico. In the first letter, scribbled on the back of a menu, he writes:

> Perhaps you have experienced the singular charm of long conversation with senoritas with only about 12 words in common understanding between you. I allude to A---, a young Cuban sailor . . . whom I met one evening after the Alhambra in Park Central. Immaculate, ardent, and delicately restrained—I have learned much about love which I did not think existed. What delicate relations may bloom from the humble—it is hard to exaggerate. (*Letters*, 275)

Or, we might say—Crane can only exaggerate: homosexuality is here once again a revelation. If this brief passage suggests that twelve words are sufficient for communication and liaison, however, it seems impossible to read the letter he wrote two days later as anything other than a sublimation of the desire he felt for Hispanic men:

> I am now, more than ever anxious to learn the most beautiful language in the world. And I suddenly conceive it as a necessary preparation for my next piece of work just apprehended in the form of a blank verse tragedy of Aztec mythology—for which I shall have to study the obscure calendars of dead kings. (*Letters*, 276)

When Crane went to Mexico on his Guggenheim in 1931, and continually tried while there to work on a proposed epic about the conquest of Mexico, his interests were still perhaps primarily erotic.[21]

In a letter written much earlier in his life, when he was still living in Cleveland, we can see that Crane equated the sublimation of homosexuality with literary pursuits, and we can see that homosexuality was an absolutely contradictory position for him. This letter traces in excessive detail (the homosexual consumed by signs) not only the object of homosexual desire but also the ways in which the homoerotic was frustrated for Crane and sublimated in intellectual pursuits (The elisions below are in the text of Weber's edition):

> Those who have wept in the darkness sometimes are rewarded with stray leaves blown inadvertently. Since your last I have [had] one of those experiences that come,—ever, but which are almost sufficient in their very incompleteness. . . . ----has manifested charming traits before, but there has always been an older brother around. Last night—it sounds silly enough to tell (but not in view of his real beauty)—O, it was only a matter of light affectionate stray touches—and half-hinted speech. But these were genuine and in that sense among the few things I can remember happily. With ---- you must think of someone . . . with a face not too thin, but with faun precision of line and feature. Crisp ears, a little pointed, fine and docile hair almost golden, yet darker,—eyes that are a little heavy—but wide apart and usually a little narrowed,—aristocratic (English) jaws, and a mouth that [is] just mobile enough to suggest voluptuousness. A strong rather slender figure, negligently carried, that is perfect from flanks that hold an easy persistence to shoulders that are soft yet full and hard. A smooth and rather olive skin that is cool—at first.
>
> Excuse this long catalog—I admit it is mainly for my own satisfaction, and I am drunk now and in such state my satisfactions are

> always lengthy. . . . The climax will be all too easily reached,—But my gratitude is enduring—if only for that *once*, at least, something beautiful approached me and as though it were the most natural thing in the world, enclosed me in his arm and pulled me to him without my slightest bid. . . . [We] who create must endure—must hold to spirit not by the mind, the intellect alone. These have no mystic possibilities. O flesh damned to hate and scorn! I have felt my cheek pressed on the desert these days and months too much. How old I am! Yet, oddly now this sense [of] age . . . is gaining me altogether unique love and happiness. I feel I have been thru much of this again and again before. I long to go to India and stay always. Meditation on the sun is all there is. Not that this isn't enough! I mean I find my imagination more sufficient all the time. The work of the workaday world is what I dislike. I spend my evenings in music and sometimes ecstasy. I've been writing a lot lately. -/-/ I'm bringing much into contemporary verse that is new. I'm on a synthesis of America and its structural identity now, called *The Bridge*. (*Letters*, 126–27)

Crane went, of course, not to India but to New York, where he did not succeed in escaping altogether the cycles of desire, and his "synthesis of America and its structural identity" would be another seven years coming to light. But we may note in passing two important things: first, that creative and "mystic possibilities" cannot reside only in the mind and must answer as well to the "ecstasy" of the flesh, but that homosexual flesh is constructed as an untenable site for aesthetic ecstasy and is therefore "damned to hate and scorn." Happiness is imaginable most powerfully as an "imagination," an escape from this contradictory problem of inspiration and incarnation. But we see here, too, how voluble Crane can be about the homoerotic when unconstrained by audience and social taboo (his drunkenness licenses him to write what he will). The letter is a primary example of Crane forcibly mistaking his project for poetry: as if it could be an escape from what he called in one of the letters to Munson quoted above "the money complex" (read also: the Oedipus complex), "the workaday world" and that historical materiality where the homosexual body was "damned to hate and scorn."

But Crane lived and wrote under any number of censures around homosexuality, and these ideological repressions produced its meaning for him as a hopelessly contradictory field of self-knowledge. In the spring of 1923, Crane left Cleveland for New York, and with that move both his homosexual life and literary career were altered, but in February of that year (before the move) he wrote to Munson in no uncertain terms about the societal strictures against homosexuality he was beginning to see as a key factor in his experience of it:

> I am in a very unfavorable mood, and just after having congratulated myself strongly on security against future outbreaks of the affections. You see, for two or three years I have not been attacked in this way [either an overstatement or a confession of the strength of this "attack"]. A recent evening at a concert some glances of such a very stirring response and beauty threw me into such an hour of agony as I supposed I was beyond feeling ever again. The mere senses can be handled without such effects, but I discover I am as powerless as ever against those higher and certainly hopeless manifestations of the flesh. O God that I should have to live within these American restrictions forever, where one cannot whisper a word, not at least exchange a few words! In such cases they almost suffice, you know! Passions of this kind completely derail me from anything creative for days,—and that's the worst of it. (*Letters*, 121–22)

Here in the course of seven sentences, Crane produces a classic gloss on the contradictory features of closeted homosexuality: the battle for internal control of homosexual desire meets frustration at the external injunctions against its appearance; the supposedly debilitating effects of homosexual desire confront the need to elevate them beyond the "hopeless manifestations of the flesh."

As an artist, and as a homosexual, Crane had outgrown the "American restrictions" of Cleveland by 1923, and he seems to have experienced New York as quite a liberation. In December 1922, he saw Isadora Duncan tell her Cleveland audience to go home and read *Calamus*. Crane remarks, "Ninety-nine percent of them had never heard of Whitman. . . . Glorious to see her there with her right breast and nipple quite exposed, telling the audience that the truth was not pretty, that it was really indecent" (*Letters*, 109). In New York, he no longer suffered in a city ignorant of the indecency of truth, and New York had a profound transformational effect on Crane, offering an environment for homosexual expression unparalleled in previous American history and available in almost no other place in North America. In his popular history of gay culture, *Culture Clash*, Michael Bronski suggests that Harlem was one of the centers for this, that it provided not only a haven for black artists but also a homosexual milieu for both blacks and whites. Only the racism of gay culture and the homophobia of African-American culture, Bronski suggests, have kept us ignorant of the profound intertextuality between the Harlem Renaissance and the birth of American gay culture. Bronski suggests that we see the careers and texts of Countee Cullen, Langston Hughes, Ma Rainey, and other blues singers as significant documents in the history of gay America, and although his own sexual practices seem to have been largely restricted to other blacks, Countee Cullen's "Tableau" clearly suggests the challenge homosexuality could offer to strict racial divisions within American culture:

Locked arm in arm they cross the way,
  The black boy and the white,
The golden splendor of the day,
  The sable pride of night.

From lowered blinds the dark folk stare,
  And here the fair folk talk,
Indignant that these two should dare
  In unison to walk.

Oblivious to look and word
  They pass, and see no wonder
That lightning brilliant as a sword
  Should blaze the path of thunder.
(*On These I Stand*, 7)

Similarly, Arnold Rampersad's recent, compendious biography of Langston Hughes not only suggests how central the homosexual elements of Harlem were to the movements fostered there in the twenties but is also perhaps the best record we have to date of the homosexual formations in any community in America before World War II.

Since the relationship itself was the most important of his adult life, it is not surprising that the most significant texts to come out of Crane's experience of homosexual New York are the letters and poems written in celebration of his relation with Emil Opffer; in them, homosexuality becomes a trope for identity that grounds itself in a theory of incarnation beyond language, thereby solving both the dialectic of mind/body and the relation between literature and the flesh damned to hate and scorn. When Crane moved to 110 Columbia Heights—Opffer's family home—in April 1924, he had found the kindest stranger he was to find in his life. Two points have traditionally been made about that move: one, that it was to the address from which Washington Roebling oversaw the construction of the Brooklyn Bridge, a fact that suggests an intensity bordering on the obsessive in Crane's project of writing *The Bridge—unless* one knows that it was his lover's home, a fact not usually mentioned. Second, as is evident in the quotation from Unterecker that suggests nothing "dirty" in the attachment between the two men, critics have always been eager to explain the relation between Crane and Opffer as something other than a homosexual one. It can be called platonic; their personalities can be described as bisexual rather than homosexual; it can remain unexamined because it was a "transitory" and therefore unimportant event that did not result in a permanent monogamous relationship: in all of the above instances, the centrality of the experience to Crane's life and to his subsequent work can be ignored or altered to suit the needs of critical ideologies about the homosexual. Critics often point to the previously mentioned letter Crane wrote Waldo Frank (21 April 1924) as evidence of the way in which this relationship transcended (and therefore had no part in) sexuality. In a passage that is something of a touchstone in the criticism, Crane wrote:

> I say that I have seen the Word made Flesh. I mean nothing less, and I know now that there is such a thing as indestructibility. In the deepest sense, where flesh became transformed through intensity of response to counter-response, where sex was beaten out, where a purity of joy was reached that included tears. (*Letters*, 181)

On the surface this might seem to suggest a platonic relationship between Opffer and Crane, but there are several problems with such a reading. Such a claim, for instance, would not see the substantially masochistic trace in the phrase "where sex was beaten out" (or see that one of Crane's favorite ritualistic metaphors for passion—drumbeats—might also be a gloss to this). More importantly, however, the platonic reading of the relationship implies that there is no homoeroticism here, that homosexuality is not homosexual unless genital sexual activity is involved. That notion needs to be questioned both because of what we know about the continuum of desire and because of the suggestion in Crane's own letters that homosexual satisfaction may reside in something other than genital intercourse ("O, it was only a matter of light affectionate stray touches—and half-hinted speech. But these were genuine and in that sense among the few things I can remember happily"). The real issue, however, is the context in which such readings are produced, for they ignore the discourse of homosexuality as we find it in other passages from Crane: the rhetoric of annunciation here is completely in keeping with Crane's other descriptions of homosexual elation. In any case, it should not be the relationship that holds our interest but the textuality through which it is recorded and interpreted.

A fuller quotation from the letter is helpful, for we see in it that this relationship strikes Crane like others have but with a force greater than that of any other recorded in his correspondence. Just as Matthiessen used the rhetoric of love as an answer to an unasked question, Crane calls his bond with Emil an "answer" and sees himself as "changed—not essentially, but changed and transubstantiated as anyone is who has asked a question and been answered" (*Letters*, 182). We see in this letter the tone of rhapsody familiar from Crane's other letters, but this time he seems up against the limits of his vocabulary:

> For many days, I have gone quite dumb with something for which "happiness" must be too mild a term. At any rate, my aptitude for communication, such as it ever is!, has been limited to one person alone, and perhaps for the first time in my life (and, I can only think that it is for the last, so far is my imagination from the conception of anything more profound and lovely than this love). I have wanted to write you more than once, but it will take many letters to let you know what I mean (for myself, at least) when I say that I have seen the Word made Flesh. . . . It's true, Waldo, that so much more than my frustrations and multitude of humiliations has been answered in this reality and promise that I feel that whatever event the future holds is justified beforehand. And I have been able to give freedom and life which was acknowledged in the ecstasy of walking hand in hand across the most beautiful bridge of the world, the cables enclosing us and pulling us upward in such a dance as I have never walked and never can walk with another. (*Letters*, 181)

The religious vocabulary Crane often employed in describing sexual relationships reaches a zenith in this letter; the rhetoric of incarnation not only assuages past suffering but raises the relationship to the level of myth, justifying all past and future in one transcendent present. The Word made Flesh is a figure through which Crane may equate objective knowledge of homosexuality with its subjective experience: the socially distancing "Word," the never-settled problem of vocabulary and inscription that his generation encountered in trying to figure (and figure out) its homosexuality becomes in this rhetoric of incarnation transparent to the seemingly unmediated experience of the homosexual body. We see in this letter an empowering synthesis of the dialectic that had before paralyzed him: the flesh become the substantiation of "mystic possibilities" rather than their antithesis. Finally, it would seem to matter very little what exactly Crane and Opffer did together to produce this figuration of homosexuality. The important point is that homosexual attachment became at this juncture in time more than a personal experience for Crane—the being homosexual became something more like the homosexual Being, the sign of an authenticity that was founded outside language, organic and whole. This is not, of course, to suggest that Crane had in any sense discovered a truth in this; as the poem "Voyages" attests, this burden of being cannot be carried by any subjectivity that is as plagued by alterity as is the homosexual. But it does remind us that Crane's investment in homosexual experience as an authorization of identity was itself historically generated within a modern moment that put all identity in crisis. The pattern Fredric Jameson identifies in the more general utopian impulse of modernism holds for Crane's homosexual utopian impulse:

> Modernism and reification are parts of the same immense process which expresses the contradictory inner logic and dynamics of late capitalism. Yet . . . modernism—far from being a mere reflection of the reification of late nineteenth-century social life—is also a revolt against that reification and a symbolic act which involves whole utopian compensation for increasing dehumanization on the level of daily life . . . the experience of *anomie*, standardization, rationalizing desacralization. (*The Political Unconscious*, 42)

What we see over and over in Crane's letters—and what we will see in "Voyages" as well—is that this homosexual dream of perfect metaphysical union is not so much a reflected heterosexual ideal as it is the compensation for having wept in the darkness, for the loss of meaning in a world governed by spiritually bankrupt institutions.

If it holds out the promise of escape from institutional identity, however, homosexuality cannot in practice deliver on that promise. It is, however, "inclusive" for Crane, it brings one a wider, more authoritative vision of self and of community. The letter to Frank turns to a description of the harbor ("the glorious dance of the river directly beyond the back window of the room I am to have") and "the skyline of Manhattan, midnight, morning or evening—rain, snow or sun." The city has become for Crane "Jerusalem and Ninevah"—the city of faith *and* the city of pleasure, "all related and in actual contact with the changelessness of the many waters that surround it" (*Letters*, 182). Writing to his mother a few weeks later, Crane offered a number of lyrical descriptions of the cityscape, and noted that it was "particularly fine to feel the greatest city in the world from enough distance, as I do here, to see its larger proportions. . . . Yes, this location is the best one on all counts for me" (*Letters*, 183). There is something coy in this, of course, since the letter explains his new address without telling her that the beneficient effects of this new perspective have been brought about by love. But he does say that he is now able again to work on his poetry: "For the first time in many many weeks I am beginning to further elaborate my plans for my *Bridge* poem" (*Letters*, 183–84), and as the final chapter of this study suggests, homosexuality became one of the attempted centers of that poem.

It is in "Voyages," his sequence in celebration of this bond with Emil, that Crane attempted his most sustained literary inscription of homosexual relations as the incarnation of "the Word made Flesh"—a figure that creates multiplicities of intersubjectivity, as in the stanza from "Voyages IV" analyzed in chapter 2:

> In signature of the incarnate word
> The harbor shoulders to resign in mingling
> Mutual blood, transpiring as foreknown
> And widening noon within your breast for gathering
> All bright insinuations that my years have caught
> For islands where must lead inviolably
> Blue latitudes and levels of your eyes.
>
> (*Poems*, 38)

Here homosexual love carries the burden of producing an unmediated intersubjectivity where "all bright insinuations" of one lover (and note the "sin" in the center of that word) are gathered in the breast of the other, where all things are not merely intermingled but are actually part of one another—two men, the sea and harbor, past and future, word and thing, spirit and flesh: all become One in this metaphysics. Robert Combs has written that "Voyages" traces "the glory of value in the world and the impossibility of sustaining it" (*Vision of the Voyage*, 96), and we must see that the inability to sustain homosexuality as an absolute value in the text of "Voyages" results from two things: (a) the value the text ascribes to homosexuality is not congruent with the culture's more general devaluation of it; (b) that value is ultimately incompatible with Crane's other privileged term of absolute value, "poetry."

Most critics are able to mention the homosexual union that occasioned Crane's writing of "Voyages," but most dismiss the possibility of reading it as a homosexual text, insisting instead on its supposedly universal qualities, unaware of how "the universal" substitutes for and legitimates in such circumstances only "the heterosexual." The following comments written in 1963 by Samuel Hazo identify for us how necessary it once was for criticism to disallow the homosexual reference in the poem and the means through which the critic accomplished this as a reasonable practice:

> Whatever influence Crane's homosexual relationship with a particular sailor may have had upon the composition of "Voyages" is a point best left to psychological disquisition. There is nothing in the poems that explicitly betrays a perversion of the impulses of love, and there is no thematic reason that would lead a reader to relate the love imagery, where it does exist, to a source homosexual in nature. Consequently, a reasonable reader could find no compelling factors in the six parts of "Voyages" that would suggest that he consider the impulses of love in any but a heterosexual sense, regardless of the relationship that may have prompted them and regardless of the person to whom they may have been directed. (*Smithereen'd Apart*, 56)

Not only must we reject altogether the philosophy of "the text that speaks for itself" and the chimera of the "reasonable reader" that legitimate Hazo's heterosexist stand, but our understanding of the vocabulary of being through which Crane articulated his homosexuality and through which he imagined the ecstatic union of "Voyages" makes it clear that there *are* in fact numerous references to homosexuality in the text. What I propose in the following reading of the text ignores this injunction not to read it homosexually; in fact, my reading is designed precisely to examine what Crane understands as the meaning of homosexual love and how homosexual subjectivity expresses itself in this text.

If "Voyages" is the Crane text where the metaphysical value of homosexuality is most carefully examined, its quest to inscribe homosexuality as a site of timeless and unmediated being seems most successful in sections II, III, and IV: there the homosexual subjects of the poem seem enthralled in an ecstatic union that makes their sexuality a threshold to transcendent value and truth. But the sequence as a whole finally presents such a triumphant homosexuality as a historical impossibility, and closes with an image of mythic and disembodied desire. The turning point in this progress has most often been seen as "Voyages V," where the lovers have for some unstated reason been "overtaken" and defeated by a "tyranny of moonlight." It is tempting to read the poem only as biographical narrative, and to explain the failure of section V as mirroring the fact that Crane and Opffer had ceased to be lovers by the time of its writing. But this "failure" should be seen as more than a reflection of Crane's biography and as different from a universal truth about human attachment (i.e., that desire is always opaque, unsettling, and impossible of fulfillment). Finally, the parting of "Voyages V" is a mark of the failure of this love only if we privilege as successful and "truly" meaningful only those relationships that result in a permanent sexual bond, criteria that would invalidate many types of relationships, including most homosexual relationships in the past, caught as they were in an economy of the forbidden and the secretive. In any case, the sequence ends by reinscribing its adventure in terms of a heterosexual courtly love where by definition one accepts separation from the object of desire, and the object of desire has itself been transformed from a person into a place, a site of union and fulfilled desire, "Belle Isle." The problematic of homosexual desire is thus relocated in metaphor and implied to be no different from other desires: it is an island of individual consciousness, experience, and hope in an otherwise indifferent sea of eternity. Our task in understanding the necessity of this poem is less to critique its closing nostalgia for unity in an "imaged Word" than to understand the homosexual referents that are erased in it.

The sequence opens with a brief and relatively unimportant poem written a number of years before the others. The language in the poem is flat—especially by comparison to the rest of the sequence, which is perhaps the most insistently difficult text in a difficult corpus—and it seems to have been included as a preface to "Voyages" because of its warning to "brilliant kids" playing on a beach: "there is a line / You must not cross nor ever trust beyond it / Spry cordage of your bodies to caresses / . . . from too wide a breast" (*Poems*, 35), the line of homosexual identification. It sets the symbolist vocabulary of the text—life is fragilely conducted on the shores of a great, indifferent ocean (the poem's closing line: "The bottom of the sea is cruel"), and perhaps the most interesting thing one can do with the poem is to claim that it represents a rewriting of the conclusion to Wordsworth's "Ode: Intimations of Immortality," with its children laughing on an inland shore. But the tone of remorse and postadolescent wisdom in this opening poem is the only false note in the entire "Voyages" sequence, and one suspects that Crane used it only to make it possible to produce the extraordinary leap that then begins "Voyages II":

> —And yet this great wink of eternity,
> Of rimless floods, unfettered leewardings,
> Samite sheeted and processioned where
> Her undinal vast belly moonward bends,
> Laughing the wrapt inflections of our love.
> (*Poems*, 36)

The immediate effect of this transition is the reader's linguistic displacement: the stanza is overloaded with words that virtually shout their significance and yet it is syntactically incomplete. It is an exclamation that foregrounds the inexpressible fullness of love and the syntagmatic or serial drive of a consciousness wakened to the infinite connections inspired by it. The "great wink of eternity" that is human life and consciousness is literally (and figuratively) plural, seen in "rimless floods" and "unfettered leewardings." We can see the emotional transport and cognitive transformation registered in these figures of excess and movement as congruent with the rhetoric of homosexuality's transformative effect in Crane's letters. The stanza transforms the ocean from a signifier with a natural referent (in the first poem it was a cruel force of nature cast in a single, menacing role) to a figure of allegory. Its belly "vast" and "undinal" not only points toward the swelling of tides and waves but also suggests a certain pregnancy of meaning that follows from ascension to this symbolic plane. Because the sea is allegorically cognate with the lovers' own experiences of transformation, it may now be said to laugh "the wrapt inflections of [their] love"—the secret ("wrapt") raptures and inflected (transformed) signs through which they recognize one another and their home in the world. In this sudden shift from referential to symbolic language, the epistemological ground of the sequence moves away from the wisdom in nature on which the first poem was based, and a new system of value is introduced in which the spry cordage of bodies *can* be trusted to the caresses of love, in which love may actually be the foundation of the universe. If the "wink of eternity" is a brief human life, it also suggests that eternity *winks* at us—*flirts* with us—that it shows us a (however fleeting) sign of its interest in us, and that it does so in the vocabulary of romance. As in Blake, eternity is figured here as in love with the productions of time, and love as the original gesture or structure of the universe. It is thus that Crane may be properly called a mystic, and it is important to see that this transformation is predicated on a break with the warnings against and repressions of homosexual desire found in the opening poem of "Voyages."

The next stanza goes so far as to suggest that it is only love that survives the "sceptred terror" and whimsical "demeanors" of "this Sea, whose diapason" rings the death "knells" of "All but the pieties of lovers' hands." The sea has become once more the antagonist of human desire, a "real" force rather than a sign. As in the philosophic nihilism of "At Melville's Tomb," which precedes "Voyages" in the printed text of *White Buildings*, life is figured in this part of "Voyages" as balanced above an abyss into which it will inevitably fall, and the poem builds to a dark crescendo: "O my Prodigal, / Complete the dark confessions her veins spell"; "And hasten . . . / Hasten, while they are true,—sleep, death, desire, / Close round one instant in one floating flower." It is important to see that there *is* a "floating flower" here—the flower a figure not only of romance but also of figuration itself, as Lee Edelman has rightly suggested; it serves therefore as an assertion of meaning in the face of this imminent and incontrovertible nothingness. This assertion of absolute meaning is evidence of what Robert Combs calls Crane's "drive to penetrate illusion, to accept the oblivion toward which we move, and at the same time to celebrate life as beautiful and pleasurable" (*Vision of the Voyage*, 84). We need only add that it is *homosexual* life, the life of Sea-sons, that Crane imagines here as the voyage toward a being triumphant over nothingness. This assertion continues and closes the stanza:

> Bind us in time, O Seasons clear, and awe.
> O minstrel galleons of Carib fire,
> Bequeath us to no earthly shore until
> Is answered in the vortex of our grave
> The seal's wide spindrift gaze toward paradise.
> (*Poems*, 36)

The poet asks to be bound in time, both bound in a historical, material existence, and bound in a timely fashion—soon enough, before whatever is imminent overtakes him and his lover. And he asks that the voyage of love may continue for these two until they have found their answer, their own equivalent to the "seal's wide spindrift gaze toward paradise." This complex passage makes all of the following intertextual with one another: innocence (this is a wide-eyed gaze); drift (both the sea drift of Whitman and the drifting or voyaging of cruising, the drifting of the self as a floating flower or signifier);[22] the privileged homosexual gaze; a full mystical awareness (whatever knowledge comes to one in the "vortex of our grave" and in the horizon of a paradisal understanding).

Written in time, the homosexual subject is claimed in "Voyages III" to have "infinite consanguinity" with his other, and with that "wink of eternity" that now pays homage to his love. Everything occurs within a horizon of intersubjectivity:

> Infinite consanguinity it bears—
> This tendered theme of you that light
> Retrieves from sea plains where the sky
> Resigns a breast that every wave enthrones;
> While ribboned water lanes I wind
> Are laved and scattered with no stroke
> Wide from your side, whereto this hour
> The sea lifts, also, reliquary hands.
>
> (*Poems*, 37)

The natural world is no longer an enemy; light retrieves from the sea plains not the "dark confessions" of "Voyages II" but the "tendered theme" of love, and the sky and sea are mutually inflected (one resigns to the other only to be enthroned by it). The "water lanes I wind" are *not* the "sentences" or "sceptred terror" of the sea in "Voyages II" but are prepared for celebration and for love: they are "ribboned," "laved." There is no distance between the lover and his beloved—no need to "hasten" in this poem—there is "no stroke / Wide from your side." And the problem of time has also been temporarily suspended, for this perfect intersubjectivity produces the illusion of a present moment with the ritual aura of eternal meaning: "this hour, / The sea lifts, also, reliquary hands." This momentary respite from the cruelty of the world springs from the erotic, figured here as harbor:

> And so, admitted through black swollen gates
> That must arrest all distance otherwise,—

> Past whirling pillars and lithe pediments,
> Light wrestling there incessantly with light,
> Star kissing star through wave on wave onto
> Your body rocking!
>
> (*Poems*, 37)

This threshold image, surely subterranean and supernatural, an anal rather than vaginal harbor for masculine desire, turns the lover's body into a cosmos, glosses what the letter to Frank said was "flesh transformed by intensity of response to counterresponse." Here the homosexual body becomes a trope for the ordered universe, for identity (note the sameness of dialectic here), and—perhaps most significantly—for immortality:

> and where death, if shed,
> Presumes no carnage, but this single change,—
> Upon the steep floor flung from dawn to dawn
> The silken skilled transmemberment of song;
>
> Permit me voyage, love, into your hands . . .
>
> (*Poems*, 37)

These final lines take seriously the threat of death from sections I and II, but they imagine it as unable to alter the value of the bond between the lovers. Death is simply a "single change" wherein they will be enabled to sing from dawn to dawn to one another across the steep floor of the universe—this is not Crane at some naive point of Shelleyan reverie but the reversal of a discursive construction of homosexuality as death and dessication.[23] The final line alludes to Christ's commending of his spirit into his father's hands immediately before his death, and it would seem that this last stanza imagines a similar transcendental moment. We know that the affair with Opffer is for Crane a vision of "the Word made Flesh," and that it provided him with knowledge that "there is such a thing as indestructibility." It seems therefore in keeping with Crane's imagination of homosexuality to read a mystical power in these final phrases that grounds the significance of its religious discourse in the material, erotic body rather than in transcendence of it.

"Voyages IV" introduces the problem of distance, the lovers now possibly separate from one another geographically if not emotionally; in the face of that danger, it proclaims the poem itself as another "incarnate word" that will, in Robert Martin's words, "preserve the moment of sexual union long after the original passion is gone" (*The Homosexual Tradition*, 133). Almost every moment in it refers to its own composition, and the speaker claims that the poem retains, from the "floating flower" of the initial "inclusive" burst of love,

> All fragrance irrefragibly, and claim
> Madly meeting logically in this hour
> And region that is ours to wreathe again,
> Portending eyes and lips and making told
> The chancel port and portion of our June—
> (*Poems*, 38)

Despite the near hysteria of this passage (we read "and" five times in five lines, and the adverbs seem out of control), we can see that the poem names itself the (re)union of the lovers, producing a textual "region that is ours to wreathe again . . ./The chancel port and portion of our June," that place where eyes and lips read and speak verse, where madness and logic meet without contest.[24] "Voyages IV" asks whether one may fashion poetic immortality out of the "fatal tides" of homosexual love, and its final stanza asserts the poet's ability to lead his lover's eyes inviolably to some intersubjective yet universal truth through the act of reading and writing the poem itself; just as the lover first brought him inviolably to a transcendent self-knowledge, the poem annotates a world "In signature of the incarnate word" where the "islands" of verse and consciousness "must lead inviolably / Blue latitudes and levels of your eyes,—." The following quatrain from an early draft of the poem, "Belle Isle," condenses in a slightly less obscure fashion than does the final draft of "Voyages IV" the problematic of the "fever pitch" of homosexual transubstantiation and bliss:

> That sharp joy, brighter than the deck,
> that instant white death of all pain,—
> how could we keep than [that?] emanation
> constant and whole within the brain!
> (Weber, *Hart Crane*, 391)

In the final version of "Voyages" this keeping of the emanation of love (here the orgasmic "instant white death of all pain" can certainly not be literally sustained) becomes less unlikely, and the poem ends with the following poised couplet that suggests the poem *can* represent and maintain the emanation or essence of the lovers' relationship:

> In this expectant, still exclaim receive
> The secret oar and petals of all love.
> (*Poems*, 38)

In the "secret oar and petals," which are interestingly phallic and labial (anal?) as sexual images *and* are images of the phallic and figurative capacities of language if one reads the referent here ("this") as the poem itself, we find the poem's claim to capture the essence of the lovers' relationship.

But the insistent rhetoric of "IV" anticipates the difficulties of "V," where the lovers are overtaken by "deaf moonlight" and are bereft of language, having "no cry" with which to alter or protest the fate of their separation, and it is difficult not to see "Voyages IV" as already a denial of that separation, as the space where Crane overloads the metamorphic possibilities of homosexual union until it expresses the highest reality:

> No stream of greater love advancing now
> Than, singing, this mortality alone
> Through clay aflow immortally to you.
> (*Poems*, 38)

If we read against that insistence, and see the poem as possible evidence of writing's inability to make itself a "signature of the incarnate word," we must nevertheless see that it attempts to inscribe a hymn to the imperishable, transcendent union of two men. Even more than "Voyages III," it approaches the unspeakable in this respect, and it is only our position outside its urgencies that allows us to see it less as the "secret oar and petals of all love" than as a secret "or," a private, equivocal naming rather than a transcendent metaphysical reality.

If sections II and VI of "Voyages" present a potentially comforting maternal body of history on which time inscribes the lovers, "Voyages V" imagines its opposite as a patriarchal power that punishes them even though it is itself absent. The poem may not consciously refigure Coleridge's "Frost at Midnight," but like that poem its opening implies that the cold and dead world external to the speaker (and to both lovers) reflects an internal void they now experience: even their dreams are revealed not as fulfillments of desire but as indices of the impossible abyss between desire and satisfaction (they are only the "shred ends of remembered stars"). The former medium of love—the constant movement of language through "Adagios of islands" (II)—becomes, in this frozen world, the "tyranny of moonlight" "loved / And changed," and the trope of horizon in this poem is not intertextual with the mutual inflections of love (as it has been before in the figure of harbors whose waves resign and ships enthrone the sky) but is marked as brittle and hard, a sign of insuperable difference and distance:

Meticulous, past midnight in clear rime,
Infrangible and lonely, smooth as though cast
Together in one merciless white blade—
The bay estuaries fleck the hard sky limits.

—As if too brittle or too clear to touch!
The cables of our sleep so swiftly filed,
Already hang, shred ends from remembered stars.
One frozen trackless smile . . . What words
Can strangle this deaf moonlight? For we

Are overtaken. Now no cry, no sword
Can fasten or deflect this tidal wedge,
Slow tyranny of moonlight, moonlight loved
And changed . . .

(*Poems*, 39)

One is invited to read the poem as a dramatic monologue (perhaps the only appearance of that convention in all of Crane's more mature lyrics): the lovers have been aroused from sleep, the cables of which (a figure in which dreams are seen as telegrams) now hang from remembered stars. There begins a brief and cryptic exchange of words:

"There's

Nothing like this in the world," you say,
Knowing I cannot touch your hand and look
Too, into that godless cleft of sky
Where nothing turns but dead sands flashing.

"—And never to quite understand!" No,
In all the argosy of your bright hair I dreamed
Nothing so flagless as this piracy.

(*Poems*, 39)

The referent behind this final extraordinary image remains unspecified, and suggests, among other things, that the lover is armed only with platitudes in the face of this abysmal landscape, platitudes that neither comfort the speaker nor fulfill his desire to "strangle this deaf moonlight." Sherman Paul has suggested that there is a trace of sexual absence or abstinence in the word "flagless" (*Hart's Bridge*, 158)—that perhaps this is the betrayal or piracy mentioned. But we need to see that the treachery here, if treachery there be, lies in what the speaker sees as the lover's manipulation or exploitation of an incompatibility of knowledges—not so much the different knowledges of the two lovers but the different authorizations of knowledge each might invoke: the speaker has been presented with a cruel choice, "Knowing I cannot touch your hand and look / Too, into that godless cleft of sky." The "godless cleft" figures the supersession of that whole religious discourse of incarnation through which Crane and the text have understood this relationship as meaningful. In the crisis which is modernity, one may choose the flesh *or* the word, the hand of the lover or the godless cleft above, but they cannot be brought together. The contradiction hidden in Crane's discourse of the Word made Flesh—that the word is always already a "godless cleft," a sign of absence and castration—returns from its repression here, and the poem closes with an acknowledgment of the insuperable difference between the lovers, one not to be bridged by words. In something like a Viking farewell, Crane imagines his lover in a different realm of consciousness, asleep or perhaps claimed by his own inescapable history, but clearly passing on to further tides beyond his ken:

> Draw in your head, alone and too tall here.
> Your eyes already in the slant of drifting foam;
> Your breath sealed by the ghosts I do not know:
> Draw in your head and sleep the long way home.
> (*Poems*, 39)

This act leaves the poet alone in his search for a "Still fervid covenant" of love, an "imaged Word" that will hold "Hushed willows anchored in its glow," strong images of phallic satisfaction. The final section of "Voyages" presents this as an unabandoned quest for "what name, unspoke, / I cannot claim," for that figure that will adequately capture what the text has searched for as the unmediated and transformative possibilities of homosexuality. The poem figures its writer as a "derelict and blinded guest," "Waiting, afire" for "Some splintered garland" of words that will serve as an analog to "Creation's blithe and petalled word," but the emotional force of the passage seems to suggest that such a felicity is not to be forthcoming within human history. With the introduction of the poem's "lounged goddess," we arrive at a closure that is written in a heterosexual vocabulary and that quite honestly announces itself as a mythology. If the perfect fusion of subject and object promised in the rhetoric of incarnation has proven false, the text maintains its utopian impulse at the end through a conventional rhetoric of subject and object fixed along an axis of specularity ("Conceding dialogue with eyes / That smile unsearchable repose"). The poem and the sequence end in the following two stanzas, often read as examples of Crane's naive Romanticism:

> Still fervid covenant, Belle Isle,
> —Unfolded floating dais before
> Which rainbows twine continual hair—
> Belle Isle, white echo of the oar!
>
> The imaged Word, it is, that holds
> Hushed willows anchored in its glow.
> It is the unbetrayable reply
> Whose accent no farewell can know.
>
> (*Poems*, 40–41)

But the text here does not find some literally other place to be the proper site for homosexual desire: Belle Isle is no more literal a place than Cythere in Baudelaire's quite different imagining of heterosexual desire in "Un Voyage à Cythere." That poem ends, "Ah! Seigneur! donnez-moi la force et le courage / De contempler mon coeur et mon corps sans dégoût" (*Oeuvres Complètes*, 1: 119), something we have seen Crane express in his letters if not in "Voyages," and Baudelaire's poem as a whole exposes the idealistic vision of an "Isle of Venus" (itself a barely concealed metaphor for the vulva, of course, as well as for the island of representation that is the poem) as the "Eldorado banal de tous les vieux garçons," "une pauvre terre," "superbe fantôme." What Crane is searching for in the figure of "Belle Isle," unlike "cette île triste et noire" well known and exhausted "dans les chansons" (1: 118), is an island that has not yet made its way into song—the island of homosexual desire, and this is expressed in the closing stanzas of "Voyages VI" less as a place than as an attitude toward language.

This chapter has attempted to trace the discursive rhetoric through which homosexuality became visible and meaningful for Crane, and

"Voyages" places that search in the context of a particular poetic sequence. In sections II, III, and IV, language is imagined as transparent to desire, as itself a liquid medium (like the sea) wherein transformations and intersubjectivities might be authoritatively constructed; "Voyages V," on the other hand, imagines language as a problem—words destroy rather than confirm the relationship in that poem. In the very last lines of "Voyages VI," Crane rehabilitates language as an "unfolded floating dais," an echo of the "floating flower" in "Voyages II" and surely a sign of its continual ability to unfold rather than refuse meanings. It is on this site, dedicated to the spectrum of ecstasy (its "rainbows") and to the textuality of desire (the word "twine" suggests the braided-ness, the inter-woven-ness of desire), that we finally find "the imaged Word," the poem's final instance of "the Word made Flesh." There is, of course, some reason to doubt whether any word or lover's "reply" (even a poem) is truly "unbetrayable" after the "piracy" noted in "Voyages V," but it would seem that the figure of the "imaged Word" is not so much indicative of a naive notion of language's transparency to meaning as it is a signifier for desire that, once written, remains henceforth legible even if its literal or initial referent remains unrecoverable.

In that sense, the ending of "Voyages" is supremely radical rather than recuperative: it imagines the continuance of homosexual desire despite the "failure" of an individual relationship and thus refuses the apparent wisdom of its opening poem and affirms a commitment to homosexuality even in the face of the cruelty that marks the bottom of life. What is most important to our understanding of this finale is that this is figured as echoes and accents, the diacritical markings of language. These closing figures serve the supremely important rhetorical and political function of allowing the text to present homosexual desire within the field of language understood now not as a medium of incarnation but as one of difference, of diacritics, of writings. In that sense, Crane's "covenant" with homosexual desire is "still fervid." Some of its best moments are still forthcoming.

4
The Homosexual Lyric

Only in lyric poetry do these direct, sudden flashes of the substance become like lost original manuscripts suddenly made legible; only in lyric poetry is the subject, the vehicle of such experiences, transformed into the sole carrier of meaning, the only true reality.

GEORG LUKACS
The Theory of the Novel

"VOYAGES" terms itself the "secret oar and petals of all love" because homosexual love is in some sense the open secret of modern sexuality, and Crane's analysis of it in the poem never goes beyond what Fredric Jameson has described as "the Utopian vocation . . . of libidinal gratification" (*The Political Unconscious*, 63). "Voyages" imagines sexuality as a distinct and distinctly meaningful realm of cultural life and stakes its concern within that realm. It could not come into being as it is (as Jameson points out the Freudian project could not) without the precondition of "the autonomization of sexuality": "The precondition for the articulation and analysis of the mechanisms of desire . . . lies in the preliminary isolation of sexual experience, which enables its constitutive features to carry a wider symbolic meaning. . . . Its symbolic possibilities are dependent on its preliminary exclusion from the social field" (*The Political Unconscious*, 64). "Voyages" pursues its transcendental agenda with virtually no external reference, with little or no regard to the material conditions of articulation that Crane occasionally shows in his letters to be crucial to his understanding of his homosexuality. "Voyages" also provides evidence of the utter incompatibility of poetry and homosexual inquiry; it represents the victory of the relatively conservative agenda of poetry over any more sustained or radical questioning of homosexuality's marginal status in the erotics of modernity. It does, however, have the radical political effect of casting homosexuality as a problematic within the languages of culture rather than as a simple question of typology.

This chapter will examine in more detail how homosexuality invested itself as the problem of language for Crane—not as the second chapter did, through the question of cultural semiotics, but through an inquiry into how homosexuality and the difficult navigations it announced for the subject affected Crane's imagination of the lyric form as a genre of self-presentation. If former critical theory imagined the lyric as the poetry of a single, unified voice, and imagined the task of criticism as elaboration and reproduction of that voice (somehow without the heresy of paraphrase, where the voice of the critic intervened), more recent critical theory suggests that the lyric interest in voice is itself a trope. As Jonathan Culler writes, "The fundamental aspect of lyric writing" is "to produce an apparently phenomenal world through the figure of voice" ("Changes in the Study of the Lyric," 50). To think of poetry in this manner is to make an irrevocable break with that older model of poetic and psychological realism cited by M. H. Adams as the metaphysical pattern of the Romantic lyric. Those lyrics, Abrams suggests,

> present a determinate speaker in a particularized, and usually a localized, outdoor setting, whom we overhear as he carries on, in a fluent vernacular which rises easily to a more formal speech, a sustained colloquy, sometimes with himself or with the outer scene, but more frequently with a silent human auditor, present or absent. . . . In the course of this meditation the lyric speaker achieves an insight, faces up to a tragic loss, comes to a moral decision, or resolves an emotional problem. Often the poem rounds upon itself to end where it began, at the outer scene, but with an altered mood and deepened understanding which is the result of the intervening meditation. ("Structure of the Greater Romantic Lyric," 201)

Clearly we can rearticulate Abrams's notions to accommodate a great deal of modern and postmodern poetry that is not at all concerned with localized, outdoor settings nor always turning upon forms of personal crisis ("alienation, dejection, the loss of a 'celestial light' or 'glory' in experiencing the created world" [Abrams, 227]). But Crane's poetry often refuses these categories. His more difficult, "mature" verse in particular (that written in the years 1923–26) breaks the conventions of Romantic lyric, as Allen Grossman has shown, by situating the reader internal to the process of the poem rather than constructing him or her as the imagined auditor. As Grossman suggests, Crane does not figure authenticity of voice by staging the speaker of the poem dramatically at a distance from some more originary voice or presence; that is, his poems do not present their subject(s) in relation to the unrepeatable, as Wordsworth recalls the leech gatherer's speech, Stevens overhears the woman by the sea, or Keats hears the nightingale. Crane's poems, according to Grossman, are attempts to record the unmediated speech, sea, song, *presence* of poetry itself (Hart Crane and Poetry," 240–45). We recognize the impossible agenda of this, of course, but, as such, we must think of Crane's as abstract peoms—abstract in the same sense as Stein's prose or Arthur Dove's landscapes. And what their abstraction foregrounds most strongly as the problem of the lyric—and as the problem of the modern as well—is the textuality of subjectivity.

We might think of Crane's lyrics from this period as constituting one of the most interesting records of homosexual autobiography in the history of literature. From relatively early homosexual poems such as "Possessions" and "Recitative" (1923) through more advanced inquiries into the problematic of homosexual intersubjectivity such as "Voyages" (written in 1924 and 1925) to later and more symbolic autobiographical texts such as "Passage" (late summer 1925) and "Repose of Rivers" (1926), Crane's lyrics test the structures of identity in a way that makes them theoretical investigations of the subject and not simple exercises in recall and interpretation. Certainly we do not want to posit an evolution into an appropriate or ideologically correct attitude toward homosexuality in Crane's record of lyric autobiography, but there is an arc of development in it that moves from an early, almost intuitive or preideological thinking about subjective homosexual experience toward an insight into the ways in which that experience was mediated by forces and terms bent on constructing it as an unacceptable cultural practice. At this latter point, Crane understands homosexuality not as a subjective experience but as a subjectivity, as part of what Althusser calls "the ideological *recognition* function" ("Ideology," 172); we see this, for instance, in the letter to Winters, and we will see it as well in a number of the poems. According to Althusser, the individual recognizes and misrecognizes himself as "*really*" or "*not really*" constituted in certain ways according to the interpellations of ideology:

> *all ideology hails or interpellates concrete individuals as concrete subjects*, by the functioning of the category of the subject. . . . Ideology 'acts' or 'functions' in such a way that it 'recruits' subjects among the individuals (it recruits them all), or 'transforms' the individuals into

> subjects (it transforms them all) by that very precise operation which I have called *interpellation* or hailing, and which can be imagined along the lines of the most commonplace everyday police (or other) hailing: 'Hey, you there!' ("Idealogy," 173–74)

We have seen in the last chapter how Crane was interpellated or hailed by the subjectivity of homosexuality, how he argued against the dominant ideological assertions about that subjectivity, and how his reimagination of it, at the close of "Voyages," for instance, was nevertheless always already written within its confines—to imagine meaningful and lasting union was already to imagine heterosexually. In this chapter we will see how the traditional lyric interest in persona, individuality, and voice is concretely realized in Crane's homosexual lyrics as interpellation into ideology—specifically, the ideological contest between homosexuality and poetic authority.

The material in the previous chapter helps to explain some of the avoidances of homosexuality in Crane's text, such as the discursive instability that assured that homosexuality would appear in culture only through other, "legitimate" discourses, or the prejudices of his literary friends against the ethical or cultural effectivity of the homosexual. There is evidence to suggest, however, that even beyond these intellectual issues, Crane feared censorship and so may have suppressed the homosexual elements in his published work. Writing to Munson as early as March 1923, Crane concedes,

> I discover that I have been all-too-easy all along in letting out announcements of my sexual predilections. Not that anything unpleasant has happened or is imminent. But it does put me into obligatory relations to a certain extent with "those who know," and this irks me to think of sometimes. . . . I find the ordinary business of earning a living entirely too stringent to want to add any prejudices against me *of that nature* [italics in original]. (*Letters*, 129–30)

This does not refer specifically to the intricacies of publishing, but Crane certainly found that business too stringent to want to add any prejudices against him of any nature. And as he became more public a figure, his need to be more discreet about his sexuality increased. In this, he is not unlike Willa Cather, who (in Sharon O'Brien's words):

> could never declare her lesbianism publicly. . . . And in her fiction she never wrote directly of the attachments between women that

> were the emotional center of her life. However "natural" they may finally have seemed to her, Cather knew she could not name them to a twentieth-century audience. (*Willa Cather*, 137)

Arnold Rampersad's biography of Langston Hughes, on the other hand, makes it clear that the very existence of periodicals such as *Crisis* and *Opportunity* called forth from Hughes more consciously radical verse than he otherwise produced, helping him construct a persona as spokesman for black experience in America.

We can see Crane's impatience with the publishing industry in his brief interactions with Marianne Moore. Moore, who returned "Passage" to Crane because of its "lack of simplicity and cumulative force," completely altered "The Wine Menagerie" and published it in *The Dial* under the title "Again." In accepting it, she removed the first two stanzas of the poem entirely and made other changes that Crane did not take well. It may seem of little consequence to have this happen to a single poem, but in a corpus such as Crane's it is equivalent to deleting or rewriting one-fourth of a novel by Faulkner, let us say, before publishing it. Crane allowed Moore this liberty because he was in desperate need of both cash (he received twenty dollars on publication of "Again") and some kind of literary validation. When Moore accepted a later poem without change, Crane voiced his displeasure at her earlier editing: "This time she didn't even suggest running the last line backward" (*Letters*, 255). But Moore was not the only literary authority Crane seemed unable to please; one of his famous prose statements (where he outlines his poetics as a "logic of metaphor") was written to Harriet Monroe in an attempt to explain to her that his poetry was not nonsense, that it was in fact grounded in an explicable theory of language. But it seems he feared offending more than the standards of style: writing to Tate in the early months of 1927, he complained about the strict morality of current editorial practices:

> I've had to submit ["The Dance"] to Marianne Moore recently, as my only present hope of a little cash. But she probably will object to the word "breasts," or some such detail. It's really ghastly. I wonder how much longer our market will be in the grip of two such hysterical virgins as *The Dial* and *Poetry*!

> what strange people these . . . [editorial elision] are. Always in a flutter for fear bowels will be mentioned, forever carrying on a tradition

> that both Poe and Whitman spent half their lives railing against—and calling themselves "liberals." (*Letters*, 289, 290)

If this seems merely the complaint of someone on the outside looking in, we should remember that Crane's paranoia about literary censorship was a reality he and other writers of his day lived with. In a world that seized *The Well of Loneliness* because of its lesbian content, in a nation that prosecuted *The Little Review* for its publication of *Ulysses* (this incident came home to him especially strongly because Margaret Anderson's "defense" of Joyce appeared in the same issue of *The Little Review* as Crane's first publication in that journal) and that closed New York theaters where lesbian and gay plays appeared,[1] Crane perhaps had justification for his fears. His letters from Ohio refer several times to the "*Ulysses* situation"—"terrible to think on" (*Letters*, 72). "It is my opinion that some fanatic will kill Joyce sometime soon for the wonderful things said in *Ulysses*" (*Letters*, 95). His friend Gorham Munson had had to sneak Crane's presubscribed copy of the book into the United States in the bottom of a trunk, and Crane clearly sees the suppression of Joyce's work as symptomatic of a more generalized threat to freedom of expression: "De Gourmont's *Une Coeur Virginal* has just been published here (trans. Aldous Huxley), and I have snatched it up against its imminent suppression along with *Jurgen* and other masterpieces. . . . I cannot see his *Physique d'Amour*, translated by Pound and to be published by Boni and Liveright, will ever get beyond the printer's hands" (*Letters*, 73). Thus we should see that when Crane writes to Munson in February 1923 about "these American restrictions [on homosexuality] . . . where one cannot whisper a word" (*Letters*, 122), he refers perhaps to written as well as spoken forms of communication.

Despite this, Crane's early work includes a number of poems in which he makes homosexuality visible and important to the text, suggesting that his later literary suppression of overt references to homosexuality was a choice conditioned in part by his need to appear literarily respectable. As Tate recalled, "Hart had a sort of megalomania: he wanted to be The Great American Poet" (quoted in Unterecker, *Voyager*, 431), and the only way he could fulfill that ambition was by conforming to the overwhelmingly heterosexual conventions and expectations of the literary. Aesthetic experimentation, of course, was a sign of his seriousness as a modern artist, but homosexuality needed to remain obscure—a "private," "personal" issue of no relevance to art—

if one were to be taken seriously by those with the power to evaluate and promote one's work. I would like to compare these early texts ("C 33," "Episode of Hands," and "Modern Craft") with those written in New York during the high period of Crane's mature and difficult verse ("Possessions," "Passage," "The Wine Menagerie") to suggest how the development of a stylistic density that marks his most ambitious work balances an effacement of homosexuality as the central subject of his lyric concern. My claim is not that homosexuality disappears from his work (we have already seen its powerful presence in "Voyages" and "Recitative," both written in the later period), but that it becomes textually obscure, hidden in a multitude of oblique references that encode it as the authorizing secret of the text.

"C 33" was Crane's first published poem, a tribute to Oscar Wilde, whom he describes as having "woven rose-vines / About the empty heart of night." The inheritance Crane claims through Wilde is one of homosexual betrayal, personal suffering, and aesthetic posturing, but the title itself, which refers to the number on Wilde's cell in Reading Gaol,[2] suggests as well the oblique nature of homosexual reference in Crane's literary work even at this early point. Only those in the know—and there could not have been many—would take the title's meaning and therefore identify the poem as a homosexual text. "C 33" is what it describes Wilde's verse to be, "song of minor, broken strain," and it is most important for us as an index of Crane's response to Wilde's trial as a critical moment in the history of homosexuality. We see in it the ideological lesson Wilde offered a young man like Crane—that "searing sophistry" is no defense against suffering, implying that the arch pose is vanity and that one ought to account *de profundis* rather than from the surface. The need to "forget all blight" at the poem's close is clearly the need to forget that one is homosexual, too, and Crane accomplishes that in "C 33" through appeal to a madonna figure whose "gold head / And wavering shoulders" are meant to establish an economy of sympathy. Although he does not condemn Wilde, as did Willa Cather, Crane's poem clearly suggests that he felt (as did Wilde himself) some need for salvation from artistic and homosexual alienation at this point in his life and that the central figure through which he understood his historical link to Wilde was that of imprisonment.

"Episode of Hands," another early poem of Crane's, is atypical of this early work, for it depicts in a naturalistic fashion—more like Sandburg or Masters than Wilde or Rimbaud—a simple narrative of male bonding and its effect on the poet. "Episode of Hands" depicts the brief moment when a "factory owner's son" bandages the hand of a worker bleeding from an accident in the factory (Crane was, of course, a factory owner's son), and the poem begins with the embarrassment the two feel in being thrown into this atypical masculine relation: "The unexpected interest made him flush." It ends, however, in a warm and gentle union between the two men: "And as the bandage knot was tightened / The two men smiled into each other's eyes." Crane uses the smile as a sign of union and interpersonal knowledge throughout his career, and it is important to see that he implies a healing of both men in this smile, for the owner's son is allowed a reprieve from his alienating position *as* the owner's son. The "knot" brings the two together in a new relation: the "factory sounds and factory thoughts / Were banished from him [the son] by that larger, quieter hand / That lay in his." Crane offers this assessment of the worker's hand, making the trace of its labor an inspiration rather than an alienation:

> The knots and notches,—many in the wide
> Deep hand that lay in his,—seemed beautiful.
> They were like the marks of wild ponies' play,—
> Bunches of new green breaking the hard turf.

The central stanza depicting the actual moment of bandaging is the most interesting, however; here the owner's son is made aware of the beauty of his own hands through his connection to the worker's:

> And as the fingers of the factory owner's son,
> That knew a grip for books and tennis
> As well as one for iron and leather,—
> As his taut, spare fingers wound the gauze
> Around the thick bed of the wound,
> His own hands seemed to him
> Like wings of butterflies
> Flickering in sunlight over summer fields.
> (*Poems*, 141)

The simile of the wings almost certainly borrows from the character Wings Biddlebaum in Sherwood Anderson's short story "Hands," for Anderson was one of Crane's preferred American writers, and "Hands," the opening story of *Winesburg, Ohio,* is one of the most visible statements on American attitudes toward homosexuality before the twenties. In the story, as in Crane's poem, it is touch, the supposed escape from language, that signals the escape from conventional gender expectations: "By the caress that was in his fingers he expressed himself. . . . Under the caress of his hands, doubt and disbelief went out of the minds of the boys and they began also to dream" (*Winesburg*, 32). The change that occurs through this touch is appropriately imaged in both texts through the most standard figure for metamorphosis—the butterfly.

This is the first instance in Crane's work of the rhetoric of homosexual transformation, and the poem is constructed entirely of simile and metonymy except for one moment. That moment, the metaphor in the central line of the text—"the thick bed of the wound"—is all the more important for its singularity. The word "bed" suggests that the union between these two men has an erotic component, and it is only after this metaphorical and sublimated appearance of the homoerotic that the hands are transformed, the owner's son's becoming "Like wings of butterflies," and the worker's "like the marks of wild ponies' play." Although only obliquely acknowledged, homosexuality is not only that which ties the healing knot between worker and son but also the origin of metaphor in the poem.

If one reads the wound in "Episode of Hands" as structurally linked to homosexuality, as others of Crane's poems would invite us to do, that wound is also healed in the poem's closure, for the close makes homosexuality the positive center of an affectionate and literally healing exchange (and a healing that is neither a "cure" or repression, as is implied in the madonna figure of "C 33"). It represents instead the worker's acceptance of the son's "unexpected interest." The knot of solidarity between them comes from their *not* being defined any longer in the hierarchical relations of partriarchal masculinity and capitalist economy; rather, the poem ends with the sign of homosexual recognition: a knowing, smiling gaze. It is not surprising that Crane investigates homosexuality through this trope of wounding. In the discourse of psychoanalysis, it is structurally linked to castration, to lack or wounding,[3] and it was no doubt often a condition of suffering for Crane and others of his generation, making the metaphor appear natural in its appeal. But if we understand two further things about pain, it becomes clear that there are other possible links between wounding and homosexuality in Crane's text. In *The Body in Pain*, Elaine Scarry suggests that pain places us at the limits of language, at a level of experience that knows no object except the body (we do not experience pain "of," "about," or "for" something as we hunger for or fear a, b, or c), and it places us as well at a level of experience that can produce no signifier (according to Scarry, pain literally destroys language). Both of these structural readings of pain make its connection to homosexuality more significant for Crane, for homosexuality, like pain, had a troubled, almost nonexistent relation to referential language; it was both unmediated and unnamable. And it is possible as well that in Crane's case homosexuality was a matter of masochistic pleasure, of knowing the body as the site on which self-empowerment was written as pain.

The rhetoric of pain appears quite frequently in his late, fragmentary work, but in none of his early poems is it as clear as in the last line of "Modern Craft." There he makes the rather startling confession, "My modern love were / Charred at a stake in younger times than ours" (*Poems*, 132)—a line whose power of surprise derives from its frankness and from its break with the earlier subjects of the poem. This rather feeble protest about the burning of homosexuals in former historical periods occurs in the final lines of a poem largely taken up with a description of an indifferent and sexually jaded female muse who seems to possess a power and authority the poet does not. In fact, she seems to invert the conventions of musology, writing him rather than being written by him, and she exposes him (to himself, at least) as a poseur, a Hamlet who is unable to act and unable to affect her despite his knowledge of her:

> Though I have touched her flesh of moons,
> Still she sits gestureless and mute,
> Drowning cool pearls in alcohol.
> O blameless shyness;—innocence dissolute!
>
> She hazards jet; wears tiger-lilies;—
> And bolts herself within a jewelled belt.
> Too many palms have grazed her shoulders:
> Surely she must have felt.
>
> Ophelia had such eyes; but she
> Even, sank in love and choked with flowers.
> This burns and is not burnt . . .
>
> (*Poems*, 132)

Sherman Paul has suggested that this represents "an encounter with a prostitute," and then amends that to say that she is "less an object of the poet's interest than an object for the play of his own feelings" (*Hart's*

Bridge, 20). But what the poet seems in fact to recognize here is her utter conventionality: not only may she function (within one old script of homosexual etiology) as the rejecting female, the powerful woman who is uninterested in (or contemptuous of) the male, but it may in fact prove more powerfully and certainly more historically accurate to read her as a figure of cross-dressing, a series of contradictions, a female muse only in her ability to masquerade as one. And this reading is bolstered not only by the poem's immediate turn to the question of past homosexual persecutions (implying that this "modern craft," while alienating, is better than burning at the stake) but also by John D'Emilio and Estelle B. Freedman's suggestion that, in addition to the location of meeting places in "sites of moral ambiguity" or "transient relationships" (such as waterfronts, theaters, etc.), there was one prominent feature to the "inchoate subculture" of pre-1920 homosexuality: transvestism (*Intimate Matters,* 227–28).[4]

When we turn from these early works to Crane's more mature poems we find a remarkable difference in style, and since form is always in a determinate relation to ideology, this difference should not be seen as coincidental. The works in question were written during the period when Crane wrote both "Voyages" and "Recitative," a time during which mentors and editors alike wrestled with Crane's work and tried (sometimes unsuccessfully) to understand its significance. This was also the period (1923–26) during which homosexuality was an integrative factor in Crane's intellectual life—not merely one facet of his personality, but the center of a dense, incarnational metaphysics where the Word became Flesh. Of the celebrated difficulty of the poems of this period, R. W. B. Lewis has written,

> the lyrics of 1923–26 contain some of the most notoriously difficult verses of modern times. To some readers, Crane's lyrics have seemed so impenetrable as to arouse suspicion of fraudulence. . . . [I]t is still possible for perfectly honest critics to come up with radically different interpretations of particular stanzas or even entire poems. . . . But I am sure that when the poems (that is, the post-"Faustus and Helen" poems) are read as a group, as the product of a single large phase of Crane's creative career, many (not all) of their difficulties evaporate. (*The Poetry of Hart Crane,* 124–25)

Lewis is not exactly correct. The difficulties of these poems remain entrenched, their meanings indeterminate, shifting radically as one reads.

As the second chapter of this study suggested, that is in part due to a homosexual semiotic that is determined to refuse closure. But all the difficulties of these poems cannot be attributed to homosexuality, for their semiotic density is often directly related to Crane's other interests in modern art and literature.

Crane's indebtedness to the discourses of modernism has been documented elsewhere, and includes subjects as well as styles: his interest in machinery and technology, for instance, an interest shared by a large number of artists, photographers, and writers; his linguistic density, which is his verbal equivalent of montage or cubist effect—the attempt to create simultaneity of reference and perspective in one synchronic structure. But perhaps the most "modern" development in Crane's work was his refiguration of mimesis. Crane does not represent external objects or even internalized processes and meditations in the manner Abrams suggests is conventional for Romantic poetry and that we find as the first assumption of Eliot's poetry. It is true that the city or the machine might enter Crane's work, but they enter it as objects enter the visual field in Steiglitz's photographs, for instance, as structure, idea, abstraction.[5] Crane differs from Williams, Eliot, and Moore (and most of the writers who have taught us to read modernist texts) in that his work is not dependent upon representation in the same way as theirs. I will not take the time here to quibble about Williams's or Stevens's many variations on the abstract and the concrete (such as *Kora in Hell*, which seems experimental and antimimetic in ways analogous to Crane's antimimetic work).[6] We should perhaps think of Crane's work as having most in common with Constructivist or conceptual art, for it is often more presentational than representational in its effect, breaking the planes and contours of illusion and making one aware of the fact that it is written work—not an imitation of a "real" interior monologue nor a description of a "real" world but a piece of language that foregrounds its textuality. As Suzanne Clarke Doeren has suggested, Crane's poetry is one where "a language system takes over the subject" ("Hart Crane," 159), where there is no illusion that language functions transparently to signify the internal state of mind of a speaker or writer. Crane's is perhaps the first lyric poetry in English (and perhaps the only poetry in English until Charles Olson's or John Ashbery's) that is designed to be read as a constructed verbal artifact rather than as mimetic of any natural discourse.[7] The lyric focus in Crane seems, finally, to be neither the minimal unit of the image, as in Imagist work, nor the maximal unit of the poem conceived as organic whole, as in Romantic lyrics or dramatic monologues that trace psychologized themes. Lyricality in Crane is that point where language breaks its transparency and forces the reader to authorize his relation to it, and for Crane this characteristically occurs on intermediate levels of meaning: in syntax and semantics. Doeren writes that "Crane's poems seem to come into existence at the point where . . . a subject becomes some other form of language: a verb, an object, a preposition" (83), and it is precisely in this use of language as a thick, palpable medium for construction that Crane's texts take their place beside other modernist experiments with aesthetic media.

The standard reading of Crane's deviation from poetic norms draws on prose statements such as the following, written for a proposed symposium in *Broom:* "It is as though a poem gave the reader as he left it a single, new *word*, never before spoken and impossible to actually enunciate, but self-evident as an active principle in the reader's consciousness henceforward" (*Poems*, 221). Crane's poems are explicitly tied to this search for the "new word," for what he terms in "The Wine Menagerie" "new anatomies" of the "new thresholds" on which humanity stands. But it is important to see that if Crane's poems are initiatory and almost literally liminal, they are not unconstructed moments. Just as the silences of homosexuality are not unstructured but are a set of conditions that mark the relation of homosexuality to other cultural practices, the antistructural quality of Crane's difficult poems nevertheless maps a set of differential relations for the production of meaning. Crane's characteristic poems seem interested neither in a literally transcribed homosexual reality nor in an imaginary realm completely interiorized and private (the assumption behind dismissals by Moore and others that the poems were no doubt meaningful but too obscure to be read); rather, Crane's most characteristic texts are interested in linguistic meaning and subjectivity as they occur through the difficulty of textuality.

"Chaplinesque" (1921) is an interim text that provides useful contrast to the early homosexual poems discussed above and the difficult, prophetic poems of 1923–26 that come after it. It seems to have been particularly pleasing to Crane, and he was confounded by his friends' confused responses to it. Stylistically it is a step toward the dense semiosis that attends Crane's full development; thematically it is a rather sentimental and even maudlin poem that suggests the poignancy of innocence in a world that crushes it (the Chaplin thematic). On its surface, the poem would appear to have nothing to do with homosexuality,[8] but it marks the beginning of Crane's disintegration of the speaking subject (although that subject appears here as "we"), and it is on this point of pronominal identification that we can begin to see the discursive outcomes of Crane's poetic response to homosexuality. The poem opens:

> We make our meek adjustments,
> Contented with such random consolations
> As the wind deposits
> In slithered and too ample pockets.
> (*Poems*, 11)

So much depends in this case not on chickens, rain, and wheelbarrows, but on who steps in to define and fill the vacuum of that "we." Who makes meek adjustment to the world? Who, later in the poem, will defy the law and "Dally the doom of that inevitable thumb / That slowly chafes its puckered index toward us"? Who "can still love the world, who find / A famished kitten on the step, and know / Recesses for it from the fury of the street"? For whom does Chaplin speak? For whom does the poem speak?

In discussing this poem, R. W. B. Lewis acknowledges that the text is (in its own words) "evasive," but Lewis does not imagine that one of the things evaded here is a more direct address to the social condition of the homosexual subject. This is not to suggest that "Chaplinesque" is intentionally "about" that subject but is, rather, to suggest that one of the strongest referents of subjectivity for Crane in 1921 was his experience as a homosexual—that the "we" of "Chaplinesque" is constructed in sight of the practice of homosexuality, its alienations and consequent, compensatory nostalgias. The poem is, that is, *and perhaps despite its intentions*, an allegory of homosexual desire and its articulation within the "American restrictions" of the Midwest ca. 1921. The next to last stanza tries to find virtue in the meek adjustment and "smirk" or "dull squint" of "innocence" and "surprise" with which this subject meets the "inevitable thumb" of the law (patriarchal repressions), and it suggests that a subjectivity grounded in desire always exceeds those social mechanisms and technologies that seek to control or euphemize it—the heart lives on:

> And yet these fine collapses are not lies
> More than the pirouettes of any pliant cane;
> Our obsequies are, in a way, no enterprise.

> We can evade you, and all else but the heart:
> What blame to us if the heart live on.
>
> (*Poems*, 11)

The "fine collapses" of obsequy, euphemism, and poetry are not lies, Crane claims, and he locates the authority for their "truth" in the heart—signifying here both a center of consciousness and the center of desire. It is social pressure ("enterprise" picks up here on a whole discourse of antimaterialist writing in the period) which forces the lie: the "victim" of that pressure remains blameless in his own heart.

Crane has not by any means made a full transition into the advanced poetry of a decentered subjectivity in "Chaplinesque." The poem ends with a rather trite assertion of transformation that seems a restatement of Emerson's claim that he was everywhere defeated yet born to victory:

> The game enforces smirks; but we have seen
> The moon in lonely alleys make
> A grail of laughter of an empty ash can,
> And through all sound of gaiety and quest
> Have heard a kitten in the wilderness.
>
> (*Poems*, 11)

In some sense the preposterousness of the final image marks a limit to Crane's naturalized Romanticism (how far from "The Tyger!"); two years later, when composing "Possessions," his rhetoric of transformation will be truly apocalyptic. But the closure marked here is also part of the poem's homosexual textuality, for the homosexual's heart needs to be defended as blameless, and the reality of its consolations asserted: loneliness in cruisey alleyways can become laughter; a genuine tenderness can be located amid the hubbub "of gaiety and quest." The tenor of this final stanza is clearly of a piece with the more optimistic moments in Crane's letters from Cleveland, and it provides in its reconstruction of a homosexual "we" something Crane felt sorely lacking at this time: a community in which he could discuss the contours of his existence, the "fine collapses" of his life, as if they were not inherently illegitimate as subjects for poetry.

Crane's investigation of homosexuality as cognate to the textual indeterminacy of subjectivity is nowhere as openly displayed as in the 1923 poem "Possessions." Of those poems written in this period, "Possessions" is the one that most makes a critical consideration of its homosexual referents unavoidable. Robert Martin has called it "the first poem of the modern urban homosexual in search of sex, his hesitations the result of fear and self-oppression" (*The Homosexual Tradition*, 128). But it is important to our understanding of both Crane and his construction of homosexuality as a possibility and an impossibility of meaning to see that "Possessions" does not dramatize that search in a straightforward fashion. It does not present an individual confronting or ruminating on this as a psychic or social problem. "Possessions" employs the first-person pronoun, and there is some attempt to locate that person within a landscape that produces him as meaningful, but it is not by any means a dramatic monologue. Crane employs the "I" here not so much to relate an individual's experience as to provide a field for those emotional and intellectual conflicts that do battle through him. Thus, Martin's claim that this is "the first poem of the modern urban homosexual in search of sex" is only partially correct. The problematic nature of the search for sex is only part of the poem's concern, and this is how Crane's text differs from Whitman's *Calamus*, for instance, or from a John Ashbery poem about cruising, "The Ongoing Story," both of which see homosexuality as transparent to the individual and not as a system in which the individual's meaning and desire are already written for him. In "City of Orgies," for instance, Whitman claims it is the "frequent and swift flash of eyes offering me love" that "repay me" (*Leaves of Grass*, 126), and while there are poems in *Calamus* such as "Of the Terrible Doubt of Appearances" and "Earth, My Likeness" that suggest some difficulty in the expression of homosexual desire, Whitman's more typical texts on homosexuality locate it internal to the subject and transparent to his real self. Ashbery's "The Ongoing Story," which is not perhaps representative of his most skeptical interrogations of identity, locates the act of cruising as one stable field in a life otherwise uninterpretable and unstable: "It's as though I'd been left with the empty street / A few seconds after the bus pulled out." Personal and poetic closure are achieved in the following:

> you,
> In your deliberate distinctness, whom I love and gladly
> Agree to walk into the night with,
> Your realness is real to me though I would never take any of it
> Just to see how it grows. A knowledge that people live close by is,
> I think, enough. And even if only first names are ever exchanged
> The people who own them seem rock-true and marvelously self-sufficient.
> (*A Wave*, 11)

In the context of the poem—and in the context of Ashbery's entire oeuvre—there is perhaps some irony in this comfort which defines reality as the realness of others. Certainly the marvelous self-sufficiency of others offered at the close of the poem is proven to be an illusion by the knowledge elsewhere evident in it that one's own self-sufficiency is a fiction. But the poem does not destabilize the reading subject as does Crane's "Possessions."[9] Crane's investigation of homosexuality, which occurs historically somewhere between the mystical naiveté of Whitman discovering the homoeroticism that is identical to his "self" and the inside joke of Ashbery's New York, where everything—including homosexuality—has always been known all along, is settled on a historical threshold where desire is no longer a secret excitement securely anchored within a Romantic self but is not yet a cultural cliché enabling only parody. "Possessions" presents homosexuality as a text but it understands the subject as lost within that text.

A closer inspection of the poem suggests that what is rejected from the outset in "Possessions" is less the practice of homosexuality than the constricting representations of it available to the homosexual and to the homosexual poet. In an almost polemical fashion, "Possessions" rejects the rhetorical construction of homosexuality as a "fixed stone of lust" and replaces it at the poem's close with a more idealized vision of "bright stones wherein our smiling plays." The poem is an attempt to depict homosexual existence as more than a "Record of rage and partial appetites," this last phrase nicely balanced to suggest that desire is both determined (one always favors or is partial to something) and fragmentary (desire is also partial and never whole; it never makes one whole, especially if it is taboo). But if homosexuality inscribes one as the field of rage and partial appetite, dividing the subject from proper knowledge of himself in his possession of sexual object after sexual object, the poem insists that this is preparatory to an "inclusive" moment when a "pure possession . . . / Whose heart is fire" will—as in the golden halo effect of Crane's letters—transform possessor and possessed into a single being.

A diachronic reading of the poem does not neatly display what I have here suggested is the poem's impact; the poem seems alternately to come into and go out of focus, to hesitate, as Martin suggests, and part of that hesitation or indeterminacy is due to its skewed syntax. If Crane claimed this text to be an example of how he "work[ed] hard for a more perfect lucidity" (*Letters*, 176), it is not immediately possible to grant that this poem exemplifies that work. Although the poem is brief and its major outlines are clear, there is considerable obscurity in specific passages and in the relation of details to the larger structure. Without intending it, Robert Combs suggests that the poem is an allegory of homosexual desire: "The difficulty of this poem lies chiefly in the way Crane delays interpretational clues which serve gradually to orient the reader. . . . 'Trust,' 'rain,' and 'key' in the first stanza are like elements in a mysterious allegory that seem to need interpretation by the last word 'lust.'" (65).[10] It would seem to be Crane's strategy to keep syntactic relations, as homosexual desire itself remains, indeterminate in the opening of the poem. We can see only textual units, possible events, attitudes, and locations that exist in juxtaposition but without any continuity or englobing frame of reference. It is a world of contiguous and accidental relations:

Witness now this trust! The rain
That steals softly direction
And the key, ready to hand—sifting
One moment in sacrifice (the direst)
Through a thousand nights the flesh
Assaults outright for bolts that linger
Hidden,—O undirected as the sky
That through its black foam has no eyes
For this fixed stone of lust. . . .
(*Poems,* 18)

We see here only an act of implied entry; "the key, ready to hand," is a phallic object employed to cross some threshold, but that threshold remains undefined (although this act of unlocking certainly bristles with sexual innuendoes and is linked figuratively to the erotic "bolts that linger / Hidden"). The desire in this opening is overwhelming in its sequential duration ("a thousand nights") and in the intensity of its passion ("the flesh / Assaults outright"), and it occurs under a vacuous yet menacing sky that certainly draws its significance from religious injunctions that traditionally have "[had] no eyes" for homosexuality. If one accepts the pun on "eyes," this "black foam" of heaven at once names and negates homosexual identity, it robs one of one's "I," and its rain (reign) "steals softly direction" until one does not know which way one is going. This moment, "sift[ed]" from a thousand, occurs within the context of cosmic alienation, and one of its meanings as a "moment in sacrifice" would appear to be that the homosexual sacrifices himself on a "fixed stone," a pagan altar of lust.

If the first stanza articulates homosexuality as a broken syntax, the second stanza asks the reader to contemplate the magnitude of such displaced meaning when it is cast across the course of a lifetime (signified here as the accumulation of "an hour").

> Accumulate such moments to an hour:
> Account the total of this trembling tabulation.
> I know the screen, the distant flying taps
> And stabbing medley that sways—
> And the mercy, feminine, that stays
> As though prepared.
>
> (*Poems*, 18)

There is in this stanza little referential clarity; although it is possible to say that something in the last four lines seems to assuage the emptiness of the "trembling tabulation," it is not possible to say what exactly that is. It is a "screen," "distant flying taps," a "stabbing medley that sways," and "mercy, feminine, that stays / As though prepared." We see in the vocabulary of distance a vague outline perhaps of longing or romance, in the stabbing medley that sways a sense perhaps of poignancy and seduction. And if mercy is feminine, that suggestion is perhaps less surprising than its appearance here, an appearance that makes the alienation of the first stanza even more overtly masculine in retrospect. How that mercy stays and for what or how it is prepared seem indecipherable; "stays" can mean both "remains" and "supports," and "prepared" could mean, to follow out the religious imagery of the preceding stanza, "preordained," prepared from before. In any case, this second stanza suggests alternatives to the opening of the poem: intersubjectivity and mercy are presented as being "real" qualities of homosexuality meant to counter its representation as nothing more than predatory lust.

The third stanza accepts the heavy burden of interpretation in the phrases "fixed stone of lust" and "take up the stone." But it does so without speech, "As quiet as you can make a man," and assigns that burden to an individual "Wounded by apprehensions out of speech."

> And I, entering, take up the stone
> As quiet as you can make a man . . .
> In Bleecker Street, still trenchant in a void,
> Wounded by apprehensions out of speech,

I hold it up against a disk of light—
I turning, turning on smoked forking spires,
The city's stubborn lives, desires.
(*Poems*, 18)

The difficult, unspeakable quality of homosexuality stands clearly behind this construction. Nevertheless, the poet "hold[s] . . . up against a disk of light" this stone that represents the "city's stubborn lives, desires." If the "turning, turning on smoked forking spires" seems to suggest a demonic skewering appropriate to Bosch's *Garden of Earthly Delights* (and thus to be a continuation of the vocabulary of punishment and wounding that surrounds homosexuality), we need to see as well that this refers to the poet's textual production. The "forking spires" (both phallic and religious aspirations) are the double-pronged instrument of writing he uses to hold this topic up for inspection. Crane's "General Aims and Theories," which postdates this poem by two years but is nonetheless relevant to this text, may serve as a gloss on how Crane conceives the poet's civic function:

> It seems to me that a poet will accidentally define his time well enough simply by reacting honestly and to the full extent of his sensibilities to the states of passion, experience, and rumination that fate forces on him, first hand. He must, of course, have a sufficiently universal basis of experience to make his imagination selective and valuable. His picture of the "period," then, will simply be a by-product of his curiosity and the relation of his experience to a postulated "eternity." (*Poems*, 218)

What we see in this image of the stone of lust held up to the light makes a claim for the poet's relevance similar to that offered in "General Aims and Theories": "Possessions" examines homosexuality (the "stubborn lives, desires" of the city that are at stake here as the "passion" and "experience" fate forced on Crane) against the background of "a postulated 'eternity'" in order to define it for this time. No longer an unshakable paradigm or "fixed stone" of lust, homosexuality begins here to be figured contiguously—in the syntagmatic placing of one term against another. Thus, Crane reverses not only the meaning of homosexuality as a "fixed stone of lust" but (perhaps more significantly) the location of meaning in the fixity of metaphor and paradigm, that possibility of unshakable meaning out of which the poem's initial sense of alienation arose.

The opening lines of the last stanza quite clearly locate the dilemma of homosexuality (on the "horns" of which one is tossed) within a problematic of language and representation.

> Tossed on these horns, who bleeding dies,
> Lacks all but piteous admissions to be spilt
> Upon the page whose blind sum finally burns
> Record of rage and partial appetites.
> The pure possession, the inclusive cloud
> Whose heart is fire shall come,—the white wind rase
> All but bright stones wherein our smiling plays.
> (*Poems,* 18)

If homosexuality as a "fixed stone of lust" is traditionally figured as a wound or lack (both of which tropes appear in the poem), what it seems most crucially to lack are "piteous admissions . . . spilt / Upon the page." Although these admissions are "piteous," and the homosexual still cloaked in the rhetoric of guilt, more open textual representations would allow some challenge to negative paradigms of the private and public implications of the homosexual life. Such representations, when themselves tabulated, would (unlike the trembling moments at the beginning of the poem) "finally [burn]" the "Record of rage and partial appetites" that are the legacy of the paradigm of lust. This image of burning transforms the demonic language of the text; the "pure possession" or "inclusive cloud / Whose heart is fire shall come" and possess or repossess the now dispossessed homosexual man. The figure of the "bright stones wherein our smiling plays" also reverses the punishing god (and the altar of sacrifice) from the opening stanza and replaces it with a vision that can only be called, according to the poem's terms, "feminine." In the poem's final lines we see on a cosmic scale the "mercy, feminine, that stays / As though prepared" that has been the homosexual's internalized source of comfort and trust up to this point, that longed-for inclusive cloud that sanctions homosexual desire. What "Possessions" finds in "trust" is neither transcendence of the body nor foreclosure of homosexual desire but their positive integration into myth. What the poem seeks is a visionary love that can accommodate the homosexual and no longer isolate him as an example of lust.

Written two years after "Possessions," "Passage" presents a narrative of poetic coming to power. The poem does not explicitly examine the discursive problems of homosexuality, but in tracing a problematic development or rite of passage into self-awareness, "Passage" is an instance of homosexual autobiography. It is perhaps the most well made of Crane's shorter, visionary lyrics, and its success is due in part to the fact that it brackets homosexuality as a textual problem and therefore avoids the difficulties of articulation seen in "Possessions" or "Recitative." But in its revision of two Whitman texts, "Passage to India" and "Out of the Cradle Endlessly Rocking," it engages the question of homosexual autobiography, depicting the self as literally textual—a book—alienated from any transcendental, Emersonian illusion of transparency, self-reliance, or fructifying presence. The poem trades on metaphors familiar to readers of modern American poetry from Stevens's "The Idea of Order at Key West" (which also refigures "Out of the Cradle"), but here the speaker himself "hear[s] the sea" and attempts to present to the reader knowledge of an unmediated vision. "Passage" is "The Idea of Order" without the woman by the sea or the inescapable mediation that provides the logic of epistemology in Stevens.

But if the poem is built upon a desire for self-discovery and passage into mature and unmediated power,[11] its promise of "an improved infancy" cannot be redeemed. In Emersonian terms, the self succumbs to Necessity—for Crane, this has to do with the inescapable otherness of the "I." "Passage" unwrites a naive Romantic subjectivity in its rejection of the trope of recovered memory and writes instead a subject divided from himself, forced to thieve his life in a writing where textuality and difference intervene. Unlike the cognitive ego privileged by memorial Romantic texts such as Wordsworth's, the subject in "Passage" does not recover an originary self-knowledge and -authorization but is actually annihilated by his "too well-known biography." The speechlessness etymologically implied in the "improved infancy" that inaugurates the poet's quest is exposed in the end as an impossibility; man is condemned to speech, to a written life where desire is not transparent to its object but is opaque and mediated even when the object of desire is self-knowledge. Crane took as the epigraph for *White Buildings* the apocalyptic line closing section IV of Rimbaud's "Enfance": "Ce ne peut être que la fin du monde, en avançant," and we know that the apocalyptics of Rimbaud center most heavily in the subject, the "I" about whom he wrote "je est un autre." The section of "Enfance" Crane quoted is in fact a map of slippages and unsettled identities leading not to some resolution of crisis but dissolving in a forbidding and inhuman wasteland:

> Je suis le saint. . . . Je suis le savant. . . . Je suis le piéton de la grand'route. . . . Je serais bien l'enfant abandonné sur la jetée partie à la haute mer, le petit valet suivant l'allée dont le front touche le ciel.
>
> Les sentiers sont après. Les monticules se couvrent de genêts. L'air est immobile. Que les oiseaux et les sources sont loin! Ce ne peut être que la fin du monde, en avançant. (*Oeuvres complètes*, 124)

Crane's "Passage" shares with "Enfance" this vocabulary of abandonment, this symbolic landscape and its stifling atmosphere, and the distant, unachievable goal of an identity confirmed in the regularity of social conventions; there is perhaps no better gloss on Crane's reading of the subject's construction in the gaps and aporiae of language than Rimbaud's reading of it.

But Crane's refigurations in "Passage" are aimed primarily at Whitman's myth of undefeated self-presence and transcendental knowledge. The differences between the "glittering abyss" of subjectivity in Crane's poem and Whitman's "outsetting bard" who "do[es] not forget" in "Out of the Cradle" (*Leaves of Grass*, 251, 253) could not be more striking. Although the Whitman poem investigates the condition of matelessness, and claims that the originary song is "Death, death, death, death, death" (*Leaves of Grass*, 253), the poem is not "The Raven," and the message of the bird in the poem is not "Nevermore." Everything in Whitman's text is recoverable. In "Passage," the final lines suggest that nothing is: "What fountains did I hear? what icy speeches? / Memory, committed to the page, had broke." I do not wish to underestimate the power of difficulty of Whitman's version of poetic authorization, but the urgent homosexual and demonic possibilities of Whitman's Other, who arouses "the fire, the sweet hell within, / The unknown want, the destiny of me," seem (finally) tamed in the text by that later, remembering bard, who claims: "never more shall I cease perpetuating you" (*Leaves of Grass*, 252). The Other in "Passage" is a thief whose appropriation of one's autobiography suggests that he has never ceased perpetuating the "I," but that that "I" will never remember itself except through the writing of this unnamable Other who, in fact, dismembers it.

Like "Out of the Cradle," the poem's first inspiration occurs in hearing the sea, and the opening of the poem (which, it has been said, can only be intoned) introduces a subject and landscape mythic in their simplicity:

Where the cedar leaf divides the sky
I heard the sea.
In sapphire arenas of the hills
I was promised an improved infancy.
(*Poems*, 21)

This "improved infancy" represents less a recovered past than a completely new one, a secure return to the origin of knowledge and self-authorization that has before been unavailable to the speaker. This would truly be an identity defined in mythic rather than historical or personal terms ("sapphire" is a sign of the sublime in Crane), and the ritual of self-purification such quests have traditionally required begins here with the speaker jettisoning memory—an action which figures his removal from history:

Sulking, sanctioning the sun,
My memory I left in a ravine,—
Casual louse that tissues the buckwheat,
Aprons rocks, congregates pears
In moonlit bushels
And wakens alleys with a hidden cough.
(*Poems*, 21)

This stanza presents difficulties of the kind that make Crane's poetry "obscure" even to his most attentive readers: the odd choice of qualities assigned to memory; the reason for the speaker "sulking" at the promise of "an improved infancy." But the stanza may be navigated. Sulking signifies something about the solitary nature of the journey toward self-reliance that lies before the speaker—and the notion of authorization that accrues to "sanctioning the sun" may be read as heliotropic (that is, as an authorization of metaphor as nature) or as the sanctioning of a poetic "son." A number of significant qualities are assigned to the memory the speaker leaves behind, not the least of which is its random or "casual" nature, but more important than the specific meaning we might wish to assign to the odd phrases "tissues the buckwheat," "Aprons rocks," and "congregates pears" (noting their sociality and their linguistic thickness) is the realization that their most egregiously arbitrary construction foregrounds the memorial as the idiosyncratic rather than as an "improved," more universally meaningful mode of knowledge.[12]

The journey the speaker undertakes requires passage through a demanding waste land toward a landscape of plenitude, but even while that promised land is in sight, the "chimney-sooted heart of man" claims him, and he finds it impossible to escape the burdens of personal and cultural history (and desire). At this point the text employs images from the discourse of religion, and it is difficult not to see in the failures of this passage some implication of inescapable evil—that which, in Emerson's words, makes man the dwarf of himself and a god in ruins:

> Dangerously the summer burned
> (I had joined the entrainments of the wind).
> The shadows of boulders lengthened my back:
> In the bronze gongs of my cheeks
> The rain dried without odour.
>
> "It is not long, it is not long;
> See where the red and black
> Vine-stanchioned valleys—": but the wind
> Died speaking through the ages that you know
> And hug, chimney-sooted heart of man!
>
> So was I turned about and back, much as your smoke
> Compiles a too well-known biography.
>
> (*Poems*, 21)

The mythic journey has great rewards: the lord's vineyard, an improved infancy; it both promises and requires loss of self: memory is left behind, the senses do not avail ("The rain dried without odour"), and the body itself begins to disappear into the wind or to metamorphose into the instruments of its own ritualized meaning ("the bronze gongs of my cheeks"). Finally, however, the embodiedness of man, and in this case his specific industrial moment (his "chimney-sooted heart"), makes the journey to transcendence through a loss of self impossible. The pilgrim is "turned about and back" in just the same way that the passionate "smoke" of the heart "Compiles a too well-known biography" that cannot be unwritten. What cannot be escaped is the very thing that defines the speaker's subjectivity: the "experience and rumination that fate forces on him [the poet], first hand" (*Poems*, 218).

"Passage" suggests at this point the incompatibility of metaphysical quest with homosexual experience (certainly Crane's "too well-known" if too-little-understood "biography"), but the speaker does not collapse;

rather, he returns "To argue with the laurel," to produce poetry despite the absence of some transcendental authority. There he finds "a thief beneath [the laurel], my stolen book in hand" and the book is not the Book of Life he had sought but the book of death, of writing: the "too well-known biography" itself. It would perhaps be comforting to believe that some "real" Other has stolen the text of one's life from oneself—that Emil kept Crane from the promised land of homosexual bliss; that Eliot kept Crane from the poetic authority he deserved.[13] But the preceding stanza has suggested that it is an internal flaw, the "chimney-sooted heart of man" itself, that is responsible for failure in the quest for self-possession: the speaker returns to the scene of his abandoned memory to confront himself in the evening, the (historical) lateness or modernity of his life:

> The evening was a spear in the ravine
> That throve through very oak. And had I walked
> The dozen particular decimals of time?
> Touching an opening laurel, I found
> A thief beneath, my stolen book in hand.
>
> "Why are you back here—smiling an iron coffin?"
> "To argue with the laurel," I replied:
> "Am justified in transience, fleeing
> Under the constant wonder of your eyes—."
>
> (*Poems*, 21)

If the poet is to be "justified" he will not be justified in a religious sense, for that would assign him a transcendental being, one with too fixed an identity. In "Passage," he is justified only "in transience," in the materiality of history, the materiality of the signifier, the materiality of the body.

Like "Possessions," "Passage" ends in apocalypse. It does not, however, promise some new order to come but records the annihilation of the single identity. The thief, like one of the Fates cutting the thread of life, closes the book, and all is lost to the poet. His memories are irrecoverably closed in a book no longer open, and the only animated figure that remains at the end of the poem is a serpent on an empty beach:

> He closed the book. And from the Ptolemies
> Sand troughed us in a glittering abyss.
> A serpent swam a vertex to the sun

> —On unpaced beaches leaned its tongue and drummed.
> What fountains did I hear? what icy speeches?
> Memory, committed to the page, had broke.
>
> (*Poems*, 21)

The serpent, usually an image of time in Crane because the shedding of its skin can be used to figure the progressive moments of history, evokes connotations of evil here as well. It suggests the inhuman nature of the universe, like the barren world that ends H. G. Wells's *Time Machine*. The "unpaced beaches" are both the as-yet-unwritten pages of history and a natural slate on which humans can make no inscription: only the snake signifies, man does not. His books and arguments with the laurel—"from the Ptolemies"—only magnify his cosmic irrelevance, are only so much sand in the "glittering abyss" of time. In Coleridge's gloss on "Kubla Khan" it is awakening from sleep that seals one's loss of inspiration—the fountains and icy speeches of Xanadu cannot be recovered and inscribed; in "Passage," writing is the figure for waking to such a loss. In this poem there is only the written text of life, and that text may only be stolen from others if it is to be owned at all.

One cannot overstate how far short of its desire for self-authorization "Passage" falls; it is as nihilistic as "Voyages" is ecstatic. It places an extreme deconstructive pressure on the subject of autobiography, and as a homosexual autobiography is perhaps unmatched in the canon of American poetry in its unwillingness to credit some myth or other of compensation. The poetry of Frank O'Hara usually refuses the myths of personal transcendence as well, and even the compensation of self-knowledge is withheld from the subject in his work. Despite the fact that it does so in such a materially and historically contingent manner that one never reads ontology in its appearance, O'Hara's text so enshrines the personality of its author as the source of meaning that it can hardly be said to pressure the subject to the extreme that Crane's work does. Even in poems like "Mayakovsky" or "Joe's Jacket," where the speaking/writing subject imagines himself as existing only in the mediations of others, or in his elegies to himself and others ("The 'Unfinished,'" "In Memory of My Feelings," "The Day Lady Died"), where knowledge is only ever knowledge of the conditions of late arrival, the processes of mediation are usually resolved by the poem's close through the consolation of concrete social structures such as friendship, love, and pity, or by one of the ironic, authoritative poses of modernity such as self-deprecation or camp. In the end, the solidity of isolation (the reified notion of a supreme personal fiction) marks the difference between Crane's response to the problem of the subject and the response one finds in O'Hara: Crane is never self-deprecating even when he is being most skeptical about the value of the self. And that difference is itself connected to the quite different historical situations of the two writers: not only the difference between New York homosexuality in 1920 and 1960 but also (and perhaps more importantly) the difference between Crane's almost desperate stake in the formally literary and O'Hara's coy refusal of it.

"The Wine Menagerie," like "Passage" written during the summer of 1925, is more clearly concerned with the issue of homosexuality although it appears in the poem as a more generalized problem of pleasure and frenzy, as drunkenness and sexual ecstasy, two somatic states linked for Crane and, in his particular case, both illegal.[14] It might be thought of as both more and less autobiographical than "Passage"—more, in that its drama is set in a modern bar rather than on some symbolic plane, thereby allowing Crane to confront the specters of alcoholism and sexual instability that were two of the thieves of his life; less, in that it does not trace an archetypal pattern of self-authorization and devotes less of its attention to the experience of an identifiable individual. "The Wine Menagerie" takes its place in a sequence of American poems about poetic authority that figure inspiration as inebriation (a sequence that includes Emerson's "Bacchus," Dickinson's "I taste a liquor never brewed," and Ashbery's "As One Put Drunk into the Packet-Boat"), but sex is also tested as a poetic inspiration and as a source of social meaning in "The Wine Menagerie," something not seen in the other poems mentioned here. Although alcohol sanctions vision in his text, Crane's is not an originary libation of "remembering wine" as in Emerson (as "Passage" suggests, remembrance fails in Crane). Nor is his inebriate "of Air," a diminutive "little Tippler," as in Dickinson; rather, it is a "leopard ranging always in the brow," a potentially violent and predatory thing, a creature from the abyss of a bottomless desire. And sexual desire is also violent and bestial here, a struggle for supremacy. Certainly one wishes to grant the complex and often overwhelming displacement of subjectivity that often overtakes both Emerson and Dickinson, but in Crane the syntagmatic drive of desire threatens to destroy all social contracts altogether. The ego given over only to the pursuit of desire can never be satisfied, and as Robert Combs suggests in a reading of "Voyages" that is applicable here, "the heart is insatiable"

(*Vision of the Voyage*, 104) in Crane. It is not that Emerson and Dickinson haven't their nihilistic moments—quite the contrary. But in Crane the nihilism seems more perverse, for in his text the nihilistic moment is not so much the fear that life comes to nothing as it is the insistence that the something it comes to is cruelty ("The bottom of the sea is cruel").

The poem begins with a general proposition about alcohol's ability to induce a visionary moment, and this gradually centers on the speaker.[15] But his identity is adduced to be only an effect of alcohol; he becomes a label that decanters "Wear . . . in crescents on their bellies" and he is "conscripted to" or written according to *their* "glow":

> Invariably when wine redeems the sight,
> Narrowing the mustard scansions of the eyes,
> A leopard ranging always in the brow
> Asserts a vision in the slumbering gaze.
>
> Then glozening decanters that reflect the street
> Wear me in crescents on their bellies. Slow
> Applause flows into liquid cynosures:
> —I am conscripted to their shadows' glow.
>
> (*Poems*, 23)

"Slow / Applause flows into liquid cynosures," obscure as it is, points as well to this surrender of identity to the "cynosure" or guiding star of alcohol, its liquidity much like the "justified" transience of identity in "Passage." The slow applause seems not to be a literal clapping of hands but the gradual granting of assent (we "applaud" qualities and efforts in a metaphorical usage of the word), and this would refer to the speaker's gradual flow into the state of alcoholic vision. Slowly, he becomes what the "glozening decanters" write him to be. These are not "glistening" decanters. "Glozening" means, primarily, "glossing," commenting upon, making a marginal note; it means secondarily "flattery," or deceit. And "decanters" has an obsolete reference to "decantate," to repeat or sing over and over again. So in the poem's opening, we have glossed the otherness of inspiration, the emptying out of self into the cynosure of alcohol which comments upon, makes marginal note of "the street" and reflects the self in its "shadows' glow." "The Wine Menagerie," as others of Crane's difficult texts, confronts us with the linguistic construction of the speaking subject, in this case with the *specific*, uncanny scandal of the speaking animal.

The "I" that is conscripted to this "shadows' glow" becomes an implied point of view through the rest of the poem but remains invisible in the next five stanzas; alcohol provides only a perspective, and as the world becomes more physical or embodied (to the point where even decanters have bellies), the subject of the second stanza surrenders its body and becomes more spiritualized. As I have suggested, the poem investigates the problem of physical passion, and since homosexuality existed within the ideology of Crane's day as a misuse or abuse of the body, the only way to comment authoritatively upon the problem of physical passion was to become pure gaze, to imagine the world as a spectacle spread before and reproduced through a disembodied voice whose very disembodiment announced it as authentic. The speaking/writing subject of "The Wine Menagerie" is a "glozening decanter" who sings at the margin of society, and the vision offered (by) this purified voice is one of violent, almost abusive sexuality where sexual partners "take" one another and "unmake" the world:

> Against the imitation onyx wainscoting
> (Painted emulsion of snow, eggs, yarn, coal, manure)
> Regard the forceps of the smile that takes her.
> Percussive sweat is spreading to his hair. Mallets,
> Her eyes, unmake an instant of the world. . . .
>
> (*Poems*, 23)

The details in the wainscoting—and its imitation quality—supply a tacky interior that mirrors the desire of those subjects written in it. What the disembodied subject of the poem sees acted out before him, in the fantasy of his eroticized vision, is the sexual interplay between a man and a woman imagined as necessarily predatory. This is sexuality interpreted according to that "direst" moment in "Possessions," where "the flesh / Assaults outright," and here it assaults equally the categories of the male and female.

This reductive vision of the world is its "unmaking" in a profound sense, for if the poem posits authenticity as disembodiment, then sexuality is inescapably animal, instinctual, and inauthentic. One cannot trust it—either as a desire or as a response; duplicity is its mode, and the despair that follows from this seems to prompt the question of the next stanza:

> What is it in this heap the serpent pries—
> Whose skin, facsimile of time, unskeins

Octagon, sapphire transepts round the eyes;
—From whom some whispered carillon assures
Speed to the arrow into feathered skies?
(*Poems*, 23)

The language here obscurely traces the question of what in such a world, one where authentic vision and sexual desire will be ever at odds, would allow for a relation between people that was more than an exercise in predation (phrases such as "whispered carillon" and "feathered skies" suggesting, in Crane's usual iconography of bells and flight, metaphysical and transcendental triumphs). But the serpent is the central figure here—it is the indifferent and inhuman figure that signifies the Otherness of experience at the end of "Passage," and it certainly brings with it here the theological interpretation of that Otherness as sin, a reading of homosexual desire almost inescapable for a man of Crane's culture. The serpent seems in control of "this heap" (the world), and in the act of sloughing its skin the serpent "unskeins" or unwrites the eternal mysteries of vision ("Octagon, sapphire transepts round the eyes") just as the woman's eyes, "Mallets, / . . . unmake . . . the world" in the previous stanza. History is, in this scenario, a continual reenactment of the fall from visionary presence, and the conscription into alcohol at the poem's opening becomes in retrospect one of the only means available for the recovery of such originary vision.

The poem has to this point addressed a metaphysical problem rather than a dramatic or autobiographical question: how to place the question of value in an alienating material world that claims powerful priorities of meaning. As the beginning of a solution to this problem, Crane turns, not surprisingly, to an image of a young boy:

Sharp to the windowpane guile drags a face,
And as the alcove of her jealousy recedes
An urchin who has left the snow
Nudges a cannister across the bar
While August meadows somewhere clasp his brow.
(*Poems*, 23)

Here, the female figure from the wainscot scene above "recedes" and with her recedes the overwhelming vision of life as a drama of guile and jealousy: the negative legacies of desire.[16] Certainly the figure of the urchin is potentially sentimental if not mawkish, but if we read him as a figure like the ragged Dick of Horatio Alger or as a figure from the sexually pure but purely homosexual reveries of J. M. Barrie, we can perhaps imagine his function in the structure of the poem differently. He represents not escape from the alienating condition of embodiment nor nostalgia for some presexual innocence but a recognition that sexual desire need not take the form of predation. Similarly, we might ask ourselves here why the presexual holds such an appeal for a gay man in Crane's era, and how it can function as a figure for unalienated identity (Sharon O'Brien suggests that Willa Cather's idealization of childhood as a pregendered and therefore unalienating autobiographical space is directly related to her alienation as a sexual adult).

An inquiry into the authenticity available through sexual intersubjectivity frames the remainder of the poem, and the next stanza bespeaks Crane's wish to locate a productive energy in the erotic. The sexual, in the following passages, becomes not an end in itself but a means to the end of intersubjective knowledges imagined as beyond the consciousness of those individuals involved; alcohol provides the distance, the Otherness, the "competence" necessary to the articulation of this "truth." As such, the stake of the writing/speaking subject in pleasure is figured as more than personal gratification:

> Each chamber, transept, coins some squint,
> Remorseless line, minting their separate wills—
> Poor streaked bodies wreathing up and out,
> Unwitting the stigma that each turn repeals:
> Between black tusks the roses shine!
>
> New thresholds, new anatomies! Wine talons
> Build freedom up about me and distill
> This competence—to travel in a tear
> Sparkling alone, within another's will.
>
> Until my blood dreams a receptive smile
> Wherein new purities are snared.
>
> (*Poems*, 24)

The first two lines extend and to some extent refigure images from earlier in the poem, and it is clear that this first stanza suggests the "unwitting" outcome of sexual encounters to be of more value than the poem has heretofore imagined their conscious motivations and outcomes to be. This alternative interpretation of Eros implies that the poor streaked body is only the instrument of some larger power even when it considers itself most in its own service. This follows from sexual discourses of Crane's era, de Gourmont's *Physique de l'amour,* for instance, which Pound translated and Crane mentions in his letters. In that text, the universe is depicted as erotically and mysteriously charged, reproducing itself as matter and life force through unwitting and completely arbitrary acts of individual species. Crane casts this as a matter of coinage, a familiar metaphor for metaphor, suggesting that sexuality makes something new by exposing or producing a relation that has not been known or understood before. The black tusks and roses may themselves not be freshly minted metaphors, but they suggest that love can shine through the darkness of desire. The exclamation "New thresholds, new anatomies!" suggests a number of possible readings, but perhaps the most interesting of them is the naming of the body as a threshold, as an entry—be it through sexual pleasure or through drunkenness—into an intersubjectivity that is as far removed from Otherness as one can imagine. The "receptive smile / Wherein new purities are snared," despite the figure of trapping in "snared," proclaims the outcome of desire pure, innocent of any charges of predation.

But the very image of the threshold suggests an ultimate dichotomy of flesh and spirit in this system of value, reproducing a romance of the spirit that finally sees the flesh as a barrier rather than a threshold. The poem understands this if the speaking/writing subject does not: it sees its homosexual subject alone, dreaming of an Other who will make his body a threshold of purity while heterosexual figures, however "unwitting," actually achieve it in the privacy of their chambers. The perfect union that has eluded Crane in all his efforts—the union of the word made flesh, of self with self-authorization—is recorded here as the drunken fantasy of the homosexual poet dreaming of "a receptive smile." His blood may authorize this dream as transparent and internally produced, as "*really*" the image of his desire, but it eventuates only in a recognition of the agony of isolation which surrounds homosexual desire in history. "Every tongue in hell" proclaims the contradiction between the expectations of desire and the impossibility of their fulfillment, how the animal "tooth implicit of the world" belies the now brittle dreams of personal freedom and erotic purity:

> Until my blood dreams a receptive smile
> Wherein new purities are snared; where chimes
> Before some flame of gaunt repose a shell

Tolled once, perhaps, by every tongue in hell.
—Anguished, the wit that cries out of me:

"Alas,—these frozen billows of your skill!
Invent new dominoes of love and bile . . .
Ruddy, the tooth implicit of the world
Has followed you. Though in the end you know
And count some dim inheritance of sand,
How much yet meets the treason of the snow.

"Rise from the dates and crumbs. And walk away,
Stepping over Holofernes' shins—
Beyond the wall, whose severed head floats by
With Baptist John's. Their whispering begins.

"—And fold your exile on your back again;
Petrushka's valentine pivots on its pin."

(*Poems,* 24)

"Wit" is the problem here, the rational understanding that pierces the comforting "blood" illusions of alcohol and sexual romance, and while the exact meaning of phrases such as "dim inheritance of sand" and "treason of the snow" is not clear, their structural significance is. The world has intervened between the subject and his desire, and the dream of transcendence and homoerotic purity is lost in the understanding that desire is socially constructed by "the tooth implicit of the world" and (in the case of homosexual desire) will be betrayed by the "treason" of a heterosexual world. The final images of dismembered men have led Lewis to comment on the apparent gynophobia at the poem's close in particularly unenlightened terms—"a real-life sense of woman as lethal, as wanting in fact to cut one's head off, is patently homosexual in origin" (*The Poetry of Hart Crane,* 339n). In addition to rejecting the "patent" claim here (this fear and homosexuality are *not* covalent), we need to remember that the poem is not "real-life" and that the morals pointed by these three figures are significantly different: Holofernes' death is due to his desire for Judith, and it is considered a just punishment for an illicit lust; John's death, on the other hand, is due to the lust of Salome and is considered unjust, he the martyr to another's desire; Petrushka, who is not dismembered but hanged, is a martyr not to anyone's lust per se, but to a romance of class inaccessibility where he can only inscribe his desire as courtly devotion indulged at a distance, as the very type of idealization Crane's "wit" understands as an impossible ideal in this world. Thus, these images return us to the problematic in which the poem is grounded: the problematic of idealized desire as a rejection of the body.

The poem attempts one of the more poised moments of closure in any Crane text: the image of the valentine on a pin echos in an interesting declension the Cupid's arrow from the poem's first half and thus refers to the romantic desire for "a receptive smile" and "new purities." The figure of exile as folded wings brings to a close the poem's discourse of flight, and the injunction to "walk away" from the bar (and the wall whereon is mounted the severed head) brings the poem around to a threshold of a realistic exit. But the poem's end does not really provide satisfactory closure. For one thing, the grammar of the conclusion is faulty: "whose" has no antecedent, for instance, and the final lines are therefore in some sense disturbing and wrong; they are not properly articulated. Secondly, a new element appears in the phrase "Their whispering begins," and we have no way to understand this except to imagine it as a figure for the subject's alienation from the majority of society—as if the poem had suddenly turned literal in this figure of other bar patrons whispering about a man who sits alone and cries—perhaps aloud! ("the wit that cries out of me")—about the poverty of his loneliness. But even more unresolved is the poem's final consideration of the problematic of flesh and spirit. Beginning with the contention that vision was pure spirit and that the flesh could be transcended through gaze and voice, the poem then turned to a consideration of what vision that gaze found only to find that it was fleshly desire. And here at the poem's close we are asked to see the flesh once again as inescapably at odds with truth, as something to be dismembered, forgotten, or walked away from.

The poem is built on a contradictory attitude toward the body that cannot be overwritten because it is the constitutive contradiction of the speaking/writing homosexual subject, the "real" issue through which he encounters and recognizes himself as "real." It is not surprising that readers have concurred with Marianne Moore and found "The Wine Menagerie" confusing, and its confusion springs from the inability of its speaking/writing subject to reconcile his desire for sexual freedom and experience with his desire for something more than physical gratification. The grace of intoxication, such as it is, is twofold: it substitutes for an even more unacceptable use of the body than inebriation and provides a means to pleasure that can seem pure of homosexual motivations; and it can (secretly) become the threshold of a new anatomy of homosexual desire, allowing freedom or license to what is otherwise repressed. This, finally, is the way I choose to read the final exile of the piece—as the homosexual taking upon himself his exile in a world of heterosexual romance, where whispers and hopeless longings (like Petrushka's) surround him. It is only thus that the poem achieves the poise it reaches for. Cowley writes of Crane's pattern of intoxicated homosexual cruising that he would leave and enter "the last phase of his party . . . when he cruised the waterfront looking for sailors" (*Second Flowering*, 215). It is that phase of the Crane party "The Wine Menagerie" prepares us for: when the illusions of heterosexual superiority and of imminent (and immanent) perfect homosexual romance have both been destroyed by "wit," there is nothing left but "the tonsiling" (*Letters*, 241), the exile of spinning one's heart on a very different pin.

Written in the summer of 1926, after both "Voyages" and "The Wine Menagerie" had tested and rejected the premise of being's authentication through homosexual experience, and long after the first elations and hopes in his relationship with Emil Opffer had led to disappointment, "Repose of Rivers" nonetheless asserts the centrality of homosexuality in authorizing a modern identity and a modern poetics. As Robert Martin has suggested, "Repose of Rivers" is a "major autobiographical statement" that "dramatizes the difficulties of coming to terms with sexuality and the final surmounting of those difficulties" (*The Homosexual Tradition*, 142). But Crane's point in the poem is not so much to represent the subjective experiences one traditionally associates with the autobiographical or coming-out text; rather, the poem concentrates on finding a model of homosexual subjectivity that moves beyond the family romance and its strict duality of masculine and feminine identities. "Repose" does not depict an actual relationship between two men; it focuses instead on the problem of homosexual self-authorization as an issue of internal resolution where one comes to maturity through a rejection of Oedipal models of development and an adoption of homosexual ones. Harold Bloom, in a rare instance of address to material difference, identifies the text as a record of "the poetic maturation that follows homosexual self-acceptance" (*Agon*, 258). The homosexual text in the poem is obscure, but certainly Martin and Bloom are right to read it as a text of homosexual authorization. Martin traces the reference to Whitman in its discourse of marshes, in its phallic image of the flag, and particularly in its allusion to Whitman's "Once I Pass'd Through a Populous City," a poem made infamous as a homosexual text when Emory Holloway published its preheterosexual, manuscript version in *The Dial* in 1920. As Martin suggests, "Whitman helped Crane understand the sexual origin of art and gave him the confidence to write poems as a tribute to his own loves and so preserve them from time and loss" (*The Homosexual Tradition*, 148).

The poem presents the search for an authentic identity as a process of losing the active, masculine will; the speaker seeks a horizontal "repose" wherein all his acts and utterances would be guaranteed authenticity. But according to the poem's terms, this must be an authenticity invested in something that is beyond the stake of the personal; occasioning the poem's autobiographical urgency is its perception that authentic identity cannot be housed in ego-formation, tainted as that is by Oedipal paradigms and repressions. For the poem, recovery of memory occurs only through the loss or transcendence of the ego signified here as an emptying out:

> The willows carried a slow sound,
> A sarabande the wind mowed on the mead.
> I could never remember
> That seething, steady leveling of the marshes
> Till age had brought me to the sea.
> (*Poems*, 46)

The memory recovered here is not, of course, some specific thing the speaker has forgotten, but a faculty—the ability to hear, and consequently the ability to speak, genuinely. The trope of authentic utterance as sea-speech of death comes from Whitman's autobiographical "Out of the Cradle," and as in Blake or Emerson, memory figures not recall but forgetting, the active forgetting of what has intervened between the subject and his original, originary relation to the universe, the "seething, steady leveling of the marshes" and their liminal grace.

The poem offers three sets of specific memories, the first two of which provide insufficient memorial instruction, the last of which represents passage into maturity. The first of these is the "remembrance of steep alcoves / Where cypresses shared the noon's / Tyranny" and "mammoth turtles climbing sulphur dreams / Yielded, while sun-silt rippled them / Asunder . . ." This heliocentric and tyrannical noon "drew me into hades almost," the speaker reports, and it would seem that this hades is a natural world, Vegetable in Blake's sense, both phallic and reproductive (the image of the turtles suggestive of sea turtles ashore in the season of mating). Unlike the reposeful leveling the poem equates with maturity, this is a world organized in hierarchies and by power, its only dimension verticality. Finally, it is possible to see the tyranny of the sun—as it occasionally becomes in Stevens—as a trope for the overpowering but false authority of patriarchal reality, and this stanza of the poem breaks off in ellipsis after the word "Asunder," allowing absence to resonate, allowing this castrated vision to speak itself as an indictment of the processes of division and competition (of Oedipal masculinity) it enshrines.

A more maternal memory, horizontal, provides the second set of images:

> How much I would have bartered! the black gorge
> And all the singular nestings in the hills
> Where beavers learn stitch and tooth.
> The pond I entered once and quickly fled—
> I remember now its singing willow rim.
>
> (*Poems*, 46)

The image of the dammed pond "quickly fled" suggests that these memories, too, are necessarily repressed and abandoned despite their pleasurable connotations. The feminine "nestings" and "gorge" (which I would read here as the maternal, since the poem sets itself as a developmental narrative) are something the speaker feels strongly drawn toward—enough so as to barter much for them; and yet, there is something castrating here as well, something unnamed which comes across in the image of the beaver pond produced through the felling of trees. And yet we do not want here merely to repeat the theory that homosexuality is produced by fear of women, by attraction-repulsion dynamics centering around the imago; I use "castration" to signify here the failure of either parental side of the Oedipal triangle to offer the homosexual son a model for his life. This maternal memory provides the appearance of that sound of willows the poem's closure will supersede (and therefore validate as that thing that requires supersession), but this does not so much establish likeness as it suggests that the "final" solution to the question of identity for the homosexual man is other than his common stake with the feminine or the maternal.

The third set of memories are the focus of Martin's contention for reading this as Crane's rewriting of "Once I Pass'd Through a Populous City," the city on the delta at gulf gates certainly seeming—referentially—to be New Orleans, the site of Whitman's "coming out" in his text.[17] This city—the privileged site of homosexual knowledge—provides the arena for acquiring that experience the poem has been leading toward, that experience through whose later reason memory may acquire its true value. The emphasis in this stanza is not on a specific coming-out experience, whatever that might have been (although the third line does have a hot, homosexual sound), but on the finality that is invested in that experience:

> And finally, in that memory all things nurse;
> After the city that I finally passed
> With scalding unguents spread and smoking darts
> The monsoon cut across the delta
> At gulf gates . . . There, beyond the dykes
>
> I heard wind flaking sapphire, like this summer,
> And willows could not hold more steady sound.
> (*Poems*, 46).

The speaker achieves here a new authority in his subjectivity—defined neither through identification with the father or the mother but according to the homosexual authority of the city and the homosexual author (Whitman). And by figuring this as "that memory all things nurse," the poem suggests both that this memory nurses or nurtures all things and that all things have led into this memory. It also suggests that this authentic identity is perhaps ever-new, always rediscovered—that even future memories may return to it for nurturance. This figure of nursing memory suggests the repose of a horizontal, syntagmatic relation to desire (the "seething, steady leveling of the marshes" rather than "noon's / Tyranny") and a source from which identity flows rather than one in which it is repressed (no longer the pond behind the dam). (It would be impossible not to comment on the word "dykes" in this context. Crane means it here most obviously as a conceptual rhyme with the dammed pond, as that which he has moved beyond. And yet we know—from its appearance in Carl Van Vechten's *Nigger Heaven*—that the word also signified "female homosexual" in the slang of Crane's era, and it signifies in that sense in the poem, too. He has moved "beyond" the "dyke-ness," the slangy, pejorative notion of homosexuality; he has moved beyond the condition of homosexual-as-woman; he has moved beyond an image of repression. And yet he has not moved beyond the deep subterfuge of such linguistic equivocation, nor beyond the need to distance himself from the lesbian.)

If we can easily deconstruct this repose as only a pose or a re-posing of what has been inscribed, or if we see in it already the shape of death (the river empties into the sea, finding its repose only in its nonbeing), we have to see as well that "Repose of Rivers" is the most fervent and well-crafted of Crane's attempts to make homosexuality the center of poetic consciousness. He refuses to surrender his right to a threshold of consciousness that is legitimate, and the difference between this poem and "Passage" would seem to be that this text takes homosexual experience as authentic whereas the former had sought an "Authentic" experience from which the homosexual would always be excluded.

The experimental lyrics written from 1923 to 1926 constitute a record of the development of homosexual subjectivity unlike any other in modern letters; with an increasing urgency, from "Possessions" through "Voyages" and "Legend" to "Passage" and "The Wine Menagerie," they present the search for an authentic voice and an ideological recognition of homosexual speech and writing, and—with an increasing clarity—the frustrations and barriers to that project. They record the dialectical unfolding of Crane's thought about the homosexual subject and poetry, and they articulate a number of important points about the ideology under which that thought took shape. First, these poems announce that homosexuality may not appear in autobiography "in person," as it were: we see this in its literal disappearance from "Passage," for instance, and in the highly coded discourses through which it appears as the universal problem of lust in "The Wine Menagerie" and as the universal problem of identity development in "Repose of Rivers." Secondly, a diachronic reading of these poems, which I have conducted here with only a few omissions, traces the disintegration of a consciousness such as Crane's, a disintegration not made necessary by enforced homophobia but one certainly encouraged by it. Especially when we understand that Crane inhabited flatly contradictory sites of culture as both a homosexual and a poet, we must read the disintegration of the speaking/writing subject in "The Wine Menagerie" as fully produced within an ideology that made the homosexual poet's subjectivity a bizarre dialectic of anguish and ecstasy. But the final poem in this progression, "Repose of Rivers," marks Crane's refusal to surrender the homosexual subject in the lyric; if it asserts a poise he never actually sustained in his life, and if his life had by the summer of 1926 already become a plague from which he would not escape (the nasty details of which one may gather from almost all his biographers and from the memoirs of countless friends), the poem nevertheless bravely signals Crane's refusal to surrender his project for homosexual centrality. As Adorno suggests, "The greatness of works of art lies solely in their power to let those things be heard which ideology conceals" ("Lyric Poetry and Society," 57), and the greatness of Crane's lyrics, written, it is not hyperbolic to say, at the cost of his life, is that they allow homosexual subjectivity to be heard as an authentic experience, as "wind flaking sapphire."

5
The Homosexual Sublime

▾

One has a profound, if irrational, instinct in favour of the theory that the union of man and woman makes for the greatest satisfaction, the most complete happiness. But the sight of the two people getting into the taxi and the satisfaction it gave me made me also ask whether there are two sexes in the mind corresponding to the sexes in the body, and whether they also require to be united in order to get complete satisfaction and happiness.

VIRGINIA WOOLF
A Room of One's Own

JANE GALLOP has suggested that "any text can be read as either body (site of contradictory drives and heterogeneous matter) or Law" (*The Daughter's Seduction*, 62), and we might remember that the writing of texts also pulls language in both of these directions. In the lyric poems he wrote between 1923 and 1926, Crane produced a volume of writing that directs its reader to consider it as body, as the site of contradictory drives and heterogeneous matter. In this, we see an instance of what I will be calling here the sublime, that difficult writing that confronts the reader with what Jean-François Lyotard has described as the "real sublime sentiment" of postmodernity, "the unpresentable in presentation itself" (*The Post-Modern Condition*, 81). Crane, of course, is concerned with the sublimity of modernity rather than postmodernity, but the dialectic of the sublime in his writing forces an encounter with the unpresentable, not the least of which is the unpresentability ("unpresentable" in all of its senses) of homosexuality. When he sought longer, more inclusive and authoritative cultural statements than these lyrics, when he directed his writing, that is, toward Law, Crane did not abandon homosexuality as the site from which the texts were produced. He did, however, find himself addressing a set of problems identified with and defined by a long tradition of prophetic writing in America, the most important of which in relation to his work was the discourse of transcendentalism. In taking up that discourse, Crane encountered a number of obstacles to a clear writing of homosexuality, including: its enormous privileging of Oedipal heterosexuality; its tropes of marriage and union as figures of dialectical resolution; its erasure of the sublime historical and material displacements of homosexual desire and its reinscription of a centered, dematerialized transcendent subject.

If we substitute the terms of homosexual desire for the unnamable Otherness of sublimity in the following description from Fredric Jameson, we find described the kind of decentered subjectivity written into the lyrics examined in chapter 4:

> The aesthetic reception of the sublime is then something like a pleasure in pain. . . . What can be retained from this description [once the "aesthetic" is rejected as a transcendent category of experience] is the notion of the sublime as a relationship of the individual subject to some fitfully or only intermittently visible force which, enormous and systematized, reduces the individual to helplessness or to that ontological marginalization which structuralism and poststructuralism have described as a "decentering" where the ego becomes little more than an "effect of structure." ("Baudelaire as Modernist and Postmodernist," 262)

Especially in texts such as "The Wine Menagerie" and "Passage," subjectivity is "little more than an 'effect of structure,'" and we might see Crane's erotic and poetic interest in dismemberment as an aesthetic pleasure in pain that marks one of the theaters of the sublime. But if this decentering of the subject marks one sublime moment in Crane (and, Jameson implies, in others as well), the more usual structure of the sublime provides not only for the disintegration of order and being but for their reintegration as well. The sublime has tended to trace an encounter with some overwhelming and potentially annihilating force and an affirmation of the mind's unity and power to synthesize itself and that force, to incorporate difference at a "higher" dialectical level. Thomas Weiskel's *The Romantic Sublime* examines in great detail the intertextuality of the psychoanalytic discourse of the Oedipal and the Romantic discourse of the sublime; Harold Bloom has offered a reading of "the American sublime" that can be summarized as an encounter between "I and the Abyss" (in *Poetry and Repression*); Patricia Yeager has written "Toward a Female Sublime," where the dialectical process of incorporation is not read as an Oedipal contest of difference but as a symbiotic fusion of identities: each of these reads the sublime as a movement toward synthesis, height, strength. According to Bruce Clarke, sublimation, the third term of the dialectic of the sublime, "tends to restore continuity, sealing gaps and blending together what the sublime puts apart, although at the price of a certain displacement of aim or substitution of object" ("Wordsworth's Departed Swans," 360). For Clarke, the sublime is the mark of an only "momentary intense experience of a discontinuity between desire and the possibility of its fulfillment" (360).

The homosexual discourse in Crane (in his letters and poems) expresses itself negatively; again and again, it is figured as an epistemological gap or broken continuity. This may still operate as the sublime, for the nihilism provides what Neil Hertz defines as a key to the sublime: "a powerful apprehension" of "the figurativeness of every instance of the figurative" (*The End of the Line*, 18), a broken episteme that must then be restored. The more obvious healing movement of sublimation, on the other hand (and this can be seen in a poem such as "The Broken Tower," with its turn to a female Other who restores the poet to a "healed," "original," and "pure" condition), is figured as a restored, perhaps originary, and privileged heterosexuality, or as the act of textual composition itself, the process of adhesive unification that makes the text appear "whole." In *The Pleasure of the Text* Roland Barthes makes an apposite distinction between the text of pleasure (the text of sublimation where social order, balance, and beauty reign) and the text of bliss (the text of sublimity where fracture, asymmetry, and the abyss are the affective correlatives):

> Text of pleasure: the text that contents, fills, grants euphoria; the text that comes from culture and does not break with it, is linked to a *comfortable* practice of reading. Text of bliss: the text that imposes a state of loss, the text that discomforts (perhaps to the point of a certain boredom), unsettles the reader's historical, cultural, psychological assumptions, the consistency of his tastes, values, memories, brings to a crisis his relation with language. (14)

In Barthes's text, pleasure is an affect of cathexis, the psychoanalytic principle of binding energy. In Crane's work this receives its ultimate linguistic and social expression in the figure of marriage. "For the Marriage of Faustus and Helen" employs the trope precisely in order to secure the sociality of the text (it seems, as we shall see, to have been conceived as an anti-wasteland piece, as an endorsement of contemporary culture intended to offer unity rather than fragmentation as the "truth" of modernity). Bliss in Barthes is castration; it lies beyond the pleasure principle in "shock, disturbance, even loss, which are proper to ecstasy, to bliss" (*The Pleasure of the Text*, 19). This is found in Crane in the masochistic vocabulary of desire and in the trope of dismemberment. Crane's texts vacillate almost exactly between these two poles of textual construction, seeking on the one hand what Jean-François Lyotard calls "the solace of good forms" (*The Post-Modern Condition*, 81) and on the other denying a "*comfortable* practice of reading."

Certainly the body has always offered itself as an accommodating site for sublimity; as Neil Hertz points out, Longinus cites Sappho's "phainetai moi" ode as an instance of the sublime for bringing together "'as a single body' . . . the names of the fragments of her natural body, seen as the debris of a shattering erotic experience that had brought her, in the words of the ode, 'only a little short of death'" (*The End of the Line*, 4–5). By the early twentieth century, however, the body had become the site of a different order of technological understanding. As Foucault has remarked:

> Sexuality must not be thought of as a kind of natural given which power tries to hold in check, or as an obscure domain which knowledge tries gradually to uncover. It is the name that can be given to a historical construct: not a furtive reality that is difficult to grasp, but a great surface network in which the stimulation of bodies, the intensification of pleasures, the incitement to discourse, the formation of special knowledges, the strengthening of controls and resistances, are linked to one another, in accordance with a few major strategies of knowledge and power. (*The History of Sexuality*, 105–06)

This newly sexualized body became the site of that disruption between Nature and Culture, between the subject and its object of knowledge or desire, that marks one of the classic dialectics of the sublime, and in its particular, disruptive relation to both Culture and Nature, homosexuality could foreground this division in a way that heterosexuality occasionally could not because of *its* (i.e., heterosexuality's) easy recuperation into the paradigm of the natural. In Hertz's reading of the sublime, "blockage" is central: the mind, brought up against structures it cannot accommodate, does, as in Wordsworth's encounter with the blind beggar in *The Prelude*, "turn around / As with the might of waters" on confronting some Other who may externalize in a single figure the epistemological impossibility it has encountered. If, as Hertz suggests, "the self cannot simply think but must read the confirmation of its own integrity, which is only legible in a specular structure" (*The End of the Line*, 54), the homosexual body may function as a locus of the sublime in modernity not because it is in any way natural for it to do so but precisely because of the increasing ideological disruptions it is asked both to signify and elide: that body becomes the figure of opacity and Otherness for the culture and the subjectivity it gives rise to.

If we try to see how the discourse of American transcendentalism ordinarily sublimates homoerotic desire, we would do well to look first at *Walden* and how Law appears there as the force in control of the body's heterogeneous drives. In *Walden* there are a number of homo*social* if not homo*sexual* moments, and the closest Thoreau may come to expressed sexual desire of any sort is in his idyllic days with the Canadian woodsman. Class difference becomes the screen that intervenes and makes expression of affection between the two consciously unthinkable for Thoreau, and yet we are treated to the spectacle of their reading aloud together passages from the *Iliad* whose tenor is homosexual mourning (Achilles weeping for Patroclus). If we orient ourselves in this passage according to the fascination with mourning in the chapter "Sounds," and according to *Walden*'s more general insistence upon the refusal of mourning in its homonymic paeans to "morning"—*and* if we remember that reading is one of the few acts Thoreau affirms as authentic—we have, it seems, found a seam of the homotextual unconscious in *Walden*. But what we see in Thoreau's discourse on reading is that *difference* can only be stated as a likeness to sexual difference, and that reading, rather than being a homosexual act, is in fact an Oedipal one, one in which allegiance to the father suppresses the power of the mother:

> There is a memorable interval between the spoken and the written language, the language heard and the language read. The one is commonly transitory, a sound, a tongue, a dialect merely, almost brutish, and we learn it unconsciously, like the brutes, of our mothers. The other is the maturity and experience of that; if that is our mother tongue, this is our father tongue, a reserved and select expression, too significant to be heard by the ear, which we must be born again in order to speak. (92)

One could hardly ask for a more metaphysically loaded analysis of this "memorable interval," and if Thoreau seems to anticipate Derrida in privileging writing over speech, we need to remind ourselves that a deconstructive reading of that difference would annihilate (rather than reinforce) it to show that language (always already written) nevertheless can never control the tongue, the sound, the unconscious, the mother.

The discourse of the heterosexual as the natural metaphor of textual power in American transcendentalism is perhaps nowhere as pointedly evident or consciously epistemological as in Stevens's pervasive use of it. From the seemingly inescapable metaphorics of the nuclear family at the close of "The Comedian as the Letter C" to the fictions of "Notes Toward a Supreme Fiction," where in the fiction of Ozymandias and Nanzia Nunzio, he claims,

> the spouse, the bride
> is never naked. A fictive covering
> Weaves always glistening from the heart and mind,
> (*Collected Poems*, 396)

Stevens employs this figure of the female interior paramour in a trope of marriage and/or heterosexual union to investigate virtually all of the epistemological, linguistic, and natural processes in which he is interested. It is most often the *Aufhebung* in his dialectical reasoning, the last term in a process of synthesis that both naturalizes and socializes the solutions to philosophical problems. It is an image of apparent oneness that, through the magical power of the dialectic and the privileged aura of marriage (what Lacan calls the dream of the One), seems not to negate difference but to raise any problematic contradictions to a "higher" level of integration. A brief glance at various other passages from his text will provide a clearer picture of this practice. In Stevens's early "The Sense of the Sleight-of-Hand Man," for instance, as in so many of his other poems, we find the trope of marriage a "natural" analogue for other species of union:

> One's grand flights, one's Sunday baths,
> One's tootings at the weddings of the soul
> Occur as they occur.
> (*Collected Poems*, 222)

The silliness of "Sunday baths" strikes just the right note for deflating the ritual aspects of any spiritualized epithelamial impulse, and clearly Stevens's transcendentalism is never free of the possibility of deflation. But despite this it would seem that espousal is not a trope of ridicule in Stevens—if anything, it is among his most honored. The irony in this passage accrues to the notion of soul and to the self-delusion that enables us to think our "grand flights" experiences of an order that will not

not prove illusory; it does not accrue to the image of wedding. In fact, the poem ends with a series of quite sincere marriage images that represent the quest for existential meaning:

It may be that the ignorant man, alone
Has any chance to mate his life with life
That is the sensual, pearly spouse, the life
That is fluent in even the wintriest bronze.
(*Collected Poems*, 222)

What we remember in reading such passages is that the dialectical structure of Western thought accommodates the heterosexual as naturally as it does day and night, the imagined and the real; it has been one of the founding binary oppositions of Western culture, and its figural importance is only the greater for the powerful ritualistic, economic, familial, and communal instantiations through which it is still disseminated as the only "natural" sexuality:

Two things of opposite natures seem to depend
On one another, as a man depends
On a woman, day on night, the imagined

On the real. This is the origin of change.
Winter and spring, cold copulars, embrace
And forth the particulars of rapture come.
(*Collected Poems*, 392)

But certainly we need at this point in history to read againt the transparency of this figure, to see, as Luce Irigaray suggests, that the discourse of natural heterosexual differences (what she calls the "sexual *in*difference" of such systems) merely "*underlies the truth of any science, the logic of every discourse*" and "assures its coherence and its closure" (*This Sex Which Is Not One*, 69, 72) but may in no way claim itself truthful outside that discourse.

The transcendental heritage of a heterosexual sublime infuses more than the level of figure, however. It comes to Crane as an entire theory of metaphor as well—the theory of metaphoric transparency or right speech. If the heterosexual discourse of Thoreau and Emerson is an *in*semination of the world through meanings established by the father's word, Crane's discourse and the homosexual discourse it more generally indicates is a *dis*semination; Crane replaces the clear syntax of insight with one that is opaque. The concept of dissemination in Derrida implies in part an infinite postponement of closure; it is a figure for the uncontrollable slippage and infinite regress of meaning, indicating a textuality not under authorial control or critical tutelage. As Barthes puts it in "From Work to Text," "The Text is not a co-existence of meanings, but a passage, an overcrossing; thus it answers not to an interpretation, even a liberal one, but to an explosion, a dissemination" (159). The disseminated text is, therefore, an unruly one that does not know how to behave; it shoots its mouth off, so to speak, as well as shooting off from other parts of its body, so (in order) to speak.

In Crane's case, this dissemination of meaning is linked to a rhetoric of blindness and a rhetorical opacity that refuse the Emersonian imperative of transparency. In what has become *the* "locus classicus" for American poetics, Emerson writes in *Nature* of that moment when he becomes aware of his perceptual power, authority, and authenticity as a moment of emptying, of becoming transparent:

> Standing on the bare ground,—my head bathed by the blithe air uplifted into infinite space,—all mean egotism vanishes. I become a transparent eyeball; I am nothing; I see all; the currents of the Universal Being circulate through me; I am part or parcel of God. (*Complete Works*, 1: 10)

This paradox of nothingness and transcendent presence is cognate with all instances of the Romantic sublime, and like that of other Romantics, Emerson's sublime consists of an elimination of others as the ego (the Reason in Kant) withdraws from the world of social mediations and enters a singular relation with nature in which it is at first threatened by the overwhelming density and scope of this Other but finally reads the power in this excess as a figure for its own capacity. We can gloss the movement of sublimity and see how it is linked to the gendering of transcendental discourse in Crane by using Thomas Weiskel's insight into the three-part structure to the sublime in *The Romantic Sublime*: a first part in which there is symmetry and balance between the opposed terms of the sublime, be they nature/culture, inner/outer, self/other; a second part in which one or the other of those terms appears excessive; and a third part in which the balance of part 1 is restored and the imbalance of part 2 is taken as a sign of the mind's relation to a transcendent order. As we shall see, the homosexual moments in Crane fall usually in phase 2, the negative phase of this dialectic where, according to Guy

Hocquenghem's theory of homosexual desire, the categories of social habit (including identity) are disrupted by a scattering discourse of the body; the sublimation that restores balance and transcendence in phase 3 of this dialectic in Crane is more usually heterosexual—is, in fact, a sublimation of homosexual desire that restores Oedipal models of reading and social identity.

Despite his statement that poems are always miswritten, Emerson asserts the possibility of a certain transparency in language, and this metaphor comes down to a precisionist poet such as Stevens as the crux and burden of "the poems of our climate." In a world where the word is blocked, in a world of carnations rather than incarnations,[1] our "delight" is not in the harmony Emerson described but in "flawed words and stubborn sounds." We may desire "more than a world of white and snowy scents" (where "scents" carries a nice pun on the *differance* and opacity of written language), but for Stevens, meaning is a matter of fallen languages; "the imperfect is our paradise" in the linguistic as well as existential sense for him (*Collected Poems*, 194). This, too, is expressed in Emerson, in the notion that language is fugitive and must surprise us "out of our propriety" (*Complete Works*, II: 321) rather than settle us in it, but the desire in Emerson is always toward transparency, toward the following:

> Then cometh the god and converts the statues into fiery men, and by a flash of his eye burns up the veil which shrouded all things, and the meaning of the very furniture, of cup and saucer, of chair and clock and tester, is manifest. The facts which loomed so large in the fogs of yesterday,—property, climate, breeding, personal beauty and the like, have strangely changed their proportions. All that we reckoned settled shakes and rattles; and literatures, cities, climates, religions, leave their foundations and dance before our eyes. (II: 311)

In "Lachrymae Christi" we see Crane's version of the Emersonian quest to align the axes of speech and vision ("The ruin or blank that we see when we look at nature, is in our own eye. The axis of vision is not coincident with the axis of things" [I: 73]). In a characteristically oblique way that is itself one effect of rejecting theories of linguistic transparency, Crane figures the entry into unmediated vision and transparency to nature as a dismemberment of the body. If "Lachrymae Christi" is Crane's essay on the image of man as a god-in-ruin and the attempted recovery of perfect vision in nature, its main purpose is to:

recall
To music and retrieve what perjuries
Had galvanized the eyes.

But it is a poem that grounds its theory of regeneration in transgression. Where nature is violent and vampiric—

Immaculate venom binds
The fox's teeth, and swart
Thorns freshen on the year's
First blood,
(*Poems*, 19)

man can only achieve harmony with it through surrender to a discourse that legitimates the body and its violent demands. The poem changes the tears of Christ from tears of sorrow over the waste of this world into tears (and drops of blood) that signify a continuing but fructifying cycle of sacrifice; it makes the notion of sin and penitence superfluous to redemption and searches instead for an innocence that will incorporate experience. In a central parenthetical passage, the poet describes his inspiration:

(Let sphinxes from the ripe
Borage of death have cleared my tongue
Once and again; vermin and rod
No longer bind. Some sentient cloud
Of tears flocks through the tendoned loam:
Betrayed stones slowly speak.)
(*Poems*, 20)

As in "The Wine Menagerie," poetic speech is authorized here through drunkenness ("borage" and the later reference to Dionysus both suggest this), and the poet is granted clear speech. Simultaneously, the "Nazarene and tinder eyes" that burn in "undimming lattices of flame" are granted clear vision. At first it seems that these two things are located in different places: the clear speech in the poet and the clear vision in the god he speaks. But finally these two axes of vision and speech are conflated when "Names peeling from [the] eyes" of the Nazarene "Spell out in palm and pain" the vision the poet reads in nature. The god whose eyes have offered this writing is now charged (and able) to speak, and the world is reborn:

And as the nights
Strike from Thee perfect spheres,
Lift up in lilac-emerald breath the grail
Of earth again—.
(*Poems*, 20)

If this structure of transcendence sounds Christian, its tenor is not. The poem names celebration rather than penitence as the proper relation to divinity: vermin and rod no longer bind as images of fallen flesh and punishment; the world itself becomes a body, "tendoned loam." And the last stanza locates the poem's authenticity in a pagan apostrophe to a god burned at the stake. Transcendence in this poem occurs in and through the body of god dismembered in joy and given over to a cycle of sacrificial beauty, and it occurs in a final apostrophe (the figure through which lyric most powerfully suggests the presence of voice):

Thy face
From charred and riven stakes, O
Dionysus, Thy
Unmangled target smile.
(*Poems*, 20)

The homosexual reference in this vision of sacrifice is strong, as can be seen in the parallel between the image here and its appearance in more overtly homoerotic texts such as "Modern Craft" and "The Dance." The dismembered body is for Crane the eroticized body carried to its logical extreme (in "Legend," "It is to be learned— / This cleaving and this burning"). But perhaps we ought to take the poem's closing image as a figure for textuality itself, one that suggests the importance of a dismembered text.

The text presents itself in a rhetoric of unnaming, of peeling perjuries from the eyes until authentic vision has been achieved, and this is as closely related to Blake as to Emerson. Here, the "infernal method" by which Blake cleansed the doors of perception becomes a chemical distillation in which the "galvanized" coatings on the eyes are washed away in "benzine / Rinsings from the moon." In the best transcendentalist way, word and thing become transparent to one another in this moment of cleansing and man becomes transparent to his own godlike capacity. But it is important to see that the text figures this not as the male authority over a female nature but through the relation of two men whose speech and sight become coaxial. And it is especially important to see that this union ends in a ritualized enactment of the prohibitions against homosexual desire figured here as the dismemberment of the desiring body: transformation and sublimity lie in the offending flesh. It would be wrong to suggest that this dissemination, this scattering and dismembering, makes Crane's text protodeconstructive, for he did write as if language could carry truth. If Derridean dissemination turns on a fourth term that refuses the closure of triadic dialectical thought and opens the triangle of position, negation, and negation of the negation, we should see that Crane does provide a synthesizing third term at the end of "Lachrymae Christi." But the closure in this poem is not an image of marriage and transparency; rather, it is an image of dismemberment, written in a language of opacity. It is, then, an encounter with transcendental discourse that refuses the usual figures of that discourse.

If we locate Crane historically between two homosexual writers such as Whitman and Ashbery, we can see more clearly how his homosexuality is (literally, in "Lachrymae Christi") at stake in this practice. Whitman, of course, is transparently transcendentalist and presents perhaps the most difficult case for understanding that transcendentalism can be inhospitable to the erotic; Ashbery, on the other hand, is an artist of the opaque and has come to represent the archetype of postmodern poetry, arguing to no temporal or philosophical end with the transcendental vocabulary handed down to him most authoritatively from Stevens, rejecting any notion of centered subjectivity or Romantic truth outside the mazed losses of language. Although there is nothing like a formulaic evolution to be invoked here, Crane fits somewhere between these two writers in his attitude toward the body's relation to language. His interest in the body has something to do with modernity and its research into the trope of structure (his work is akin, that is, to the work of Eliot, Pound, Stevens, Moore, Williams, Stein, and others in its self-conscious investigation of structuring principles). But the specific urgency with which that trope is eroticized in Crane's text would have to do, it seems, with the decentering pressures homosexuality placed on identity in the early decades of this century. In Crane's text, as in that of Whitman, the homosexual body is a site of sublimity if not of transcendent or cosmic knowledge, and, as in Ashbery's text, Crane's practice of dissemination is grounded in the body's occlusion of the perfect transparency of speech.

In one of the famous passages opening "Song of Myself," Whitman enacts a moment of transparent sexual union between two men that has always been read as a figure for the union between his body and his soul. However one reads the passage—as religion, as pornography, or as the fruitful area where they cannot be distinguished—since only the soul in the Emersonian text is "Me," the body being relegated to the Other, the "Not-Me," we might describe this as going down on the Not-Me:

> I mind how once we lay such a transparent summer
> morning,
> How you settled your head athwart my hips and gently
> turn'd over upon me,
> And parted the shirt from my bosom-bone, and plunged
> your tongue to my bare-stript heart,
> And reach'd till you felt my beard, and reach'd till you
> held my feet.
>
> (*Leaves of Grass*, 33)

The erotic thrill of this passage rests at least in part in the coy non-concealment of fellatio as an act of licking the heart. But we can see that one reaches to feel a beard not when one's head is at chest level. Both "bosom-bone" and "bare-stript heart" are unmistakable substitutions for the penis. As the initiating moment in the erotic narcissism of Whitman's text, the importance of this passage cannot be overemphasized. In consequence of it, the Whitmanian speaker realizes nothing less than the "peace and knowledge that pass all the argument of the earth," the benediction or blessedness of self-understanding. In Whitman, the homosexual body is a gateway to an authoritative self-knowledge that cannot be gainsaid by others and their arguments, and it is important to see that through his narcissistic and genital understanding of sexuality, Whitman is able to sexualize the Emersonian notion of transcendence. For the first time in American letters, the body becomes the site of its own excess and then (through this) the site of its authority to reunite man with the dwarf of himself (in the form of other men, as well).

But if Whitman's body becomes the threshold of transcendent meanings, we find a very different text in Ashbery, one where the body is languageless and opaque. And yet, the very inarticulability of the body may become the sign of its authority within a postmodern economy of the sublime. The following is from "No Way of Knowing:"

The body is what this is all about and it disperses
In sheeted fragments, all somewhere around
But difficult to read correctly since there is
No common vantage point, no point of view
Like the "I" in a novel. . . .
                                        This stubble-field
Of witnessings . . .
                                        was always alive with its own
Rigid binary system of inducing truths
From starved knowledge of them. It has worked
And will go on working. All attempts to influence
The working are parallelism, undulating, writhing
Sometimes but kept to the domain of metaphor.
There is no way of knowing.
(*Self-Portrait*, 56)

This is not Ashbery's most supple verse, but it is nonetheless an instructive and important passage. Unlike Whitman (or Crane, whose relation to this will be taken up below), Ashbery writes in an era of the eroded sign, and we see from this passage that he conceives the body as radically resistant to incorporation: there is no corporeal "I" and no transcendent ego, as in Whitman. For Ashbery, meaning is always a matter of absence. But to claim that "There is no way of knowing" is also to claim, of course, that one knows, and what one knows in this passage is that the body is absolutely irrecoverable through language and yet "alive with its own" languge, its own "Rigid binary system of inducing truths / From starved knowledge of them." If a certain Romantic nihilism haunts this and other texts by Ashbery, it is important to see that the body in his work is neither articulate nor inarticulate, but a "stubble-field / Of witnessings," a trope that points to absence but also to former presences. The body is not so much meaningless as it is the site of dispersed, disseminated meanings that are "in sheeted fragments, all around somewhere / But difficult to read."

Crane—like Whitman and Ashbery—figures the homosexual body as a site of self-knowledge and authentic being, as has been suggested in previous chapters. He quite consciously privileged the homoerotic as meaningful, and we see in his more ambitious sequences how the erotic body becomes heterosexual in order that the poem authorize itself within the discourse of transcendentalism. Before turning to the question of how the homosexual sublime is articulated in Crane's text, however, it would be instructive to see how that text has traditionally been read as mystical, religious, transcendental, and/or sublime, for we can see how those more traditional formulations depend upon a denial and sublimation of the homosexual that is itself already encoded in the texts in their dialectic of disruption and healed originality. In 1925, Gorham Munson wrote a review essay entitled "Hart Crane: Young Titan in the Sacred Wood" that was not accepted by any magazine at the time but eventually appeared with other essays by Munson in his collection *Destinations* (New York: 1928). Crane, however, saw it sometime shortly after it was written and responded to it vehemently as a misrepresentation of his intentions. What bothered Crane more than anything else in Munson's piece (the title alone suggests how much Munson meant it as praise) seems to have been Munson's characterization of him as "a 'mystic' on the loose" and the claim that Crane, in his poetic representation of ecstasy, ran the "risk of bringing back a distorted and poorly glimpsed vision" (50). There is no program in Crane's verse, Munson suggests, only a destabilizing quest for continual ecstatic experience; and, Munson notes, "Crane cannot maintain his feelings on this plane. He drops off until fortune gives him another ecstasy after which in turn he slumps" (51). In response to this charge of unevenness, what he called "this charge of alternate 'gutter sniping' and 'angel kissing'" (*Letters*, 239), Crane rejected the assumption in Munson's letter that some clearly delineated system of metaphysical belief need inform a modern poet's work, and he suggested that his vision of the modern world rejected systematics. In his essay "General Aims and Theories" Crane had characterized Western civilization as "so in transition from a decayed culture toward a reorganization of human evaluations that there are few common terms, general denominators of speech that are solid enough" for meaningful use by the poet (*Poems*, 218); so in this letter to Munson he suggested that the conceptual and linguistic liminality of the modern world ought to solicit from the writer doubtful speculations rather than a simple, programmatic affirmation:

> The tragic quandary (or *agon*) of the modern world derives from the paradoxes that an inadequate system of rationality forces on the living consciousness. I am not opposing any new synthesis of reasonable laws which might provide a consistent philosophical and moral program for our epoch. Neither, on the other hand, am I attempting through poetry to delineate any such system. If this "knowledge," as you call it, were so sufficiently organized as to dominate the limita-

> tions of my personal experience (consciousness) then I would probably find myself automatically writing under its "classic" power of dictation, and under that circumstance might be incidentally as philosophically "contained" as you might wish me to be. . . . But my poetry . . . must by so much lose its impact and become simply categorical. (*Letters*, 238–39)

We see in this argument with Munson a parallel to Crane's problems with Winters and Tate examined earlier: each implied that Crane lacked some necessary control, that he would have been a better poet if he had had a more stable and morally centrist vision to offer his reader. But Crane defined the modern as just this lack of absolute system, and he rejected as foolish the vogue for organized mysticism that led Munson and "a number of [his] other friends" to the "portals of the Gurdjieff Institute" where "presumably the left lobes of their brains and their right lobes respectively function (M[unson]'s favorite word) in perfect unison." In the same letter to Winters in which he defended homosexuality as a basis for cultural knowledge, Crane described Munson and these others as "hermetically sealed souls" (*Letters*, 298–99), implying that their "consistent philosophical and moral program for our epoch" was not a solution to the anomie of the modern world.

If he occasionally employed the vocabulary of mysticism in his articulation of "the relation of tradition to the contemporary creating imagination" (*Poems*, 217), Crane's mistrust of such systems is apparent throughout his life and ought to qualify any portrait of him as a "mystic on the loose." The perception of him as an undisciplined mystic has persisted, however, aided in part by his employment of traditional religious vocabularies and motifs. But, as Robert Combs has suggested, Crane's poems do not "represent an attempt to reassert the religious consciousness in an unreligious age"; rather, Combs writes, "What Crane has discovered is that the power of the mind never has depended on the absolute truth of its beliefs . . . , its genius for disagreeing with itself is its greatest strength" (*Vision of the Voyage*, x–xi).[2]

Criticism has not defined Crane's text as visionary without some justification, however; Crane himself invited this reading on occasion. Writing to Munson in June 1922, for instance, while "notoriously drunk," he confessed the following, an event that links him, through its claim for visionary experience, to Blake before him, Yeats his contemporary, and Ginsberg yet to come:

> Did I tell you of that thrilling experience last winter in the dentist's chair when under the influence of aether and *amnesia* my mind spiraled to a kind of seventh heaven of consciousness and egoistic dance among the seven spheres—and something like an objective voice kept saying to me—"You have the higher consciousness—you have the higher consciousness. This is something that very few have. This is what is called genius." A happiness, ecstatic such as I have known only twice in "inspirations" came over me. I felt the two worlds. And at once. As the bore went into my tooth I was able to follow its every revolution as detached as a spectator at a funeral. O Gorham, I have known moments in eternity. (*Letters*, 91–92)

Given this letter, and his own interest in mysticism, it is little wonder that Munson insisted on Crane's mysticism in his "Young Titan" essay or that he turned to a passage from "For the Marriage of Faustus and Helen" as one of his touchstones for Crane's work: "There is the world dimensional for / those untwisted by the love of things / irreconcilable." The "two worlds . . . at once" in Crane's ecstatic moment fits perfectly into readings that make his a Platonic or disembodied text neatly situated in a history of binary oppositions that have privileged the ideal over the real, the noumenal over the phenomenal, the mind over the body.

Certainly Crane wrote within such a metaphysical tradition, and his texts often exhibit its biases. But there are perhaps other questions to ask about the metaphysics of this text. We have seen, for instance, how the rhetoric of transcendence figures in Crane's letters about homosexuality, and we know that the body for him is a site of transfiguration and promise that can be neither escaped nor disregarded. In the letter to Waldo Frank that relates the beginning of his affair with Emil, Crane takes the sublime or religious rhetoric of homosexuality to its highest, claiming to have seen "the Word made Flesh," and to have been "kissed with a speech that is beyond words entirely" (*Letters*, 181, 183). Very early (in December, 1920), we find the rhetoric of cosmic visitation in the "NEWS!" letter: "The 'golden halo' has widened,—descended upon me (or 'us') and I've been blind with happiness and beauty for the last full week!" (*Letters*, 49), and in a letter from 20 February 1923 we see him caught in the throes of that impossible split between idealized and actual homosexual desire that was the paradox of homosexuality for his generation. He declares the "flesh damned to hate and scorn" yet the "intellect alone . . . [to] have no mystic possibilities" (*Letters*, 127). We see in Crane's letters an insistence on what Guy Hocquenghem has called the "real miracle" of homosexual encounters, the unexpectedness that makes them "a kind of predestination that is both splendid and accursed" (*Homosexual Desire*, 71), and from such evidence as those letters provide, it should be impossible to make Crane's purported mysticism something separate from the body on which was staged this intense drama of homosexual desire. In short, some of Crane's "moments in eternity" seem certainly to have been homoerotic.

Furthermore, if we look at the larger context of his claim to have been transported to the "seventh heaven of consciousness," we see an important fact about the construction of mystical transport in the letter above. As a moment in eternity, the dental-chair experience may seem rather laughable, and it occurs in a place most would identify with excruciating personal pain rather than with the body's ability to transcend pain. But Crane's reconstructed moment of ecstasy in the dental chair is truly a moment of annunciation, and if it is meant to signal the incarnation of his poetic authority, it is also structured as a sublimated moment of impregnation. As Harold Bloom and others have suggested, it is necessary to see that something is repressed in each new influx of the sublime—and what is repressed in this excerpt from Crane's early life is the body as a site of homosexual desire. A subtext of referents links the dentist's drill to both phallic erections and poetic inspiration; the bore entering the tooth is a substitution for a sexual ritual Crane noted just one paragraph before. He had been impressed by a book on Greek vases given to him by Sam Loveman "in which satyrs with great erections prance to the ceremonies of Dionysios [sic] with all the fervour of de Gourmont's descriptions of sexual sacrifice in *Physique de L'Amour*"; and these great erections are almost immediately transmuted into an "enormous power" of poetic possibility that "seems almost supernatural" in him, a sign of his own hope for a poetic career—"If this power is not too dissipated in aggravation and discouragement I may amount to something sometime" (*Letters*, 91). Finally, under the rapid sway of a "notoriously drunk" free association, the great erections and enormous power of poetic ability are condensed into this clinical penetration in which all pain (possibly the pain or wound of homosexuality we have seen before) is forgotten. The letter to Munson is founded on a dynamic of substitution—"I" for "you" in the "objective voice"; consciousness in loss of consciousness; great erections become dental drills;

and Crane's substitution of "amnesia" for "anesthesia" is interesting because it suggests the pattern of repression that leads from homosexual desire and ritual dismemberment to the transcendental sanction of poetry; it names the act of forgetting that in this case founds the sublime.

In "For the Marriage of Faustus and Helen," Crane employs a phrase that has come to provide perhaps too easy an entry into his text—"*the love of things irreconcilable*"—and as the title also indicates, Crane uses the poem to test a number of possible reconciliations, syntheses, marriages, and dialectics. But what is perhaps most interesting for our purposes is what cannot be brought together: the irreconcilable structures of homosexuality and transcendentalism. If we say that homosexuality is not overtly "present" in the text of "For the Marriage of Faustus and Helen," we need to question what counts as a textual presence. The title alone, for instance, clearly refers us to a long tradition of homosexual writers such as Marlowe who use heterosexual figures to investigate the problem of desire, and we must read Crane's interest in the erotic possibilities of modern culture as they are recorded in this text against his own transformational homosexual experiences. This is not in any sense to suggest that Crane's writing of the poem was an investigation of the question of homosexuality or that we would be truer to the spirit of the text to read it as such. It is to suggest rather that our reading of the poem ought to include an awareness of exactly how and why homosexuality is absent from a poem inscribing a myth of cultural resurrection. And we need to ask how homosexuality (structured as a sublime encounter and authentic experience) may survive its repression in the public heterosexual discourse of the text, returning (as the repressed) in another form.

I would like to return to the letter responding to Munson's essay, to Crane's contention that "the tragic quandary (or *agon*) of the modern world derives from the paradoxes that an inadequate system of rationality forces on the living consciousness," for "Faustus and Helen" casts its concerns in terms of "the modern world" and the ways in which its overstructuration blocks access to the sublime and authentic (including, I would argue, an authenticity of bodily experience that Crane located in homosexuality). Conceived as his first "major" piece, as a definitive response to and critique of *The Waste Land*, and carried with him to New York in 1923 like a passport to artistic respectability, "Faustus and Helen" was written under a set of immensely rigid and not altogether self-imposed expectations. His early letters are full of references to the conception, writing, and reception of the poem, but two letters written to Waldo Frank and Gorham Munson in the late winter of 1923 thanking them for their praise of his work focus for us the problematic marked by his desire to be a major writer despite his sexual minority. To Frank he wrote:

> Such major criticism as both you and Gorham have given my "Faustus and Helen" is the most sensitizing influence I have ever encountered. It is a new feeling, and a glorious one, to have one's inmost delicate intentions so fully recognized as your last letter to me attested. I can feel a calmness on the sidewalk—where before I felt a defiance only. . . . What delights me almost beyond words is that my natural idiom (which I have unavoidably stuck to in spite of nearly everybody's nodding, querulous head) has reached and carried to you so completely the very blood and bone of me. There is only one way of saying what comes to one in ecstasy. (*Letters*, 127–28)

And to Munson he wrote:

> The more I think about my *Bridge* poem the more thrilling its symbolic possibilities become, and since my reading of you and Frank (I recently bought *City Block*) I begin to feel myself directly connected to Whitman. I feel myself in currents that are positively awesome in their extent and possibilities. "Faustus and Helen" was only a beginning. . . . Potentially I feel myself quite fit to become a suitable *Pindar* for the dawn of the machine age. . . . Frank has done me a world of good by his last letter (which promised another soon including further points on "F. & H.") and, as I wrote him, now I feel I can walk calmly along the sidewalk whereas before I felt only defiance. . . . And now to your question about passing the good word along. I discover that I have been all-too-easy all along in letting out announcements of my sexual predilections. Not that anything unpleasant has happened or is imminent. But it does put me into obligatory relations to a certain extent with "those who know," and this irks me to think of sometimes. After all, when you're dead it doesn't matter, and this statement alone proves my immunity from any "shame" about it. But I find the ordinary business of earning a living entirely too stringent to want to add any prejudices against me *of that nature* in the minds of any publicans and sinners. Such things have such a wholesale way of leaking out! Everyone knows now about B——, H—— and others—the list too long to bother with. (*Letters*, 128–30)

Obviously, Crane doth protest a bit too much his "immunity" to "shame," and it would seem from the evidence in these two letters that Crane found himself in 1923 in an irreconcilable position: clearly his ambition to become the Pindar of his age was at odds with the public disclosure of his homosexuality. His "natural idiom," whether in writing or in walking the sidewalks, needed occasional policing, and he closed the letter to Munson with this plea: "I am all-too-free with my tongue and doubtless always shall be—but I'm going to ask you to advise and work me better with a more discreet behavior" (*Letters*, 130). It seems that Crane felt himself finally unable to afford the social luxury of "one way of saying what comes to one in ecstasy" when that ecstasy was homoerotic. Even the inspiriting presence of Whitman was not proof against the need to obscure reference to homosexuality in his work, for if Robert Martin is correct in suggesting that Crane learned from Whitman to trust his homosexuality and to inscribe it in verse, he also surely learned from Whitman to encode it so that it might be read in something other than a homosexual way.

While working on the third and final section of "Faustus and Helen," Crane wrote to Munson in January 1923:

> There is no one writing in English who can command so much respect, to my mind, as Eliot. However, I take Eliot as a point of departure toward an almost complete reverse of direction. His pessimism is amply justified, in his own case. But I would apply as much of his erudition and technique as I can absorb and assemble toward a more positive, or (if [I] must put it so in a sceptical age) ecstatic goal. I should not think of this if a kind of rhythm and ecstasy were not (at odd moments, and rare!) a very real thing to me. (*Letters*, 114–15)[3]

This context in part explains Crane's turn to a topography of heterosexual union in the poem as well as his attendance to issues of a broader cultural significance than those he had addressed in his pre-1923 work. But it also helps to explain some of the odd, uneven quality in the text. For instance, the poem borrows from Eliot a much-admired, modernist aesthetic of synecdoche and metonymy but attempts to use that for the symbolic or mythic purpose of presenting the modern as sublime, ecstatic, eternal, and whole. The off-balance quality of the poem may in part be explained as the result of this attempt to fuse an organic vision of history with a poetics in which everything is fragmented and ironic. The poem is at times written in direct echo of Prufrock:

O, I have known metallic paradises
Where cuckoos clucked to finches
Above the deft catastrophes of drums.
(*Poems*, 30)

At other times it appears in the unmistakable "style" of Hart Crane:

The siren of the springs of guilty song—
Let us take her on the incandescent wax
Striated with nuances, nervosities
That we are heir to: she is still so young,
We cannot frown upon her as she smiles,
Dipping here in this cultivated storm
Among slim skaters of the gardened skies.
(*Poems*, 31)

The telling difference here is not merely one of good or bad poetry, but raises the troubled question of authenticity.[4] These two stanzas rest back to back in the second part of "Faustus and Helen," and there is nothing in the poem to suggest that they are stylistically or epistemologically asymmetrical. The ideology of harmony and marriage rules throughout the poem although incongruities and inconsistencies such as this often provide its most interesting tensions. It is also necessary, in understanding this as a homosexual text, to see that "marriage" does not occur in the poem; in the section from which the above passages are taken, originally entitled "The Springs of Guilty Song" and the first section of the sequence's three parts to be written, the diction suggests something more like rape: "Let us take her." Similarly, although section I supposedly presents an image of Helen on a streetcar, it ends with the speaker in a posture not of marriage but of prayer (although his "Bent axle of devotion" certainly carries a phallic nuance). And the final section celebrates a union between the speaker and another man, both veterans of World War I.

If there are no marriages, per se, in the poem there are certainly unions and transcendent moments of a kind that strain intellectual credulity. As R. W. Butterfield writes, in assessing the poem's (and Crane's) intellectual "schizophrenia," "squalor and violence are confronted" in the poem, "but, though they are transcended, they are not resolved" (*The Broken Arc*, 66). Butterfield goes on to equate this dualism in the text with familiar readings of the artist's personal collapse and with the myth that sexual license leads to artistic impotence, neither of which provides a satisfactory frame for the text. But he is quite right that Crane's poem merely swerves away from the more serious issues it raises; it is a poem written as an argument, and (despite a number of more powerful textual moments that seem to undercut the assurance with which the assertion is made) it officially asserts that modernity will redeem itself. The problem in reading the poem lies in what Crane, writing of the poem in 1925, called its "scaffolding," a "series of correspondences" so schematic in their conception as to guarantee the irrefutable simplicity of the poem's message:

> When I started writing Faustus and Helen it was my intention to embody in modern terms (words, symbols, metaphors) a contemporary approximation to an ancient human culture or mythology . . . the basic emotional attitudes toward beauty that the Greeks had. And in so doing I found that I was really building a bridge between so-called classic experience and many divergent realities of our seething, confused cosmos of today, which has no formulated mythology yet for classic poetic reference or for religious exploitation.
>
> . . . I found "Helen" sitting in a street car; the Dionysian revels of her court and her seduction were transferred to a Metropolitan roof garden with a jazz orchestra; and the *katharsis* of the fall of Troy I saw approximated in the recent World War. The importance of this scaffolding may easily be exaggerated, but it gave me a series of correspondences between two widely separated worlds on which to sound some major themes of human speculation—love, beauty, death, renascence. (*Poems*, 217)

What we see in this is how easy it was for Crane to read his own poem schematically—perhaps another effect of conceiving the work as a final entry into cultural maturity and authority—and yet how even within this proposed scheme, one can read the "seething, confused cosmos" of the modern in excess of classical, Hellenic harmony. What will be interesting in our reading of the poem will not be the recovery or display of that scaffolding (which is invariably the site of a repressed homosexual desire) but the inevitable collapse of it, the particular ways in which the "divergent realities" of the modern interrupt "a contemporary approximation to an ancient human culture or mythology" of integrated sensibilities and block movement toward sublime incorporation.

In thinking about how Crane presents the peculiar divisiveness of modernity, we might keep in mind two notions from Theodor Adorno: one, that "the semblance of unity and wholeness in the world grows with the advance of reification; that is, with division" (*Prisms*, 31), and two, that "the concept of man envisioned by classicism . . . retreated into the realm of private isolated existence and its images; only there did it seem that the 'human' could be preserved" ("Lyric Poetry and Society," 67). From this point of view, it is possible to read the swerve in the poem away from a critique of the material present toward an assertion of the unity of eternity as one result of modernity's intense efforts toward reification, and to see in the trope of marriage an antidote to the insuperable disease of separation that marks the interpersonal in the modern world. Of particular interest here will be sections I and II of the sequence and the ways in which Crane investigates the problem of alienation in them, for if the official argument of "Faustus and Helen" asserts that mankind may "thresh the height / The imagination spans beyond despair," its more interesting moments are investigations of the cause, effect, structure, and difficulty of resisting that despair.

Crane began what would become the longer sequence by writing section II as a separate poem, "The Springs of Guilty Song," in which "the living consciousness" is "young" rather than old, ever-renewing. This section valorizes the modern through its ability to produce the "new," specifically, jazz. "New" and "modern" should not be read here as the same thing, however: "new" suggests something genuine that "springs," like song, from unconscious conditions and therefore escapes the overstructuration and rationality that falsify modern consciousness; it operates according to "strange harmonic laws," "Striated with [its own] nuances." "Modern," on the other hand, suggests a historical lateness, a division from authentic experience that we are only "heir to" (*Poems*, 31).[5] In this, Crane understands the problem of his modernity as Emerson (and Bloom, and Milton, according to Bloom) understands his: as the condition of late entry into the world. As Lee Edelman suggests, Crane:

> knows that no modern poetry can be uncontestably "virginal," that no creative enterprise can be free of fragmentation. The hypothesis of an unfissured poetry, a poetry unequivocally whole, would be hopelessly nostalgic, a willful mystification. Instead, Crane's poetry knows that its claims to earliness are only a fiction; it recognizes that the virginity it envisions is necessarily only a trope. (*Transmemberment of Song*, 85)[6]

In that condition, one may either wither under the burdens of history (as Eliot suggested Western culture would) or fight for a rebirth of culture (what Crane's insistence on renascence is meant to encourage). But if the first and last sections of the poem take up Eliot more directly, focusing on Western cultural icons and discourses, this middle section authenticates modernity through the figure of jazz and jazz dancing, a phenomenon Edward Brunner has suggested that we read as political much in the way the drug and music culture of the late sixties was political. Brunner claims that jazz in the twenties signified rebellion against bourgeois morality, and we can see this in Wallace Thurman's *The Blacker The Berry* as well, where the discourse of jazz unmistakably articulates a transgressive desire:

> Every one began to dance again. Body called to body, and cemented themselves together, limbs lewdly intertwined. A couple there kissing, another couple dipping to the floor, and slowly shimmying, belly to belly as they came back to an upright position. A slender dark girl with wild eyes and wilder hair stood in the center of the room, supported by the strong, lithe arms of a longshoreman. She bent her trunk backward, until her head hung below her waistline, and all the while she kept the lower portion of her body quivering like jello. (172)

We might well, it seems, read Crane's interest in this "new" form of cultural expression as in part motivated by homosexual affinities with modern urban life and its liberation of desire. And certainly one of the most hopeful notes struck here is the fact that the "Brazen hypnotics," the "Blest excursion," and "opéra bouffe" (*Poems*, 30) of this rooftop party are not indebted to any past *Western* culture. This is not renascence of old forms but invention of new ones, and ones Eliot himself was never comfortable with. Jazz is for Crane the genuine experience the first time around, and it centers in the body.

But there are issues here over which we must pause. At the end of the first stanza, Crane addresses his fellow revelers as Olympians—"Know, Olympians, we are breathless / While nigger cupids scour the stars!"—and we see in this one of the gaps over which is suspended the poem's claim for the sublimity of the present: music may make "us" breathless with its echo and training of our desire, but "we" can only be defined in opposition to the "nigger cupids" who actually produce the music that mesmerizes "us" so. The language here describes exactly the political relation between white patron and black artist in the glory days of Harlem club life, something Crane knew from his earlier visits to New York, and while Crane wishes jazz and jazz dancing ("White shadows slip across the floor;" "slim skaters of the gardened skies") to provide a metonymy for organic and self-unifying culture in postwar America, the image is drawn from a social realm where division and differentiation were strictly enforced. There could be no "Olympians" without those who served them. And even if there had not been this racial differentiation in American culture at that time—or if the word "nigger" were elided in this passage—we would still find in this poem a representation of musical production in a culture of differentiation rather than reunion. In *The Weary Blues*, Langston Hughes also makes jazz and dance the focus of his version of modernity, but a strong consciousness of the social irony and alienation confronting black Americans—even in the relatively positive landscape offered by Harlem—is never absent from his text, as in the title poem, "The Weary Blues." In Crane, jazz—as a synecdoche for all art—comes to define its own world separate from the one in which it is actually produced, and art is thus set up as the ultimate reification, inhabiting its own autonomous realm of truth that escapes the material conditions of cultural alienation. Hughes's understanding of blues is never that naive; Crane's understanding of poetry usually is.

But it is when we turn to section I of the poem (or begin there, if we are engaged in a linear reading) that we see how powerfully division rather than unity is the force of that modernity the poem is determined to celebrate. It begins with images of fragmentation and regimentation, implying that the modern world is spiritually unacceptable (there is a glance at the parable of the loaves and fishes in these opening lines):

> The mind has shown itself at times
> Too much the baked and labeled dough
> Divided by accepted multitudes.
>
> (*Poems*, 27)

One leaves the "stacked partitions of the day" and the false interpersonal relations of the business world's "stenographic smiles and stock quotations" behind and returns instead (at the end of the opening stanza) to the suburbs where life is "Virginal perhaps, less fragmentary, cool." But this is no solution to the problem of division, for it only solidifies one of the divisions that make the modern world so alienating, that between a meaningful "private life" and a meaningless but economically necessary life in the marketplace that supports it.[7] Thus, when Crane has Helen appear, it is not in this suburban landscape but in the city that is the locus of his text's concerns. Like other famous figures called forth from crowds (Wordsworth's blind beggar, Baudelaire's mourning woman in "A une passante"), she offers a specular structure through which we may read the alienations that called her forth. But any assessment that she provides a solution to those alienations must take into account the unconvincing drive for closure and reassurance that turns her from a literal woman "across an aisle," on a streetcar, "Half-riant before the jerky window frame," into a figure of the eternal feminine and her supposed virtues of transcendence. What the figure of Helen allows is a turn toward that inward "world which comes to each of us alone," validating in that process the reified human relations the poem has been written to correct.

This introductory section has a three-part structure each part of which interrogates the triangular relation between language, desire, and culture. The first part, which suggests the division and alienation at the heart of modern urban culture, critiques the use of language as a purely instrumental act, what it calls the "labeled dough," of "memoranda, baseball scores," and the "stenographic smiles and stock quotations:" these last two figures especially suggest a truncation of interpersonal relations that occurs with an instrumental theory of language and culture. But this opening moment in the poem offers a counter theory that language is the idiom of desire as well:

> Across the stacked partitions of the day—
> Across the memoranda, baseball scores,
> The stenographic smiles and stock quotations
> Smutty wings flash out equivocations.
>
> (*Poems*, 27)

The "equivications" of language, its continual excess of meaning, may well be what makes it "Smutty" or stained in the businessman's eye, but it names as well the grace and hope of desire ("The mind is brushed by sparrow wings") and a means of political resistance:

> Precision must be avoided if the economy of the One is to be unsettled. Equivocations, allusions, etc. are all flirtations: they induce

> the interlocutor to listen, to encounter, to interpret, but defer the moment of assimilation back into a familiar model. (Jane Gallop, *The Daughter's Seduction*, 78)

The yearning implied by the Icarian image of the wings suggests how meager in contrast is the earthbound world of the "asphalt, crowd," "druggist, barber and tobacconist" that next appear in the poem as more typical representations of the urban crush. It is the desire for a virginal world where the mind may be "brushed by sparrow wings" that sends workers home to suburban realms in "the graduate opacities of evening." But this is a false world of originary purity and wholeness, one that finally only exacerbates the problem of division and alienation in the modern world, as was suggested above. It is not really the virginal, unified, cool place the mythology of real estate would suggest, as satirists have not tired of showing, and this final separation of self from Other that falsely pronounces itself "less fragmentary" (Edelman emphasizes the weight of the "less" and the "perhaps" in this passage [*Transmemberment of Song*, 85]) brings from Crane the prose tag in which we find glossed the entire problematic of the poem: "*There is the world dimensional for those untwisted by the love of things irreconcilable* . . ." [italics in text]. This announces that the values of the material, physical world ("*the world dimensional*") will not provide a solution to the true problems raised in the text—that is, to the problems of irreconcilability the poem addresses. Presenting himself as by implication twisted "*by the love of things irreconcilable*," we see initiated here a familiar, disempowering scenario of the artist's retreat into sensibility as well as the echo of denigration that identifies the homosexual as twisted, as alienated from the straight, supposedly untwisted world of bourgeois normality. The only thing that can straighten out this twistedness, once one has accepted the terms of the bargain as they are articulated here, is devotion to an object of desire in which sexuality may be sublimated and purified rather than encountered. This is the Platonic trap of homosexuality, and this is the sexualizing trap of it as well: to read all alienation as at base a repression of sexual energies.

Before moving on to examine the figure of Helen and her role in the poem, we might briefly note Crane's obsession with an "ideal woman with whom he might fall in love" (Unterecker, *Voyager*, 162) in order to lay to rest one reading of this "habit" that, according to Unterecker, formed early in his life before his "acceptance" of a homosexual identity (the biographer is writing of 1919) and to some extent found itself played out even in the final affair with Peggy Baird. This psychodrama, and Crane's representation of woman as a repository of eternal value, beauty, devotion, etc., calls for at least two comments: one, it is not enough—as some have done—to read Crane's mother (Grace Hart Crane) and Hart's tangled, destructive devotion to her into these appearances. Quite clearly, one of the outcomes of homosexual self-repression is the mental production of a woman one may admire in a manner free of overt sexual elements. If a strict reading of this according to family romance would take such mental processes to a source in "the mother," and the repression of desire for her, we must see that "she" has long since become an absence, a signifier around which are clustered the traces and networks of countless other desires and their repressions as well. It gets us nowhere, either analytically or interpretively, to point to these passages in Crane as instances of a "real" mother-love; in fact, it only serves as a mask for belittling homosexual men as incompletely Oedipalized and therefore as failed heterosexual men. Such insistences also ignore the gay male fantasy of sexual desire for the father—and what a recognition of the centrality of that possibility within the family romance would do to our notion of the etiology of sexual subjectivity. Secondly, the textual pressure to produce Woman as an object of desire, beauty, eternal virtue, etc., was something so much a part of Crane's vocabulary and dialectical thought (as it has been of Western male aesthetics more generally) that its appearance in his text—while it may seem experientially false or ideologically regrettable—is not surprising. In another sense, because Crane inherited from Aestheticism and from the French Symbolists a sense of lived experience as itself an aesthetic production, a text, his more literally textual presentation of nonsexual females may have been *not* experientially false but a true representation of his life-as-text.

In any case, in the second movement of this opening section of the poem, Crane finds embodied in Helen a being who is not subject to the devalued uses of language seen in its first moments; her place as a signifier is more stable than equivocations that merely "flash out" and then disappear, mere allegories of some whole but unrecoverable desire. Her "eyes across an aisle," although "Still flickering with those prefigurations" (of "memoranda," perhaps, or "stock quotations") portend a realm of meaning that exceeds the controls of that other, daylight world and its "smutty equivocations." She is described as "Prodigal," a term that carries a trace of gender not quite appropriate here but one that places her in a narrative of loss and recovery. There is in her appearance a sense of recovery, a healing in the union she promises:

> There is some way, I think, to touch
> Those hands of yours that count the nights
> Stippled with pink and green advertisements.
> And now, before its arteries turn dark
> I would have you meet this bartered blood.
> (*Poems*, 28)

And yet even here we can read how market economy still invades and structures the appearance of desire.[8] Not forgotten here, as they will be in the third section of this opening poem, are the material conditions of the city—those "nights / Stippled with pink and green advertisements," the "arteries" that carry such as her back and forth, making human subjects the commodity trafficked and "bartered" in. And the hands are not simply the indicators of a fetishized sexuality (although part of the movement of modernity is to elide all in the sexual, the private, the personal) but are as well the signs of alienated labor and alienated modernity ("The role of the hand in production has become more modest, and the place it filled in storytelling lies waste" [Walter Benjamin, *Illuminations*, 108]); it may be her job, her pleasure, or both to "count" the nights, but the specter of instrumentality has not been exorcised here.

And yet Crane manages to assert that there is, "I think," "some way . . . to touch" her. Crane uses the urban landscape to frame the question of the value of love, and he turns to the second theory of language to appear in the poem:

> Imminent in his dream, none better knows
> The white wafer cheek of love, or offers words
> Lightly as moonlight on the eaves meets snow.
> (*Poems*, 28)

These words, themselves offered rather lightly, disperse into a whiteness on whiteness (moonlight on snow) that figures some originary wholeness beyond the "pink and green advertisements" of public nights, beyond the "smutty equivocations" of the marketplace. Language is restored in these lines to a primal unity and purity of purpose in the dialogue of lovers for whom it is a transparent medium of desire. But if this appears to solve the problem of language in the modern, alienated world, that is nothing more than an appearance, for these lines suggest that it is only in privacy, in the withdrawal into an imminent dream of one's own, that one may solve the contradictions and problems of alienation. These lines offer a communion ("white wafer" carries the trace of the host) and marriage of two spirits that is the only haven against alienation in the world "dimensional," and that union finds its highest moment in the orgasmic body:

> Reflective conversion of all things
> At your deep blush, when ecstasies thread
> The limbs and belly, when rainbows spread
> Impinging on the throat and sides . . .

But the ellipsis of orgasm leads not to reunion or reconciliation. It leads only to the "inevitable" division of Otherness that even sexual intimacy cannot overcome:

> Inevitable, the body of the world
> Weeps in inventive dust for the hiatus
> That winks above it, bluet in your breasts.
> (*Poems*, 28)

Offered as the possible solution to the anomie of modern, instrumentalized subjectivity, sexuality here betrays itself as only a threshold, only a sign of the still radical division that marks the subject. And as Carroll Smith-Rosenberg has pointed out in *Disorderly Conduct*, we cannot read the twenties discourse of sexual liberation as always in the political service of female equality: "The New Man could portray the New Woman as the enemy of liberated women because he had redefined the issue of female autonomy in sexual terms. He divorced women's rights from their political and economic context. The daughter's quest for heterosexual pleasures, not the mother's demand for political power, now personified female freedom" (282–83). In making Helen a figure of heterosexual desire, then, Crane reifies the very gender distinctions that were in turmoil in his culture and only compounds the problem by transcendentalizing that female desire, a process that reaches its conclusion in the third part of this opening section.

What defines interpersonal relations in the conclusion to this first section of the poem is not some erotic intersubjectivity nor a genuine speech between two lovers, but a relation in language considered now as "a glowing orb of praise." The literal touch that promised union is replaced by a logic of specularity and courtly devotion that enables the speaker only to "lift [his] arms" and his words to the object of his desire. What Crane's work encounters here is the "Inevitable . . . body of the world" as a body written by sexual difference, one term of which signifies access to language and the gaze (the masculine) and one of which is powerless except in its ability silently to suffer and accept (the feminine). The poem is transformed from an "Imminent . . . dream" of fulfilled desire into a prayerful worship where the speaker offers as a token of his devotion only "a lone eye riveted to [her] plane." Surely we have here that idealized woman mentioned earlier as one "solution" for the epistemologically constrained homosexual writer; *and* we have here an instance of what Lacan has identified as the courtly tradition of the One, with its dependence on the category of the not-One (the castrated feminine) and its insistence upon completely separate spheres of femininity and masculinity. But we have here a third term as well, what we might identify as a kind of crossover, where the male speaker (homosexual) does not align himself with the phallic term (although he claims a "Bent axle of devotion"); rather, he identifies with the feminine, what Eve Sedgwick (in a reading of Whitman) calls "the deeper glamor . . . of being like a woman" (*Between Men*, 205). When the speaker envisions his final reunion with Helen, it is in a desexualized space (the "eventual flame" and "white cities" where even the division of sexual difference and orgasmic loss have been superseded) where he, too, will be purified by the knowledge "which comes to each of us alone" (*Poems*, 29). Like the vamp transvestite figure in "Modern Craft," what the speaker and his object of desire share here is more than the knowledge of sexual union; it is the knowledge of sexual likeness. Both have known "The press of troubled hands," and the desire to forget that knowledge leads the poem to a Platonic theory of sexuality and language where the material divisions of culture are forgotten in "One inconspicuous, glowing orb of praise."

The final section of "Faustus and Helen," the last written, rather directly addresses the destruction and aftermath of World War I and asserts that a renascence of human culture is possible even in the wake of that experience. It is not at first clear how this relates to the issues of the first section; indeed, it never becomes clear what logic necessitates Crane's address to the war at this point except the logic of the literary marketplace and the fashion for literature about the war. But this was not only an attempt to be fashionable: certainly any writer whose ambition was to be the "Pindar for the dawn of the machine age" would address the single most disturbing episode of cultural crisis in contemporary history. But what is at work in the separation of the first and third parts of the poem, in keeping the vision of Helen on a streetcar from the vision of wartime destruction, is the ideological pressure to see and maintain a distinction between the private and public realms of existence that we have already seen as one of the divisions in the poem's first section. Supposedly, questions of interpersonal relation, sexuality, and devotion had nothing to do with the public issues of history, culture, and nation. Neither is it a coincidence that this first set of issues is cast in terms of heterosexual relations and the second in terms of male bonding. If the larger sequence is not susceptible to readings of the organic unity among its parts—such as those, for instance, that *The Waste Land* has always been called upon to support—its inhospitality to such practice is evidence of its refusal to enter a strictly symbolic or mythic plane of reference. Its vision of history and its vision of sexuality may well suffer from certain mystifications, but the text is firmly grounded in a cultural moment, and the differing myths of private and public meaning that frame its questions cannot be smoothly resolved. They are addressed in separate sections because they name one of the constitutive contradictions of the culture that produced them.

Section III offers perhaps the most explicit theory of history found in any of Crane's work—including even *The Bridge*—and it begins with an address to Paris, the "arbiter of beauty" whose desire inadvertently brought about the destruction of Troy and who will also "fall too soon," as did those "intricate slain numbers" who died in the war. The male figure who is the focus of the poem in this "motor dawn" is variously identified by the speaker as a "religious gunman," an "eternal gunman," and the "delicate ambassador" of death, and we see in him a figure not unlike those Lawrence describes as archetypal American male heroes—innocent killers. But we can see, too, that that Lawrentian image has always been one of sublimated homosexuality as well: Leatherstocking and Uncas, Queequeg and Ishmael, Huck and Jim—these figures (as Leslie Fiedler pointed out two decades ago) are thick with homoeroticism. And the substitution of Thanatos for Eros that marks this final section is itself an instance of desire. As Fredric Jameson writes in *Fables of Aggression:* "Where Eros marks a kind of realistic compromise, a consent to time and an accommodation to the inevitable rebirth and organic repetition of desire, Thanatos projects an otherwise more final solution and wills, as it were, to come so completely that desire and sex utterly cease to exist and their intolerable repetition is forever silenced" (169). Homoeroticism appears only in its sublimated, thanotic form in this final section of the poem, but the repressed desire that is displaced in that movement returns in the image of two men together in a "street / That narrows darkly into motor dawn." And it is death, considered in the cultural drive to mechanized warfare and as the repression that marks the only acceptable appearance of homosexual desire, that Crane's text must test and reject if it is to truly imagine the rebirth and repetition of culture.

This third section of the poem ends by proclaiming a final triumph of the human spirit, but its opening acknowledges the tragedy of the war and the need for some cathartic repetition of its severe dislocations:

> Let us unbind our throats of fear and pity.
>
> We even,
> Who drove speediest destruction
> In corymbulous formations of mechanics,—
> Who hurried the hill breezes, spouting malice
> Plangent over meadows, and looked down
> On rifts of torn and empty houses
> Like old women with teeth unjubilant
> That waited faintly, briefly, and in vain.
>
> (*Poems*, 32)

We are reminded here of Benjamin's essay "The Storyteller," which contains the following succinct and moving statement of how the war and its technologies dislocated human beings from the universe they had formerly inhabited. The echoes to Crane are strong:

> With the [First] World War a process began to become apparent which has not halted since then. Was it not noticeable at the end of the war that men returned from the battlefield grown silent—not richer but poorer in communicable experience? . . . And there was nothing remarkable about that. For never has experience been contradicted more thoroughly than strategic experience by tactical warfare, economic experience by inflation, bodily experience by mechanical warfare, moral experience by those in power. A generation that had

> gone to school on a horse-drawn streetcar now stood under the open sky in a countryside in which nothing remained unchanged but the clouds; and beneath those clouds, in a field of force of destructive torrents and explosions, was the tiny, fragile human body. (*Illuminations*, 84)

We are reminded as well of Freud's work with veterans recorded in *Beyond the Pleasure Principle*, where the inability to secure health in peacetime is directly related to the lack of injury: the men Freud describes cannot unbind their throats of fear and pity, cannot communicate their experience except in the symptoms of recurrent nightmare because their bodies have never found a site on which to localize the psychic trauma of the war. As Crane writes,

> We know, eternal gunman, our flesh remembers
> The tensile boughs, the nimble blue plateaus,
> The mounted, yielding cities of the air!
>
> That saddled sky that shook down vertical
> Repeated play of fire—no hypogeum
> Of wave or rock was good against one hour.
>
> (*Poems*, 32)

The strain of the language here (the odd metaphors, "saddled sky" and "nimble blue plateaus," like the words "corymbulous" and "hypogeum") speaks to the difficulty of assessing and representing so apocalyptic a change in technology and social organization as came about in the war. It is interesting that the text names the site of those changes as the body, the flesh that remembers, and that even "nimble blue plateaus," as Crane's correspondence explains it, is meant to represent the *kinesis*, the *feeling* of flight. These stanzas attempt to give voice to the private history of the nerves as they were altered by the public history of warfare—one of the subliminal projects of the whole sequence.[9]

The text dismisses personal agency in the matter of wartime destruction, claiming that its participants "did not ask for that, but have survived, / And will persist to speak again." And this speech is imagined as self-evidently authentic; the text uses the fact of survival to ground its theory of historical transcendence. "Faustus and Helen" ends with the following stanza in praise of the human imagination, a faculty inscribed as forever in excess of the material, historical conditions that produce it:

> Distinctly praise the years, whose volatile
> Blamed bleeding hands extend and thresh the height
> The imagination spans beyond despair,
> Outpacing bargain, vocable and prayer.
>
> (*Poems*, 33)

What Crane does not specify (although the language here implies materiality and physical labor) is the way in which that imagination is subject to the particular historical pressures examined in the first section of the poem and mentioned by Benjamin in the above quotation. This conclusion states flatly that imagination transcends the materiality of language; one may read the material trace of it in culture, but it remains itself a disembodied power in excess of economy, the materiality of speech ("vocable" implies only sound and not meaning), and personal entreaty (wish, desire). There is in this, as in H.D.'s discourse of resurrection and renewal in *Trilogy,* some attempt to account for the materiality of historical process, and yet "the years" are cast in a distinctly binary relation to the "imagination" or spirit in a manner that duplicates Hegel and makes history not a dialectical process but a drive toward the ideal. It is only in the tautology that the present will be the present (and therefore authentically itself if in troubled relation to the authenticities of the past) that Crane may read the issue of historical displacement. He proclaimed in "General Aims and Theories" that the present would be what the present would be, and his proclamation of the transcendentality of the modern in the conclusion of "Faustus and Helen" is related to this:

> But to fool one's self that definitions [of modernity] are being reached by merely referring frequently to skyscrapers, radio antennae, steam whistles, or other surface phenomena of our time is merely to paint a photograph. I think that what is interesting and significant will emerge only under the conditions of our submission to, and examination and assimilation of the organic effects on us of these and other fundamental factors of our experience. It can certainly not be an organic experience otherwise. (*Poems*, 219)

What the rhetoric of organicism disguises is the historical mediation of knowledge and experience (it flatly contradicts the rhetoric of recovery that otherwise operates in the poem); what it naively implies is that mental energy is always in excess of the materiality of culture, responsible for it and yet always already more complete than the fragmented "reality" it is called upon to order and reinvent.

The poem closes in three different voices: the voice of wisdom, the voice of conspiracy, and the voice of counsel:

> The lavish heart shall always have to leaven
> And spread with bells and voices, and atone
> The abating shadows of our conscript dust.
>
> . . . .
>
> Delve upward for the new and scattered wine,
> O brother-thief of time, that we recall.
> Laugh out the meager penance of their days
> Who dare not share with us the breath released.
>
> . . . .
>
> Distinctly praise the years, whose volatile
> Blamed bleeding hands extend and thresh the height
> The imagination spans beyond despair . . .
>
> (*Poems*, 33)

This combination of subject positions we call the bardic voice, the voice that knows from a distance that can only be provided by language itself and not by the subjectivity that utters it. Crane worked hard to achieve that voice, sublimating what was basically a lyric talent to the ends of cultural prophecy. To produce it, what he knew as a homosexual about the specific lessons of the lavish heart, the conspiracies of men in "breath released," the volatile instantiations of desire in time—these things had to be suppressed in order that the "universal" could speak. But in denying the homosexuality that was central to his experience, the split between the material and the ideal remained irreconcilable for him, as indeed the culture demanded that it must and as indeed "For the Marriage of Faustus and Helen" exhibits in its very structure.

"The Broken Tower," Crane's last poem, was written in Mexico during his last, often pathetic year. On a Guggenheim there, after completely alienating his friends and supporters stateside, he struck up a relationship with Peggy Baird, Malcolm Cowley's ex-wife, and finally proposed marriage to her. It does seem that their relationship, while it by no means figured an end to Crane's homosexual life, offered him a security and center that had been missing from his personal life at least since the breakup with Emil and certainly since his serious binges of sexual and alcoholic abuse had begun in the mid to late twenties. The myth of "The Broken Tower" is that it is Crane's final masterpiece—a swan song in which he recovered the powers he had squandered in those years of debauchery. Indeed, it is one of the few poems from his later years that has the psychological density and tropological depth of his more mature work. But R. W. Butterfield is correct, it seems to me, in asserting that it is not one of Crane's better performances: "It is better than anything he had written for several years," but largely because it was the first poem in years "in which Crane aesthetically believed, and which he took the trouble to fashion, to polish, to complete" (242). But if it is true, as critics have suggested, that Crane could not write a poem while not in love ("Faustus and Helen" bespeaks his love for words and with the newfound call to genius; "Voyages" of the love for Emil; *The Bridge* of his love of system more generally), it is significant that the love in which "The Broken Tower" is grounded is a love that Crane can only imagine in terms of its proof against homosexuality as an isolated spiritual, emotional decay. "The Broken Tower" is a poem that "confesses" the "failure" of homosexual life and yearns for a return to origin, purity, and wholeness: it is a poem in which life wishes to escape the allegory of language and become pure being. As such, it cannot but fail; as such it is the strongest instance of Crane's submission to the homophobic insistences of transcendental literature.

The poem traces the "disaster" of homosexuality not only in the broken phallus of the tower itself (a figure that functions in this respect similarly to the airplane that crashes in "Cape Hatteras") but also in its notion of the body as the site of wounding, as an engraved or written field that brings, contradictorily, a knowledge of both alienation and joy. If the opening stanza begins by placing its subject in exile from meaning ("feet chill on steps from hell"), the third stanza searches for an answer to this alienation:

> The bells, I say, the bells break down their tower;
> And swing I know not where. Their tongues engrave
> Membrane through marrow, my long-scattered score
> Of broken intervals . . . And I, their sexton slave!

The knowledge of the body, figured here in the bliss of "Membrane through marrow," remains, however, a "long-scattered score / Of broken intervals," a disseminated and decentered subjectivity not unlike that described by Ashbery in "No Way of Knowing." And the text is led to ask whether in a world of such disfigured knowing any of the poet's writing has been true:

> And so it was I entered the broken world
> To trace the visionary company of love, its voice
> An instant in the wind (I know not whither hurled)
> But not for long to hold each desperate choice.
>
> My word I poured. But was it cognate, scored
> Of that tribunal monarch on the air
> Whose thigh embronzes earth, strikes crystal Word
> In wounds pledged once to hope—cleft to despair?
> (*Poems*, 193)

That this is the "visionary company" of "the broken world" of homosexual love ("that corps / Of shadows in the tower, whose shoulders sway / Antiphonal carillons"), a world where (at least in Crane's history of it) one held not "each desperate choice" for long—that this registers the despair of homosexuality judged by a patriarchal and punishing Other who became the specific *critical* tribunal that judged Crane's work immoral, failed, and/or jejune: to deny this at this point is to continue to misread and obfuscate the matrix of concerns traced in Crane's text. It is not surprising, given the dynamic of heterosexual transcendence we have noted throughout this chapter, that Crane resolves this problem of alienation and brokenness by a turn to a healing female presence at the end of the poem:

> The steep encroachments of my blood left me
> No answer (could blood hold such a lofty tower
> As flings the question true?)—or is it she
> Whose sweet mortality stirs latent power?
>
> And through whose pulse I hear, counting the strokes
> My veins recall and add, revived and sure
> The angelus of wars my chest evokes:
> What I hold healed, original now, and pure. . . .
> (*Poems*, 194)

Surely critics who read this as the healing of Crane's memory of heterosexual wars (seen first in those between his mother and his father) are on to something. But clearly those memories were not the "cause" of his homosexuality (as some would have it), and so this affair with Peggy Baird (if, indeed, we read the "she" as her) cannot be read even as a potential "cure" of it. And yet the word "latent" in this context is insistent: is this Crane's claim to his own latent heterosexuality? To read it thus, it seems to me, is to read it as a suicide note—which, all warnings against such mystifications notwithstanding—it seems partly to have been. And yet it seems obvious as well that we might read the healing that occurs here as a healing of ideological alienation, the return of an "original" (since, "latent") power to write that has (since his first poems) been a site for the celebration of transformative powers of love—*including*, and not opposed to, homosexual attachment.

The poem is the final autobiographical statement of a man in the depths of a purely ideological homosexual despair, and it ends in a brief hymn to internalized affection: if the tower from the beginning announces itself as phallic, and the poem throughout traces bodily desire as problematic, Crane manages a resolution to this in the final stanzas by internalizing the tower, by placing it in the "matrix of the heart," claiming love as the "answer" his blood has heretofore lacked in its quest through the broken world, a love that grants him peace ("visible wings of silence sown / In azure circles") he has not known before. The poem closes by bringing together one of the oldest of heterosexual tropes—the marriage of sky and earth, male and female, now in perfect harmony:

> visible wings of silence sown
> In azure circles, widening as they dip
>
> The matrix of the heart, lift down the eye
> That shrines the quiet lake and swells a tower . . .
> The commodious, tall decorum of the sky
> Unseals her earth, and lifts love in its shower.
>
> (*Poems*, 194)[10]

The ultimate sign of alienation in the opening section of "Faustus and Helen" (the gap between the subject and his transcendence marked by "the body of the world" and the "hiatus / That winks above it") is refigured here *not* as a masculine/feminine union, although tower and lake, shower and matrix have strongly gendered properties. The final image, however, is one of a female presence lifting the speaker into the sky and into union with her; it is a pietà. The conclusion of the poem no longer fears the patriarchal "crystal Word" and its ability to wound; but it is a healing that is wholly maternal, something we might read not so much as a heterosexual solution to homosexual alienation as a sublime displacement of its displacements.[11]

What makes "The Broken Tower" an abysmal text is that Crane is not engaged here in questions of broad cultural formations, as he was in "For the Marriage of Faustus and Helen," where the very notion of community forced on him an (albeit oppressively) legitimated heterosexual vocabulary as the only appropriate one. "The Broken Tower" is an autobiographical statement, one intertextual with "The Wine Menagerie," "Legend," or "Voyages," and its complete surrender to the tropes of heterosexual transcendentalism must be read as an act of homosexual (and thus of) self-erasure. It is a text, therefore, in which autobiography becomes an act of death, and it was only weeks after writing it that Crane threw himself off the *Orizaba* into the waters of the Gulf of Mexico. *That*, finally, is the burden of transcendentalism taken up naively by the homosexual: homosexual desire is often repressed and signified as death in Whitman's autobiographical pieces ("Out of the Cradle," for instance), and this seems to have been the irreconcilable contradiction that Crane experienced as his homosexuality. He needed it to be, as chapter 3 suggested, a site in which the body could be legitimated, and yet he could not forego the question of "moments in eternity" where the body itself would be forgotten. The trope of dismemberment that haunts almost all of his writing of desire comes finally to signify not only the inarticulate flesh of the homosexual body and the broken discourses through which it attempts to make itself coherent. It comes to signify as well the "end" of desire in a sublimity that is both the denial of good forms and the surrender to nonbeing.

6
The Unmarried Epic

Where it finds inadequacies it does not ascribe them hastily to the individual and his psychology, which are merely the facade of the failure, but instead seeks to derive them from the irreconcilability of the object's moments.

THEODOR ADORNO
on cultural criticism, Prisms

CRANE FIRST CONCEIVED "a new longish poem under the title of *The Bridge* which carries on further the tendencies manifest in 'F and H'" (*Letters,* 118) in 1923 while still living in Cleveland. Almost from its initial conception he thought of the poem in terms that he knew were ambitious and that might prove difficult of accomplishment: writing to Munson just twelve days after his first mention of the poem, he notes that "the more outline the conception of the thing takes,—the more its final difficulties appal me" (*Letters,* 124). Six months later, in July of 1923, he wrote, "I am perfectly sure it will be finished within a year" (*Letters,* 141), but it was approximately six and a half years until Crane brought the project to closure, a period during which his conception of its purpose and of his position within American culture changed radically. As R. W. Butterfield somewhat sensationally stated in his 1969 summary of the writing of *The Bridge,*

> It was just under seven years between the conception of *The Bridge* and its completion. In February 1923 Crane had been the messenger of a free-wheeling optimism, with an intermittently megalomaniac confidence in his mission and in his poetic genius; in 1929 he was a self-contemptuous alcoholic, whose erotic ecstasies had become self-conscious barbaric lusts, whose only certainty was of his own failure and loss of talent, and whose "philosophical optimism" had been routed by a more or less steady conviction of general spiritual disintegration [in the West]. The man who completed the poem shared few beliefs with the man who had begun it. It is hardly surprising

> that the poem is not conspicuous for its coherence, its internal logic, and its consistency of development. (*The Broken Arc*, 151)

In the beginning, Crane imagined the poem as a response to the pressures of modernization, to the overwhelming cultural changes that were transforming the American landscape in the early years of the twentieth century; it was imagined, that is, as a continuation of the project of "Faustus and Helen," a celebration of the present and of America as Possibility. It was, he wrote,

> a mystical synthesis of "America." History and fact, location, etc., all have to be transfigured into abstract form that would almost function independently of its subject matter. The initial impulses of "our people" will have to be gathered up toward the climax of the bridge, symbol of our constructive future, our unique identity, in which is included also our scientific hopes and achievements of the future. (*Letters*, 142)

But as the rhetoric of abstraction implies, Crane's central trope in the poem becomes detached from its social and institutional moorings and in the process becomes so protean as to defy logic—even the logic of metaphor. The bridge came to be anything and everything Crane wished. In early 1926, he wrote to Waldo Frank that the bridge "in becoming a ship, a world, a woman, a tremendous harp (as it does finally) seems to really have a career" (*Letters*, 232), a life of its own.

To his patron Otto Kahn he sent in March 1926 the outline of a six-part structure that emphasizes how the poem "is based on the conquest of space and knowledge" in which "the theme of 'Cathay' (its riches, etc.) ultimately is transformed into a symbol of consciousness, knowledge, spiritual unity" (*Letters*, 241). Edward Brunner has commented on the heavily historical burden in this plan for the poem, suggesting that this shows the heavy influence of Allen Tate, whose own definitive statement on modern America, "Ode to the Confederate Dead," made a strong statement about the lessons of history. What Brunner does not note is how the addressee of this letter (Kahn) may have influenced the shape of its outline: Kahn was an industrial philanthropist whose "loan" of two thousand dollars enabled Crane to turn his full attention to the composition of the poem. Kahn's ideology was firmly rooted in an optimistic and spiritualized notion of American institutions and their history that Crane (perhaps) felt he should mirror in asking for more money. As such, one cannot read the letter without wondering how much Crane is begging the question when he describes the poem; what might most forcefully redirect our reading of all of these various pronouncements about the meaning and scope of the text, however, is the fact that when they were written virtually none of the poem—as it was subsequently to be published—had been composed. When Crane wrote of *The Bridge* between 1923 and 1926, it was as a fantasy text, and his fantasies about it seem to have changed dramatically in the specific details of their structure and meaning *and* to have been somewhat beyond execution, for the finished text is quite different from any of the projected ones.

The history of nonwriting on the poem is instructive, for if the symbol of the bridge seemed to Crane to have "a career," he himself did not between his first reference to it and its final appearance from Harry Crosby's Black Sun Press in 1930. Between his 1923 confidence of its swift completion and the summer of 1926 in which he actually wrote approximately two-thirds of the final text while in residence on the Isle of Pines off Cuba, the poem was more written about than written; an early version of its concluding section, "Atlantis," given the working title "Finale," was the only thing on *The Bridge* that had been composed before that summer.[1] The breakthrough in his inability to write more than the poem's (perhaps) never-earned transcendent conclusion came in 1926 after his infamous quarrel with the Tates made it imperative that he leave New York.[2] On the Isle of Pines, he at first found it impossible to write, and penned to Waldo Frank his well-known doubts about the relevance of his project:

> At present—I'm writing nothing—would that I were an efficient factory of some kind! It was unfortunate in a way to have been helped by our friend, the banker,—with my nose to the grindstone of the office I could still fancy that freedom would yield me a more sustained vision; now I know that much has been lacking all along. This is less personal than it sounds. I think that the artist more and more licks his own vomit, mistaking it for the common diet. (*Letters*, 259)
>
> The form of my poem rises out of a past that so overwhelms the present with its worth and vision that I'm at a loss to explain my delusion that there exist any real links between that past and a future destiny worthy of it. The "destiny" is long since completed, perhaps the

> little last section of my poem is a hangover echo of it—but it hangs suspended somewhere in ether like an Absalom by his hair. The bridge as a symbol today has no significance beyond an economical approach to shorter hours, quicker lunches, behaviorism and toothpicks. (*Letters*, 261)

About one month after this second passage was written, however, he had managed his breakthrough, "Proem: To Brooklyn Bridge," a text that resituates the "quicker lunches, behaviorism and toothpicks" model of the bridge within a still-emergent vision of expectancy and possibility.

A number of factors may have contributed to this breakthrough, but among the main ones was the fact that Allen Tate had agreed in the interim between these two letters to write a preface for *White Buildings* in the absence of one promised but not forthcoming from Eugene O'Neill. This news was significant for various reasons: it indicated some healing of the rift between Crane and his New York friends and it also indicated a valued colleague's approval of his work. Moreover, it came at a time when it seems that Crane felt his homosexuality alienated him from literary culture (what he calls the "elite") and made his particular artistic situation impossibly idiosyncratic: Rimbaud and Whitman seemed to him to have been worthy of a prophetic poetry in a way that he was not (*Letters*, 261). In a letter written less than a month before the "Proem" to *The Bridge*, he had surrendered himself to a cruelly disabling and isolating vision of homosexuality:

> It has been so disgusting to note the sudden turns and antics of my "friends" since I had the one little bit [of] help I ever had toward my work in the money from Kahn. Everytime I came into N.Y. from the country I'd hear new monstrosities of fables going about town as to how I was squandering money on pate de foi gras, etc. And worse whisperings. It's all been very tiresome—and I'd rather lose such elite for the old society of vagabonds and sailors—who don't enjoy chit-chat. . . . Let my lusts be my ruin, then, since all else is a fake and mockery. (*Letters*, 264)

If we grant that homophobia is implied in this letter as part of the "elite" whispering about him (and we can see from memoirs by Tate and Cowley how much it was a part of their vision of him); if we see the reference to Absalom in the letter to Frank as an allusion to his early text "Recitative," where it is a figure for the homosexual's alienation from a punitive patriarchal and capitalistic culture; if we remember that "the old society of vagabonds and sailors" came to play an unpredicted, crucial, and homosexual role in the two-thirds of *The Bridge* that Crane produced in the next few months; and if we see that Tate's authorization of Crane's poetry is in effect an authorization of a homosexual vision: then we must imagine that all these competing attitudes toward homosexuality inform both the long period of noncomposition and the breakthrough into writing in the summer of 1926.[3]

If we read "Passage" and "The Wine Menagerie" as the abysmal moments in Crane's mid-twenties writing of the homosexual, as the culminating texts of a loss of transcendent union and power, it is important to note that the first poem Crane wrote on the Isle of Pines in the summer of 1926 was "Repose of Rivers," a testament to homosexual poetic authority that reverses the despair of those two recently completed poems. Thus, we might read Crane's long period of nonwriting on *The Bridge* as due not only to some philosophical insight into the naiveté of his utopian hope for modern America but also to a more specific crisis of authority as a homosexual poet confronted with the loss of homosexuality's threshold experience of transcendence.[4] "Repose of Rivers" was followed within weeks by "To Brooklyn Bridge," the "proem" or prologue that initiated the resolution of what had kept him from writing *The Bridge* for so long.

Almost since its publication, critics have noted the poem's critique of the modern industrial and economic landscape of New York City.[5] We may see in the rapid montage of the following stanza a celebration of the city as machine, but this celebration is marked as much by its violence as by its beauty. It is distinctly opposed to the pacific reach of the bridge cables, and it is in fact nature's excess of the modern urban landscape that seems to carry value here:

> Down Wall, from girder into street noon leaks,
> A rip-tooth of the sky's acetylene;
> All afternoon the cloud-flown derricks turn . . .
> Thy cables breathe the North Atlantic still.
>
> (*Poems*, 45)

In the opening figure of the poem, sea gulls enjoy a freedom of movement unavailable to human beings:

> How many dawns, chill from his rippling rest
> The seagull's wings shall dip and pivot him,

Shedding white rings of tumult, building high
Over the chained bay waters Liberty
(*Poems*, 45)

There is in this some index of human restlessness; already a sense of weariness pervades the text—"How many dawns . . ." becomes the opening of a complaint, an appeal for respite and rest. In the act of naming freedom its desire (the wish to "be," like Liberty, un-"chained"), the text records perhaps more strongly the contradictory desire to escape from movement, to find a point of stasis that will no longer be the point of dip and pivot (just as the plea in "Voyages III," "Permit me voyage, love, into your hands," is a request for an end to the endless displacements of desire).

The problem of the modern, as it is figured at the outset of *The Bridge*, is the problem of motion,[6] the problem for the homosexual who understands himself as displaced, the fact that nothing "stays" him. The epigraph to the epic is Satan's statement of his dislocation from Job—"From going to and fro in the earth, and from walking up and down in it"—and the poem presents the ultimate effect of this dip and pivot, this rootlessness and movement (here a "speechless caravan"), as suicide:

Out of some subway scuttle, cell or loft
A bedlamite speeds to thy parapets,
Tilting there momently, shrill shirt ballooning,
A jest falls from the speechless caravan.
(*Poems*, 45)

In this figure of the bedlamite, we see one person crushed by the anonymity, the speechlessness, of what Waldo Frank called the impersonal, busy machine of New York: "The average New Yorker is caught in a Machine. He whirls along, he is dizzy, he is helpless. If he resists, the Machine will mangle him. If he does not resist, it will daze him first with its glittering reiteration, so that when the mangling comes he is past knowing. He says he is too busy, and wonders why. He means, that all preference to act is gone from him" (172). We see the problem of movement without meaning in acts of business as well ("As apparitional as sails [sales] that cross / Some page of figures to be filed away") and even in the realm of mass-marketed pleasures that manipulate aesthetics in isolated and ultimately valueless scenes of fantasy:

I think of cinemas, panoramic sleights
With multitudes bent toward some flashing scene

Never disclosed, but hastened to again,
Foretold to other eyes on the same screen.
(*Poems*, 45)[7]

The modern world is, in the first half of this poem, an altogether alienating prospect.

But the second half of the poem finds "Vibrant reprieve and pardon" from this alienation in the presence and meaning of the bridge as a symbolic object. If we are rather strongly invited to see the bridge as a sign of the possibility of reunion even in such an alienating and fragmented landscape as the opening of the poem depicts, we are also invited to see the value of the bridge as its potential to absolve the citizens of the modern city from the burden of their anonymity, that which "time cannot raise." In exceeding its own functionality, in being an object of beauty and contemplative richness as well as a means to "shorter hours," the bridge transcends the strictly utilitarian and suggests that the subject under its sway might also transcend his mere utility in culture. It becomes a figure in which the whole is more than the sum of its parts, in which one may read the "*Unfractioned* idiom" [my italics] of a non-alienated existence. If this comes close to a Coleridgean theory of the organic symbol, it is important to see that the rhetoric of the text is not organic. In echo of Blake, it proclaims, "(How could mere toil align thy choiring strings!)," and we know that "mere toil" *has* aligned its choiring strings, that part of what inspires the viewer of the bridge is the fact that it draws together the collective energy and labor of many people in a single, supremely functional and yet beautiful object. It is thus that a religious humanism attaches to the bridge, producing an idiom in which God remains "obscure as that heaven of the Jews" but which yet allows the structure of the bridge to be read as a "myth to God."

In naming the bridge a "harp and altar," and in declaring the desire that it "descend / And of the curveship lend a myth to God," the text celebrates not some mystical Ouspenskian other world but the energy of human manufacture. If the bridge is likened here to God, we are invited to read in it a structure that centers all subjectivity: as Althusser claims, God is the Subject of subjects, and in the more positive movement of the poem's second half, the bridge becomes the means to a very different form of exchange:

Under thy shadow by the piers I waited;
Only in darkness is thy shadow clear.

The City's fiery parcels all undone,
Already snow submerges an iron year. . . .
(*Poems*, 46)

This is an echo of the darkness that is Whitman's figure for difficulty in "Crossing Brooklyn Ferry," a text that "To Brooklyn Bridge" strongly evokes, and this intertext requires some explication, for it is in the reconnection to what Winters derogatorily called "the Whitmanian inspiration" that Crane brought *The Bridge* to birth. "Repose of Rivers" marks, of course, the beginning of his reclamation of Whitman as a powerful precursor, and "Crossing Brooklyn Ferry," with its synthesis of past, present, and future, allows Crane (in rewriting it) to circumvent the damaging notion that the "past . . . so overwhelms the present" as to call into question any "future destiny" (*Letters*, 261). It allows him, too, to counter Eliot, and the view of the dead crossing London Bridge in *The Waste Land* (Whitman writes, "Just as you feel when you look on the river and sky, so I felt, / Just as any of you is one of a living crowd, I was one of a crowd, / . . . Had my eyes dazzled . . . / Look'd . . . / Look'd . . . / Look'd . . ." [*Leaves of Grass*, 160–61]).[8] And with that reclamation comes a reclamation of homosexuality and the body as well, making (with Whitmanian verve) even isolation a condition of empowerment:

I too felt the curious abrupt questionings stir within me,
In the day among crowds of people sometimes they came
upon me,
In my walks home late at night or as I lay in my bed they
came upon me,
I too had been struck from the float forever held
in solution,
I too had receiv'd identity by my body,
That I was I knew was of my body, and what I should be I
knew I should be of my body.

It is not upon you alone the dark patches fall,
The dark threw its patches down upon me also.
(*Leaves of Grass*, 162)

In Crane's opening poem to *The Bridge*, the homosexual is presented as marginal, as implicitly at odds with that daylight world where bridges represent primarily the means to quicker lunches, behaviorism, and toothpicks. But through his refusal of the realm of business as somehow the "real" locus of meaning for the bridge and for those written under its sign, the text undoes the city's ability to "parcel," to fragment. For its homosexual subject, the bridge becomes a powerful scene of possibility and love (not only in providing a literal cruising place, "Under thy shadow by the piers I waited," but by offering itself as a symbol for the transformative structure of homoerotic experience as well): it becomes "Terrific threshold of the prophet's pledge / Prayer of pariah, and the lover's cry."

Before we can begin to analyze more fully how homosexuality is important to the construction of *The Bridge*, however, we need to understand a bit more about how epic poems in general are constructed, what claims they make for cultural centrality, and how one might think of the ideology or discourse of the epic as a counterideology to the discourse of homosexuality. I do not wish here to become bogged down in definitions of epic poetry: it is accepted practice to define *The Bridge* as an epic, and I have little desire to challenge that definition. The interest here is in genre only as genre takes itself as a site for the representation of gender, which means in this instance that epics should be seen as far more culturally definitive in their inscription of the values and proprieties attached to gender than are novels or romances, for instance, with their more openly contestatory relation to questions of morality, class, and ideology. As Michael Bernstein writes in *The Tale of the Tribe*, epics have as one of their differentiating features a strong stake in cultural imperatives:

> The dominant voice narrating the poem will . . . not bear the trace of a single sensibility; instead, it will function as a spokesman for values generally acknowledged as significant for communal stability and social well-being. . . . [T]he proper audience for epic is not the *individual* in his absolute inwardness but the *citizen* as participant in a collective linguistic and social nexus. . . . [E]pic speaks primarily to members of a "tribe," to listeners who recognize in the poem, social (in the broadest sense, which here includes political) as well as psychological, ethical, emotional, or aesthetic imperatives. (14)

Because it takes the definition of cultural value as its conscious center, the construction of epic is a far richer field than lyric for analyzing the textual control of difference and the social struggle among peoples, languages, manners, and values that Althusser suggests occurs throughout ideological apparatuses such as literature. Epic is, then, a text produced through the figure of voices and discourses disciplined to a single, authoritative, "tribal" understanding, and the multiple elisions and operations of power that legitimate its "collective vision" form a distinct political unconscious of the text. For instance, when Crane names Whitman's "choice / . . . to bind us throbbing with one voice" (*Poems*, 95) as that which legitimates and authorizes his own epic project, he exposes one of the important problematics in which his epic is based—the disciplining or binding of difference into unity, the production of a single, authoritative voice that in this case reduces the strong homosexual element in his filiation to Whitman to the rather weak textual trace that adheres in the word "throbbing." In this instance homosexuality is immediately sublimated, and what appears in its place is praise within a nationalist vocabulary: "New integers of Roman, Viking, Celt— / Thou, Vedic Caesar, to the greensward knelt!" (*Poems*, 95).

In turning to *The Bridge*, we are faced with a critical task that is by now quite familiar: to denaturalize our usual placements of the text in order to foreground its question as a homosexual one. This requires that we think about both the place of epic in schemes of American literary history and the place of gender in the epic. Roy Harvey Pearce's *The Continuity of American Poetry* takes account of Crane *only* within a reading of American epics (Pearce grants most of the other modernist poets in that section of his text sustained attention to the entire body of their work, but he does not to Crane), and his criteria for evaluating the long texts of American poetry—not surprisingly—ensure the invisibility of homosexuality: "This is the form and substance, the basic style, of the American epic; its strategy is to make a poem which will create rather than celebrate a hero and which will make rather than recall the history that surrounds him" (61). By taking the construction of virtual individuals as its theme, Pearce's criticism may ignore concrete, historical subjects—may, as he quite openly declares, ignore history altogether in favor of projections from a wholly internalized and self-sufficient, "heroic" consciousness. The long poem in America is for Pearce "a poem of the breadth and scope of the epic, yet without its heroically plotted articulation; a poem which, working solely as poem, would engage its reader's sensibilities in such a way as to reinvigorate and reform them and would then relate him anew to a world which, until it were poetically transubstantiated, could not give him the one thing he most wished for: humanity articulated by history" (63). In this last sentence, Pearce inscribes the purpose of literature as the negation of history, the removal of those contingencies of causality and materiality that currently block "Man's" approach to heroic liberal perfection. That such a theory has in practice produced a white, male, heterosexual American as the normative and natural center of humanist interest is at this historical moment beyond dispute, as is the inadequacy of reading anything as "solely" one genre of writing (the poem is as discursive as any other form of writing).

Other attempts to read American epics inclusively have not produced paradigms congenial to homosexuality. James E. Miller's *The American Quest for a Supreme Fiction*, which takes as its subject the "almost obsessive impulse in the American poet to write a long poem," advances a somewhat controversial (if intentionalist) homosexual reading of *The Waste Land*, and acknowledges the homosexuality in other texts such as Ginsberg's, but Miller still imagines his task as within the parameters of a nationalist criticism, as the search for a "particularly American way of conceiving or perceiving or receiving the world" (16). Furthermore, homosexuality remains the scandal of the text for Miller; his text merely speaks or does not speak the word "homosexual" but has nothing to say about what that word means in its cultural or material manifestations, why one would write about it, how it is defined, legitimated, controlled, etc. We see repeated again and again in the criticism of American epics a drive for cultural consensus that is wholly in keeping with what Sacvan Bercovitch has identified in *The Puritan Origins of the American Self* as the production of auto-American-biography, a cultural mode of self-apprehension and -authorization through the typology of nationally and spiritually representative men. Bercovitch identifies the first moment of this writing in America as Cotton Mather's *Magnalia*, and it is not difficult to imagine how the imperative to national consensus has been wholly incompatible with the projects of homosexual writing.[9] "Nation," we should remind ourselves, is not only the most privileged term of Americanist criticism but the most important system of reference for the epic as well. Certainly in the gender ideologies advanced by classic (as with classical) epic texts, the containment of homosexual desire has been crucial (see, for instance, the refusal of the homosexual subject in *Don Juan*, Williams's depiction of lesbianism as unflattering deracination in *Paterson*, Milton's heterosexual reader, Dante's castigation of homosexuals, Pound's rant—perhaps "after" Dante—against (Jews and) homosexuals as *contra naturum* in the *Cantos*, the repressive coding and implied scorn of homosexuality in *The Waste Land*, etc., etc., etc.).

Although his subject is why modern culture more generally cannot be expected to produce an epic literature, Jones Very's contentions in his prize-winning 1839 Harvard essay, "Epic Poetry," name the problematic in which Crane (like Whitman before him) is situated: "The poets of the present day who would raise the epic song cry out, like Archimedes of old, 'give us a place to stand on and we will move the world'" (1). The homosexual poet—particularly when his intentions are toward as culturally authoritative a text as epic has traditionally been expected to be—has no ground on which to stand. The competing agenda of national teleology, referentiality, and scope—as well as quite overt contestations over history, language, and ideology that found the long, culturally authoritative poem—produce a text in which homosexuality is simultaneously present and absent, forceful and impotent, concrete and virtual. The issue in epic is, finally, one of power—and Very in 1839 understood this in a way that more recent critics have not. In a discourse based wholly in a Christianized vision of redemptive history (what he calls "the ever-increasing beauty and grandeur developed by the spirit in its endless progress" [31]) Very predicts the disappearance of epic from the modern world because humanity has moved beyond a merely physical relation to the universe and now imagines its most compelling dramas as internal wars of the soul and intellect: "The wonder and interest of the world is now transferred to the mind, whose thought is action, and whose word is power" (15). Although he does not understand humanity's intrigue with power in a political sense, Very quite rightly sees that the subject matter of the epic is not warfare, or nationhood, or even personality (despite his insistence on the phenomenon of internalization). Rather, he imagines what is at stake in epic literature as power, the only possible subject for epic in the modern world, the "action made *visible* of a superior intellect on an inferior" (36). Very reads the manifestation of power as an internalized mechanism of control, discipline, and repression:

> This it is which has transferred the interest from the outward manifestation of the passions exhibited in the Iliad, to those inward struggles made by a power greater than they to control them, and cause them, instead of bursting forth like lava-torrents to devour and blast

> the face of nature, to flow on like meadow-streams of life and joy. . . . The heroism of Christianity is not seen so much in the outward act, as in the struggle of the will to control the springs of action. (27–28)

Although this way of understanding it is not within *his* power, Very sees the action of modernity as the colonization of subjectivity and the only fit topic for epic as the battle to control and inscribe desire. If Very does not politicize this struggle as a later generation might, Whitman certainly does—indeed, his insistent interest in the struggle over how desire is legitimized within culture (in addition to the specific modes of subjectivity and desire he represents) would seem to constitute Whitman's most radical contribution to the literature of America. And it is important to note here that Whitman is the authorizing precursor of Crane's homosexual epic, the only thing about *The Bridge* other than its title to be constant in every projected version of the text throughout its almost seven years of composition.

To see the text as a contestatory field of discourses, as a site on which various ideological constructions of the subject vie for legitimacy and visibility, requires analysis of the discourses that participate in its vision of its own authority as a cultural artifact rather than interpretation of its linear progress. This is less to interpret than to explain the poem, to demystify it in the sense demanded by Roland Barthes: "If the alienation of society still demands the demystification of language (and notably the language of myth), the direction this combat must take is not, is no longer, that of critical decipherment but that of *evaluation* ("Change the Object Itself," 166). And Barthes means by this *not* an evaluation of Crane's aesthetic accomplishment (i.e., as critics have previously loved to argue whether he is a good poet or a splendid failure) but an evaluation of the cultural and ideological necessity of his work. As Terry Eagleton has explained the task of criticism, "Its function is to install itself in the very incompleteness of the work in order to *theorize* it—to explain the ideological necessities of those '*not-saids*' which constitute the very principle of its identity. Its object is the *unconscious* of the work—that of which it is not, and cannot be, aware" (*Criticism and Ideology*, 89). What we will need to see is how the "not-saids" of *The Bridge*, those discourses and knowledges relegated to its unconscious, contradict its conscious intentions. Thus, we will often be reading *against* the poem's desire to present a synthesis of America, a myth for the modern age, etc., and will be inspecting the ways in which that consciousness cannot fully elide the counterdiscourse and knowledge of the homosexual although it has the power to force it into invisibility.[10]

It is a measure of how well Crane effaces his homosexuality in *The Bridge* that many would deny it any importance or presence whatsoever in the poem. But three sections in particular are apposite to a discussion of the topic: "The Harbor Dawn," a poem which takes as its subject the moment of awakening with a lover; "Cutty Sark," which depicts the rendezvous with a drunken merchant sailor in New York; and "Cape Hatteras," the most troubled section of the poem, in which Crane supposedly asserts his essential union with Whitman and the Whitmanian vision of America. In none of these instances is homosexuality allowed to assume a full and central presence in the work: it becomes the unconscious of the text, that which the text may not speak, for as a discourse it contradicts the very things the epic is called into being to address. Homosexuality is contradictory to the discourses of heterosexuality, national destiny, and commerce, for instance, in the three poems mentioned above. It is also, however, contradictory within itself, providing both moments of ecstasy and an inescapable burden of alienation, and in reading *The Bridge* we must keep in mind how the structural impossibility of these contradictions informs the poem's failure to cohere. If earlier criticism understood the poem's lack of aesthetic harmony as evidence of artistic failure, we can now understand that ideological conditions may also account for any text's myriad incompletenesses. In fact, the marginal text and the "limit text," as Barthes puts it, now fascinate us precisely because they may indicate what literature and the aesthetic cannot "properly" represent and/or accomplish. Crane's inability to figure smoothly within the parameters of the well-made literary artifact as new and ideologically confused a field as homosexuality can be thought in at least two ways other than as artistic failure: if all literature is revision, there are in such cases no clearly articulated precursor texts for the artist to refigure; one rather muddledly refigures what was only rather muddledly figured in the first place. More importantly, we might think that what is ideologically "hot" will likely rupture or disrupt aesthetics. Thus, if *Sister Carrie*, *Uncle Tom's Cabin*, and the Leatherstocking tales attempt new cultural work, as Philip Fisher suggests in *Hard Facts*, they cannot smoothly "refer" to or beautifully mirror some ideologically settled reality. With such an understanding of literary success in mind, the infamous incoherence of *The Bridge* should be seen as one of the things about it most to be trusted. That incoherence should be read as the product of the ideological impossibility the poem traces rather than as an index of the poet's failure to achieve a successful poetic synthesis of its dialectical tensions.

"The Harbor Dawn," which begins the second major section of *The Bridge* ("Powhatan's Daughter"), initiates the larger journey of the text. Situated in the present, overlooking the harbor of New York City, this lyric establishes many of the semes to be developed in the course of the entire sequence. We might think of Crane's epic as opening with a series of poems each of which actually traces a different beginning for the text. Columbus overturns the mythology of the Old World in encountering the New in "Ave Maria," the poem immediately preceding "The Harbor Dawn"; and "Van Winkle," the poem immediately after it, announces the text as a repetition of certain patterns in the history of America (and of American literature). Columbus's monologue, which has always been privileged as the opening gesture of the sequence, is a prayer addressed to the Virgin Mary, and it announces not only a discovery of the New World but also a new mythology of human desire: "[S]till one shore beyond desire" lie "kingdoms / naked in the / trembling heart" (*Poems*, 52). "Harbor Dawn," which follows this historical prologue without direct reference to Columbus or his discovery, presents one of those "kingdoms" as the literally naked modern homosexual. Human history in this poem—and in the modernity of the sequence it initiates—is under a new dispensation, not the dispensation of Columbian discovery but the dispensation of dream, desire, sleep (in this case, with another man). At this point in *The Bridge*, we can read Columbus's earlier appearance as an official "origin" in the text merely as a screen presented to hide the ideologically difficult terrain of the epic's real concern: modern homosexuality. "Harbor Dawn" begins with the speaker unable to sort external images from internal ones:

> Insistently through sleep—a tide of voices—
> They meet you listening midway in your dream,
> The long, tired sounds, fog-insulated noises:
> Gongs in white surplices, beshrouded wails,
> Far strum of fog horns . . . signals dispersed in veils.
> (*Poems*, 64)

What meets this latter-day Dante midway in his dream (this reference being one of Crane's many pointed allusions to Eliot in *The Bridge*) is not a Virgilian predecessor and guardian but "a tide of voices"—all of those voices and discourses of modernity that accost the homosexual but do not speak for him. Until Whitman arrives in "Cape Hatteras" (and Crane did not write that section of the text until 1929: Whitman arrived very late), the epic voyager of *The Bridge* is on his own amid the insistent strains of cultural demand.

Eric Sundquist points to this last phrase, "signals dispersed in veils," as an indicator of "the language of repression" ("Bringing Home the Word," 382), but what is being repressed here is not only the more general psychosexual matrix that all writing and representation represses; it is, more specifically, the particular sexual formation of homosexuality. The gender of the lover with whom the speaker awakes remains unspecified, itself a code for homosexual relations drawn from the pronomial equivocations of Whitman. But as this reading will suggest, it is willfully repressive not to see this as a moment of homosexual union (and therefore as a moment of homosexual awakening in its broader sense). The poem displaces the intimacy of waking with a lover onto the structural necessities of epic *as a public performance* by supplying marginal notes that ask: "*Is it from the soundless shore of sleep that time / recalls you to your love, there in a waking / dream to merge your seed / —with whom?*" (*Poems*, 55, 57). This question goes unanswered; the gender of the "with whom" is effaced, and there is perhaps some impulse to read this as a moment of heterosexual fertility. But a fuller consideration of the poem destroys any authority this impulse would seem to have. Crane answers his marginal question with another marginal question that exposes itself as not being an answer to the "*with whom*": "*Who is the woman with us in the dawn?*" (*Poems*, 57). The woman here is not the beloved; she is "*with*" the lovers only as an official argument of the epic, a literally marginal presence who remains trapped within an unanswered question. As the structure of the sequence develops, this female figure becomes Pocahuntus and she is subsumed under the image of the continent in a displacement of desire that is a well-worn motif in American literature. The movement here is precisely rhetorical—that is, "publicly persuasive"—and as is the case for the lovers of this poem (we will see this in the reading below), public contexts destroy private truths, the structural necessities of the epic force an effacement of the homosexual foundations of it.

Reading the poem in a homosexual context, we find that the homosexual dawn is quite tenderly depicted:

And you beside me, blessed now while sirens
Sing to us, stealthily weave us into day—
Serenely now, before day claims our eyes
Your cool arms murmurously about me lay,

While myriad snowy hands are clustering at the panes.
(*Poems*, 55)

And this moment of awakening is represented in a manner that solicits attention to its materiality as the opposite of traditional gender expectations. The lovers, barely awake, hear the beginnings of morning activity in the harbor, actions that announce the end of their harbor in one another and assert the primacy of economic harbors where other forms of male behavior take precedence:

And then a truck will lumber past the wharves
As winch engines begin throbbing on some deck;
Or a drunken stevedore's howl and thud below
Comes echoing alley-upward through dim snow.
(*Poems*, 54)

Within this context of public work and traditional masculinity, the homosexual moment is sealed off, "fog-insulated," removed from a society that will not recognize it as legitimate. It is identified as different from the usual activities of men both through the symmetrical contrast of images in the previous and following passages (light instead of alcohol is drunk by the lover, the lover's arms sing, the drunken stevedore howls, forests rather than alleyways are the site of meaning) *and* through its appearance on the page—the moment of presence and imaginative fertility in the poem is highlighted as different by indenting and italicizing it:

your hands within my hands are deeds;
my tongue upon your throat—singing
arms close; eyes wide, undoubtful
dark
drink the dawn—
a forest shudders in your hair!
(*Poems*, 56)

Vaguely asserted here, only to be lost, is the possibly masculine nature of nature. If the rhetorical strategy that identifies the virgin land of America (Pocahuntus in the larger structure of the epic) allows for the sexual despoliation of that landscape, as Annette Kolodny has suggested, that rape occurs in this instance outside the text of the poem; within "The Harbor Dawn" itself the orgasmic shudder represents pleasure given to another and not pleasure taken on his unwilling body. Reversing one familiar typography of the homosexual, Crane identifies it here with nature, and the mechanical, alcoholic, and traditionally masculine world outside it with the "*un*natural."

But the rising sun, the reigning deity or necessity of the poem, appears in collusion with economy and conventional masculinity in the poem, making them appear as "natural" as its rising. The text may imply that the hands of men within the hands of other men are just as surely "deeds" as are the hands of men on the gears of trucks or on the levers of winches, but it is important to see that the day that dawns in the poem will put an end to the possibility for such alternative meanings in the lives of men. The star under whose sign the lovers have experienced their union is replaced by the sun of the "real" world of work and masculinity, and when "day claims [their] eyes," it is a sign of their reappropriation by that daylight world and its power to enforce certain expectations of men:

> The fog leans one last moment on the sill.
> Under the mistletoe of dreams, a star—
> As though to join us at some distant hill—
> Turns in the waking west and goes to sleep.
> (*Poems*, 56)

We have, then, in "The Harbor Dawn," the poem's homosexual moment of catastrophe and loss—not only the loss of a homosexually defined existence but also the effacement of homosexuality as a reference in the text. The "waking west" in which the star turns to go to sleep, symbolic of continental imperative (and implying thereby traditional modes of American masculinity as well), will take over in the poem, placing the homosexual in the sequence under a sign of literary and cultural erasure. Thus, "The Harbor Dawn" is the moment when the homosexual enters historical displacement, the moment of beginning the poem and its quest.

It is no coincidence that, after "The Harbor Dawn," while certain stanzas of intervening poems in the sequence are presented in the voice of personal experience or confession, the tone of lyric intimacy disappears as the reigning motif of the text until the next moment of homosexual encounter, "Cutty Sark." The four poems that intervene between these two complete the "Powhatan's Daughter" section of *The Bridge* and expand that heterosexual motif which begins on the margin of "Harbor Dawn" and becomes central to the historical/continental dimensions this first section of the poem seeks to maintain. But we can see that a subtext of homosexual referents persists even in the text of "The River," one of the most consistently praised poems in the sequence and the poem that most explicitly takes up the trope of continent-as-female. In "The River," which presents a panoramic view of America from aboard the 20th Century Limited and incorporates in that view traces of the past, Crane presents hoboes, nameless men or men with first names only, those who wander the continent just as he has "trod the rumorous midnight." These are figures who, in their constitution of an underground social structure, represent an alternative to the poem's opening vision of America as dominated by commerce. Their Otherness and their anonymity recommend them as in possession of a knowledge beyond the ken of the quotidian.

> Behind
> My father's cannery works I used to see
> Rail-squatters ranged in nomad raillery,
> The ancient men—wifeless or runaway
> Hobo-trekkers that forever search
> An empire wilderness of freight and rails.
> Each seemed a child, like me, on a loose perch,
> Holding to childhood like some termless play.
> John, Jake or Charley, hopping the slow freight
> —Memphis to Tallahassee—riding the rods,
> Blind fists of nothing,· humpty-dumpty clods.
>
> Yet they touch something like a key perhaps.
> From pole to pole across the hills, the states
> —They know a body under the wide rain;
> Youngsters with eyes like fjords, old reprobates
> With racetrack jargon,—dotting immensity
> They lurk across her, knowing her yonder breast
> Snow-silvered, sumac-stained or smoky blue—
> Is past the valley-sleepers, south or west.
> —As I have trod the rumorous midnight, too.
>
> (*Poems*, 65–66)

One recognizes here an affinity between these "wifeless" men and the homosexual in whose epic they personify the wandering signifier unmoored from social structures such as family, content to pass through a world where all he knows is an anonymous "body under the wide rain." They do "touch something like a key perhaps" for that subject. But there is more than a nebulous affinity in this: it is completely possible that Crane found the male society of vagabonds (a word that appears as a code for homosexuals in the letter of July 1926 quoted above) not merely analogous to homosexuality but one of its actual sites in culture. Certainly we can see in the male vagabond a figure whose relation to culture is much like that of the wanderers fantasized by Peter Berg in *Sodomy and the Pirate Tradition*, men whose homosexual inclinations lead them into a life lived chiefly with other men. And that this may have been known as one of the components of hobo life can be seen in a number of texts available to Crane, including Hemingway's short story "The Battler" and an appendix to *Sexual Inversion* (Ellis and Symonds, 1897; reprinted, 1923) on "Homosexuality Among Tramps" by Josiah Flynt. Flynt relates the remarkable finding that:

> every hobo in the United States knows what "unnatural intercourse" means, talking about it freely, and, according to my finding, every tenth man practises it, and defends his conduct. Boys are the victims of this passion. The tramps gain possession of these boys in various ways. A common method is to stop for a while in some town, and gain acquaintance with the slum children. They tell these children all sorts of stories about life "on the road" . . . and they choose some boy who specially pleases them. By smiles and flattering caresses they let him know that the stories are meant for him alone . . . , and he begins to plan secret meetings with the man. The tramp, of course, continues to excite his imagination with stories and caresses, and some fine night there is one boy less in the town. (253)

This short treatise is remarkably interesting, not only for its repetition of the familiar narrative of adolescents seduced through nonfamiliar narratives but also for its attempt to address sexual practices it clearly sees as dangerous and unthinkable (Flynt turns to a clinical and rather euphemistic Latin to inscribe anal intercourse):

> On the road the lad is called a "prushun", and his protector a "jocker." . . . Each is compelled by hobo law to let his jocker do with him as he will, and many, I fear, learn to enjoy his treatment of them. . . . How the act of unnatural intercourse takes place is not entirely clear; the hoboes are not agreed. From what I have person-

> ally observed I should say that it is usually what they call "leg work" (intercrural), but sometimes *immissio penis in anum*, the boy in either case lying on his stomach. I have heard terrible stories of the physical results to the boy of anal intercourse. . . . Some of them [the boys] have told me that they get as much pleasure out of the affair as the jocker does. Even little fellows under ten have told me this, and I have known them to wilfully tempt their jockers to intercourse. What the pleasure consists in I cannot say. The youngsters themselves describe it as a delightful tickling sensation in the parts involved. (253)

"The River" may not literally repeat this narrative of seduction in its memory of the "hobo-trekkers," but clearly they appear as the bearers of a marginalized masculinity romanticized by the homosexual from childhood. The poem concludes by developing them into archetypal figures whose experience gathers all human aspiration and loss into itself:

> The River, spreading, flows—and spends your dream.
> What are you, lost within this tideless spell?
> You are your father's father, and the stream—
> A liquid theme that floating niggers swell.
>
> (*Poems*, 69)

The closing section of "The River" was originally written as "The Calgary Express," a dramatic monologue spoken by a Pullman porter. And as Edward Brunner points out, this last line carries in it reference to the practice of lynching in the 1920s and is not simply a nostalgic retreat into the past where one may imagine oneself connected to one's father's father. Brunner is right to suggest that this meaning still adheres in the finished text, and just as "The River" carries in it an embryonic analysis of racial difference (despite its service in the theme of a "common" historical experience of America), it carries in it the trace of homosexual difference as well despite its figure of the continent as that female presence who names all subjects under her.

"Cutty Sark," which follows "Powhatan's Daughter," is not explicitly homosexual in its content, but its depiction of a drunken sailor carries on the theme of homeless men traced in "The River." Eric Sundquist finds the sailor's meaning for the poem to be that he "enacts the insanity produced by an attempt to ravage the sacred ancestral abode" ("Bringing Home the Word," 387). But the situation itself, which is reminiscent of

Crane's life in waterfront bars from New York to California to Marseilles, suggests as well that this poem may profitably be read as a moment with homosexual meanings. Crane explicitly depicts the old sailor of the poem as suffering the consequences of a deep alienation unspecified in origin. He is rootless and drunken, displaced from history and from coherent knowledge of himself. He says at one point that "that / damned white Arctic killed my time," implying that some outside force is the agent of his alienation; but he has internalized this as his own failing: "I'm not much good at time any more keep / weakeyed watches sometimes snooze" (*Poems*, 82). This "character"—and he is one of the few fleshed out and delineated in such naturalistic detail in the poem—is a tragic case. He is alcoholic and quite unable to make narrative sense in telling the story of his life, an effect that suggests not only his drunkenness but the fragmentation that has made that drunkenness seem necessary. It is evidence of the inability to authorize one's own life, and once again the text includes details that lead our attention to the question of economics and to the place of gay men in capitalist culture:

> "I ran a donkey engine down there on the Canal
> in Panama—got tired of that—
> then Yucatan selling kitchenware—beads—
> have you seen Popocatepetl—birdless mouth
> with ashes sifting down—?
> and then the coast again . . ."
> (*Poems*, 83)

Sold on an imperialist dream of grandeur, he goes to Panama only to encounter the beginnings of a displacement and wandering that will not end. This is the record of a man who has not found his harbor, and who has, sadly, succumbed to a seemingly infinite series of disasters. It may be difficult for us to think of gay men as economically displaced, since contemporary iconography insists through its coding that gay men are affluent. But Crane himself knew that this is not necessarily or historically the case, and the poem's reference to Melville in its epigraph suggests this as well. Gay men have been ostracized, driven out of the social structures that center and anchor heterosexual existence, forced to accept the kind of lonely and exploited life personified here in the drunken sailor:

> Outside a wharf truck nearly ran him down
> —he lunged up Bowery way while the dawn

was putting the Statue of Liberty out—that
torch of hers you know—

(*Poems*, 84)

Here is a man whose life is proof against the myth of freedom that drives American self-consciousness. And if we recognize in him an avatar of the same system that produced Eliot's Phlebas the Phoenician, we can see not only how much Crane's epic is invested in an examination of the underbelly of American culture but also how hard the poem works to remain rooted in the real, resisting the tendency to write only on a symbolic plane. Even if, as James E. Miller suggests we should, we read Phlebas as Eliot's dead lover, Jean Verdenal, how much is lost in making those eyes into pearls, how little of the material alienations of modern culture *The Waste Land* actually addresses!

The second half of the poem leaves the sailor and the bar behind and presents the wandering poet of the sequence walking across Brooklyn Bridge alone musing on "clipper dreams indelible and ranging, / baronial white on lucky blue" (*Poems*, 84). The evidence just presented, of course, suggests that the realities of merchant sea life are far from their conventional depiction in romance, and one might explain this shift in the poem's tone and topic by calling it fantasy or drunken reverie. But we must always inquire into the social origins and effects of such fantasies, and we can see here that the poem's closing catalogue of the names of clipper ships suggests a heavy irony. The nostalgia in the text, buoyed by the fantasy that life at sea represents not trade and alienated labor but freedom and movement, an exotic space where male union might even be the norm: this is not in keeping with the life lived in service to such ships, as the old sailor has clearly demonstrated. And the very proper names of the ships (*Thermopylae, Black Prince, Flying Cloud*) emphasize the anonymity of those whose lives are used up on them. "Cutty Sark" ends not with the union of two men but with a rendezvous between two clipper ships, only their names mated at the end:

—where can you be
Nimbus? and you rivals two—

a long tack keeping—

Taeping?
Ariel?
(*Poems*, 85)

Rivals rather than lovers, competition and market economy replacing in the double authority of the proper and romantic name the union and private economy of desire that the poem and the sequence as a whole are destined not to recover.

The split consciousness evident in "Cutty Sark" is perhaps even more evident in "Cape Hatteras," the most troubled section of the entire sequence, the one that asserts Whitman's centrality and relevance to the modern world. Although the structural center of *The Bridge*, this section was the last Crane composed, and the one that presented him with the most difficulty in its composition—partly, it would seem, because it carries a heavy experiential burden of homosexual alienation that could not be made coherent with its more optimistic notion of the Whitmanian. Its epigraph from "Passage to India," as Robert Martin points out, stops one line short of the following: "As fill'd with friendship, love complete, the Elder Brother found, / The Younger melts in fondness in his arms" (*Leaves of Grass*, 420), and its affiliation with Whitman must be read as homosexual. As even Allen Tate realized:

> Hart had a sort of megalomania: he wanted to be The Great American Poet. I imagine he thought that by getting into the Whitman tradition, he could carry even Whitman further. And yet there's another thing we must never forget—there was the homosexual thing, too. . . . I don't think he was wholly conscious of it, but it must have had some influence. The notion of "comrades," you see, and that sort of business [elision in text]. (quoted in Unterecker's *Voyager*, 431)

One dies to know what was in that elision, but it should by now be clear that this filiation as a "homosexual thing" was something of which Crane was far more conscious than Tate. The intended message of "Cape Hatteras" seems to be that literature transcends history, and that the "pact, new bound / Of living brotherhood" (*Poems*, 93) that the text names as the central legacy of Whitman, is as potent and "still the same as when you walked the beach / Near Paumanok" (*Poems*, 89). But if we see the reverence for Whitman and the transhistorical power of literature as screens for "the homosexual thing, too," we can see in this the record of Crane's need to proclaim homosexuality a positive center for modernity as well. If we keep in mind the record of his life from 1926 (when *The Bridge* was begun in earnest) to 1929 we can see the poem as expressive of the desire that homosexual unions transcend the ravages of time and alienation that in Crane's particular case left him bitterly and alcoholically alone by the age of thirty. This in part explains how this late addition to the text is able to reclaim an integrative vision of homosexuality when the sections written earlier revealed it mostly as a marginalized Otherness (in "The Harbor Dawn") or under the collapse of homeless and anonymous wandering (in "The River" and "Cutty Sark").

Early commentators decried Whitman's influence in the poem for two reasons: according to the lights of Winters, Tate, and others, Whitman was guilty of the twin literary offenses of bad form and bad philosophy (in Winters this latter charge reaches a hysterical crescendo and Whitman's text becomes for him the destruction of all value and ethics outside personal whim and sensation). In defending Whitman in "Cape Hatteras," Crane writes a poem of fifteen stanzas each sonnetlike in form, thereby making Whitman the muse of a more formal literary inheritance. He also places this homage to Whitman in the second half of a poem the first half of which is a meditation on the negative effects of technology, taking aviation as a synecdoche for the power and the horror of industrialism. By doing this, the poem also tests and tempers the image of Whitman as a jingoistic apologist for American technology (as in "Song of the Exposition"). But as a sonnet sequence, the poem also carries the trace of a love poem, and it ends with the image of Crane and Whitman hand-in-hand, never to be parted:

> Recorders ages hence, they shall hear
> In their own veins uncancelled thy sure tread
> And read thee by the aureole 'round thy head
> Of pasture-shine, *Panis Angelicus!*
> yes, Walt,
> Afoot again, and onward without halt,—
> Not soon, nor suddenly,—no, never to let go
> My hand
> in yours,
> Walt Whitman—
> so—.
> (*Poems*, 95)

This may strike us as terribly sentimental poetry and as a homosexual union purified of any bodily referent whatsoever; but we should read the "terror" in terrible when making that assessment, for if "Cape Hatteras" traces the terror of homosexuality, Whitman in some sense resolves it for Crane. The meditation on flight that takes up the first half of the poem may refer to Crane's doubts about the legacy of technology in American culture (it ends with the crash of a plane) but it is also symbolic of the ecstatic flight and crash of homosexuality. Freud reminds us that flying is symbolic of phallic power, and the Wright brothers are not only historical figures of invention in the text; they represent as well a metonymic displacement of that other brotherhood of homosexuality the text traces. The plane that crashes is a not so subtle phallic image of the pitch and tragedy of Crane's life as a homosexual, anxiety over which we may read in a number of his late, rather unpolished texts. The late poem "The Idiot" (a rewriting of "Lenses") casts homosexuality as a voyeuristic "trespass vision," and Crane represents himself in a late poem to Emil, "The Visible The Untrue," as "the terrible puppet of my dreams" (*Poems*, 176) in these years of disintegration. "Reply" opens with the claim that "Thou canst read nothing except through appetite" (*Poems*, 177) but writes the homosexual in an inflexible ethos of shame. And "By Nilus Once I Knew" puts the quandary of the homosexual writer's troubled authority as the problem of a "Decisive grammar given unto queens" (*Poems*, 174). These are poems of a homosexual subjectivity that has lost faith in its own ability to mean, and the pact with Whitman recorded in "Cape Hatteras" thus has an urgency that initiates beyond its placement in the linear composition of *The Bridge*.

One must give some credit to Crane for this literary coming out. Until then, only Mid-western poets such as Sandburg had declared any allegiance to Whitman as a poetic precursor, and no one had before claimed *Calamus* (and its "Recorders Ages Hence," alluded to above) as his master text. Lawrence, in fact, in *Studies in Classic American Literature* (1924), interprets *Calamus* and homosexuality more generally as death wish:

> In *Calamus* [Whitman] changes his tune. He . . . sings of the mystery of manly love, the love of comrades. Over and over he says the same thing: the new world will be built on the love of comrades, the new great dynamic of life will be manly love. Out of this manly love will come the inspiration for the future.
>
> Will it though? Will it?
>
> . . . The next step is the merging of man-for-man love. And this is on the brink of death. And the death of Jonathan.

David and Jonathan. And the death of Jonathan.
It always slides into death.
The love of comrades.
Merging.

(159–60)

Even Federico Garcia Lorca's famous praise of Whitman in "Ode to Walt Whitman" so seriously qualifies its celebration of homosexual possibility that it reads now as more homophobic than positive in its construction of homosexuality. First published in Cuba in 1933, and part of the *Poet in New York* series that was a response to Lorca's years in New York City (the same years as are in question here for Crane), the "Ode" insists that there is value in homosexuality only when that affection is proletarian, "natural," or "organic." Otherwise, it is seen as predation and decadence, akin to other forms of exploitation and death blooming in industrial America:

Ah, filthy New York,
New York of cables and death.
What angel do you carry, concealed in your cheek?
. . . .
Not a moment, blood-brother, Adam, and masculine,
lone man in a sea, Walt Whitman, comely old man—
for look!—on the rooftops,
or huddled in bars,
or leaping in packs from the gutters,
or held between legs of the motorist, shuddering,
or whirling on platforms of absinthe,
the perverts, Walt Whitman, all pointing you!
. . . .
But you never went looking for the scar on the eye,
or the overcast swamp where the boys are submerged,
or the freezing saliva
or the contours, split open, like the sac of the toad,
that the perverts in taxis and terraces carry
as the moon whips them on into terrified corners.

You looked for a nude that could be like a river,
the bull and the dream that could merge.

(*Poet in New York*, 119–23)

Nowhere is Crane this strongly outspoken against other gay men, and while we cannot transparently equate the kind of homophobia informing Spanish culture with that which Crane encountered, internalized, and reproduced, there is a similar structure of sentiment in Lorca's rejection of homosexual lust and some of Crane's treatments of the same subject. Homosexuality must be qualified as a "natural" masculine affection, otherwise it is a condition of shame:

> Perverts of the world, dove-killers!
> . . . .
> No quarter! Death
> oozes out of your eyes
> and clusters gray flowers at the edge of a bog.
> No quarter! Beware!
> Let the pure, the bewildered,
> the illustrious, classic, and suppliant
> shut the festival doors in your face.
>
> (125)

It is true that Lorca is only attacking a particular kind of homosexual self-expression: "my voice is not raised / to admonish the boy who inscribes / a girl's name on his pillow," "not to shame the young man who dresses himself like a bride / in the dark of the clothes-closet . . . / or the green apparition of men / who cherish mankind and burn out their lips in the silence" (125), but surely what comes across in his text is the strong reaction *against* homosexuality as a social construction (and it seems important to remember that most readers see homosexuality as a monolithic rather than plural category, and that the figures attacked here by Lorca have stood metonymically for all homoesexuals). If Lorca's interests are more overtly political than Crane's, both consider homosexuality a problem of ethics.

The union with Whitman Crane describes in "Cape Hatteras," and the legitimacy this grants to acts of male homosexuality, must be seen, therefore, as a singularly brave attempt in the canon of modern American literature. Pound's famous poem to Whitman, "A Pact," takes up only the question of style, completely eliding the question of sexual formation and literature's position in relation to it. And yet a glance at Crane's text demonstrates how much is effaced even in the allusion to *Calamus*. In "Recorders Ages Hence," Whitman is rather explicit about his homosexuality and about what he would have people think of it:

> Come, I will take you down underneath this passive
> exterior, I will tell you what to say of me.
> Publish my name and hang up my picture as that of the
> tenderest lover.
> (*Leaves of Grass*, 121–22)

And Whitman does not make his hand-in-hand conclusion to "Recorders" a solely symbolic one, as the relation between Crane and Whitman at the end of "Cape Hatteras" must perforce be. Rather, he explicitly represents himself and his lover "wandering hand in hand, they twain / apart from other men" (*Leaves of Grass*, 122). But the Crane text buries the sexual in the literary, and praises Whitman—on the surface—for his place in a national and nationalist poetry, thus forgetting the stated desire of *Calamus* to celebrate "the institution of the dear love of comrades" (*Leaves of Grass*, 128) and offering instead this hyperbolic celebration:

> Beyond all sesames of science was thy choice
> Wherewith to bind us throbbing with one voice,
> New integers of Roman, Viking, Celt—
> Thou, Vedic Caesar, to the greensward knelt!
> (*Poems*, 95)

Not until Ginsberg took up the question of Whitman's utopian vision in the mid-1950s (in *Howl* especially) did the question of sexual experience come again to the fore of American thought in its relation to utopian energy and social critique. And not until Ginsberg's text made an interest in homosexuality part of a concerted social resistance did this reading of Whitman begin to have currency in American culture.

If we follow the trajectory of homosexuality in *The Bridge*, then, we move from a union which disappears before our eyes like a star disappearing in the dawn in its opening homosexual moment, through the loss and ironic displacements in "The River" and "Cutty Sark," to the assertion in "Cape Hatteras" that Whitman is a valid poetic, spiritual, and homosexual precursor—although this last is deeply buried in oblique allusions. Nor should this movement surprise us. It is almost inevitable given the ideologies of gender and poetry Crane labored under. And if the homoerotic content of the poem is incrementally displaced, it is so in favor of a purely literary one. Because of his appeal to social vision and his absolute denial of Otherness, Whitman becomes the only acceptable icon of homosexuality the text may admit, and the erotic content of the verse is completely replaced by a textual one. In *The Ringers in the Tower,* Harold Bloom suggests rearranging *The Bridge* according to its chronological order of composition, placing "Atlantis" at the beginning and "Cape Hatteras" at the close. Such a structure, he claims, would reveal the poem as "demonic romance, quest fulfilled to no consequence, or fulfillment revealed as parody of the goal" (3). Such a reading is exactly what emerges from a consideration of its central moments of homosexuality. In so reading the text, we trace a movement whereby the homosexual becomes progressively unspoken by the text, appearing instead as a marker in a purely literary game: that of textual allusion.

But if homosexual unions are variously disallowed on the surface of *The Bridge*, heterosexual unions prove no less illusory as the social ground of Crane's utopian vision. If the homosexual may become the homo*text*ual, and so be disciplined or controlled in "Cape Hatteras," the heterosexual remains a problematic site for Crane. "Three Songs," which follows "Cape Hatteras" in the text, is composed of three poems each of which presents a woman as the modern incarnation of three biblical types—Eve, Magdalene, the Virgin—and as we might expect, the sexual ideology informing these texts is quite convoluted. It might be argued that "Southern Cross," the first of these, is not about women at all, that it is a more disembodied meditation on the kind of cosmic loneliness fashionable in early modernist texts (here the speaker is depicted as alone at sea under "nameless" stars). But we know that such figurations are not disembodied when they inscribe the female body as the site of their meditation: the speaker's encounter with philosophical nihilism ("It is / God—your namelessness," "Slid on that backward vision / The mind is churned to spittle") is also his encounter with sexual difference. The poem begins by seeing sexual difference in very conventional terms—"The Southern Cross takes night / And lifts her girdles from her, one by one"—but immediately recognizes the abyss that separates its speaker from this display of "happy" sexuality: the poem situates its subject "wide from the slowly smoldering fire / Of lower heavens" where the cut or "vaporous scars" of a quite unstable desire inscribe sexual difference and meaning:

It is blood to remember; it is fire
To stammer back . . . it is
God—your namelessness.
(*Poems*, 98)

The poem presents a sexual displacement that shades into sexual horror, and while this was for Crane experientially homosexual, it appears here in the mediating vocabulary of heterosexist desire.

O simian Venus, homeless Eve,
Unwedded, stumbling gardenless to grieve
Windswept guitars on lonely decks forever:
Finally to answer all within one grave!
. . . .
All night the water combed you with black
Insolence. You crept out simmering, accomplished.
Water rattled that stinging coil, your
Rehearsed hair—docile, alas, from many arms.
Yes, Eve—wraith of my unloved seed!

The Cross, a phantom, buckled—dropped below the dawn,
Light drowned the lithic trillions of your spawn
(*Poems*, 99)

This is, of course, Woman as abyss—an abyss of figuration and artificiality. Nor does it meliorate the gynophobia in the passage to read this dialectic in the opposite direction and see that it figures the abyss of figuration, its artificially constructed and "rehearsed" qualities, as "feminine" in the vocabulary of deconstruction. We recognize in this a familiarly misogynistic rhetoric seen most blatantly in Crane's contemporary T. S. Eliot but certainly not limited to him or to the texts of modernism more generally. Yet if Crane couches this poem's rootlessness in the terms of rejected love ("I wanted you, nameless Woman of the South"), surely we can also say that this poem is peculiarly modern in the following way: it is the complaint of a barren man, of a homosexual for whom the "wraith of [his] unloved seed" figures the permanent dislocation—the *dissemination*—that defines his social existence. This enforced and disempowering liminality expresses itself here not as desire for a female object of desire but, curiously enough, as a kind of gender envy. The Cross, that seemingly transcendent phallus, is nothing but a "phantom," and the poem also suggests that Woman's power (which is seen only as reproductive when one reduces the question to such "archetypal" terms) is also ultimately nullified: if she may reproduce, and hence find men biologically useful but erotically undesirable, her "spawn" are "drowned" at the poem's close. While we cannot ignore the oppressive sexual ideology in this formulation (and it would seem to draw heavily on certain mystical male tracts of sexuality such as Remy de Gourmont's *Physique de l'amour*), surely we can also imagine that Crane intends the female figure here ("Unwedded, stumbling gardenless to grieve / Windswept guitars on lonely decks forever") as an icon for homosexual (and modern) homelessness.

The other two poems of this section fail adequately to provide an image of heterosexual union. "National Winter Garden" is about the display of the female body for the male gaze in burlesque, but the last two lines of its opening stanzas suggest the inadequacy of this institution, implying that it does not really satisfy desire:

> Outspoken buttocks in pink beads
> Invite the necessary cloudy clinch
> Of bandy eyes. . . . No extra mufflings here:
> The world's one flagrant, sweating cinch.
>
> And while legs waken salads in the brain
> You pick your blonde out neatly through the smoke.
> Always you wait for someone else though, always—
> (Then rush the nearest exit through the smoke).
>
> (*Poems*, 100)

The poem depicts (and implicitly critiques) the captive, contradictory position of Woman in a sexist society, the dual role of saint and whore she is asked to play: she is fetishized, ornamented, and yet curiously unerotic (except as male sadism makes violence erotic):

> And shall we call her whiter than the snow?
> Sprayed first with ruby, then with emerald sheen—
> Least tearful and least glad (who knows her smile?)
> A caught slide shows her sandstone grey between.
>
> Her eyes exist in swivellings of her teats,
> Pearls whip her hips, a drench of whirling strands.
> Her silly snake rings begin to mount, surmount
> Each other—turquoise fakes on tinselled hands.
>
> (*Poems*, 100)

This parody of female sexuality, the ritualized nonorgasm of striptease in the ruby/emerald sheen of spotlights (her true body not snow white but seen when the specularity is exposed through the failure of its apparatus ["A caught slide shows her sandstone grey between" the ruby and emerald]): this is implied as an analogy for all heterosexual relations. Exposed here as well is the paradox of that male desire that would possess only through its deployment of the gaze and the deliberate creation of an object to be renounced yet returned to again and again:

> We wait that writhing pool, her pearls collapsed,
> —All but her belly buried in the floor;
> And the lewd trounce of a final muted beat!
> We flee her spasm through a fleshless door. . . .
>
> Yet, to the empty trapeze of your flesh,
> O Magdalene, each comes back to die alone.
> Then you, the burlesque of our lust—and faith,
> Lug us back lifeward—bone by infant bone.
>
> (*Poems*, 100–01)

The tone of scathing rebuke in this poem is not, it seems to me, directed at women, but at the "we," the implied male subject-as-reader who participates in and demands this spectacle.

If Crane cannot imagine female sexuality in any other way, if women remain for him "empty trapezes of . . . flesh" "sandstone grey between," "National Winter Garden" nevertheless performs the important function of exposing the systematic debasement of women in heterosexual culture. It is positioned as the male response to female Otherness (read archetypally in "Southern Cross" and here historicized and materialized with a vengeance), and it leads into "Virginia," the final, almost overtly trivial poem of "Three Songs." This brief text does not resolve the problem of female commodification and Otherness except to counsel its somewhat infantilized subject to "Keep smiling the boss away." It presents a series of disconnected images that are meant to engender the fulsomeness of love:

> High in the noon of May
> On cornices of daffodils
> The slender violets stray.
> Crap-shooting gangs in Bleecker reign,

> Peonies with pony-manes—
> Forget-me-nots at windowpanes.
> (*Poems*, 102)

But "Virginia" presents this vision of playful devotion as a denial of sexuality, as "Keeping the boss away." The final lines may exclaim, "Out of the way-up nickel-dime tower shine, / Cathedral Mary, / shine!—," continuing the problematic of sexuality and economy that was at the heart of the debasement of women in "National Winter Garden," but this vision of transcendence still imprisons women in a worshipful devotion that is undeniably centered in the phallus. This "transcendence" is no solution to the historical problem of sexual difference.

The one moment of ecstatic sexual union that actually makes its way into the text of *The Bridge* occurs in "The Dance," that section of "Powhatan's Daughter" that attempts, as Crane wrote to Otto Kahn, to possess "the Indian and his world before it is over"; here, he says, we are on "the pure and mythical smoky soil at last!" (*Poems*, 251). While Crane means this comment to be taken as instructive to our reading of the continental and historical aspects of the text, we might also take it as instructive to our reading of the ideology of gender in it, for here we are on the pure, mythical, and smoky soil of heterosexual union and fertility seen as the natural anthropological origin of human community. The poem rehearses a sky-god/earth-goddess fertility rite, the dance of the title, and is a primal scene in both a Freudian and anthropological sense. The speaker, who takes a canoe from his village into the wilderness, observes the "swift red flesh, a winter king . . . [squire] the glacier woman down the sky" (*Poems*, 70). He watches the shaman or medicine man whose dance reenacts this creation narrative, a representative of the *berdaches* of Native American culture whose power is both coded as and derived from their transgression of gender systems:

> Dance, Maquokeeta! snake that lives before,
> That casts his pelt, and lives beyond! Sprout, horn!
> Spark, tooth! Medicine-man, relent, restore—
> Lie to us,—dance us back the tribal morn!
> (*Poems*, 73)

Eric Sundquist points out how the plea to "lie to us" in this stanza is the text's admission that the poet as medicine man lies to his reader in recovering this moment as some source of authority for the poem: "In the sacrificial dance of Maquokeeta the transformation of autobiography into myth is 'fulfilled' by the poet's enactment of the desired death of the Father and reunion with the Mother" ("Bringing Home the Word," 383).

What is perhaps more interesting in this scene, however, is the poet's relation to it, for the autobiographical subject here is depicted in the traditional iconography of homosexual martyrdom; he is something like a St. Sebastian of the American West:

> And buzzard-circleted, screamed from the stake;
> I could not pick the arrows from my side.
> Wrapped in that fire, I saw more escorts wake—
> Flickering, sprint up the hill groins like a tide.
>
> (*Poems*, 73)

We may allow the masochistic desire expressed here to pass without further analysis, for it is not the only such moment in Crane's text. The real focus here should be the way in which it situates Crane's relation to the heterosexual. The heterosexual is a formation that places him in the position of martyrdom, defined and yet denied by it. If the heterosexual rehearses "tribal morn," the homosexual is tribeless—or else affiliated with the night (as in "The Harbor Dawn" and "Cutty Sark") or with wandering tribes of marginalized men (the hoboes of "The River"). And while this dance is a lie, more convention than actuality (participating in the vogue for comparative mythology seen most evidently in Frazier's popularization by Eliot and therefore more literary than real), it is nevertheless surely the dominant mythology and a very powerful one. *It* can appear as a "nature" myth, and therefore as a natural one, allowing the heterosexual to appear as inevitable and real as sky or trees. This elides any question of the ideological formations heterosexuality is subject to, ones clearly evident elsewhere in *The Bridge* (most pointedly in "Three Songs"). Yet the text clearly presents this dominant mythology of the naturalness of heterosexuality as one which forces the ideological stigma and burden of Otherness on the homosexual: "pure mythical and smoky soil"—indeed![11]

We find, then, no successful unions or marriages in *The Bridge*. Heterosexual unions announce themselves as violent appropriations or as lies and conventionalities; homosexual ones are not allowed full presence but are elided in favor of more admissible and "important" topics. But it is in the sequence's final poem, "Atlantis," that Crane attempts his most ecstatic *readerly* marriage, and that section also is informed by the ideological constraints of gender I have been discussing here. As John Irwin has pointed out (in "Hart Crane's 'Logic of Metaphor'"), the real bridge in Brooklyn with which the poem began becomes by the conclusion of the text a completely metaphorical bridge, symbolic not only of all those bridges between people and time that the epic has attempted to build but also of the very act of creation and imagination. The bridge in "Atlantis" becomes a metaphor for metaphor, and the entire text threatens to collapse into obscurity under the burden of this textual weight. The epigraph, from Plato, "Music is then the knowledge of that which relates to love in harmony and system," alerts us to the fact that this final poem will be abstract and disembodied. But this is, as Joseph Riddel suggests, Crane's distinct desire, "to transmute the temporal self into pure space—to purify himself virtually into the form of a poem" ("Hart Crane's Poetics of Failure," 474). Unable to depict full-bodied unions throughout the poem, either homosexual or heterosexual ones, the only union imaginable for Crane is a completely figurative one, a music that has no referent, no body to become trapped in, no ideological weight (and thus, the text must beg "pardon for this history"). It is precisely this supposed escape from ideology that points to the deep ideological formation of "Atlantis." This is underscored not only by an entire history of nonreadings of *The Symposium* (the source of the poem's epigraph)[12] but also by the movement whereby the homosexual desire strongly inscribed as the model of love in Plato disappears completely from the surface of "Atlantis." It is also evident, finally, in the intense stylistics of the text.

Much has been written of the linguistic reaches of this section of the poem and of the hyperbolic extensions of language Crane employs to reach them. The bridge becomes "Tall Vision-of-the-Voyage," "Answerer," "Deity's glittering Pledge," "Psalm of Cathay," etc. (*Poems*, 115, 116), and one feels Crane stretching for that "multitudinous Verb" which will predicate these multitudinous apostrophes and make a proposition of what is otherwise only a list. The poem ends in meta-poetic language, trope upon trope, the obscurity and density of which Crane's critics have lamented. But finally this peculiarity of expression must be linked to Crane's effacement of his homosexuality as well, for as Allen Grossman points out, the use of language in Crane is intimately related to desire:

> This crowding of the frame came to constitute a trope peculiar to himself—not the modernist "ambiguity" which hierarchizes, or

> ironically totalizes a plurality of meanings—but a singularly naive rhetoric of shadowed wholeness (the impossible simultaneity of all the implications of desire) that struggles merely to include all meanings in the space of one appearance. ("Hart Crane and Poetry," 229)

This desire to include all meanings in the space of one appearance might be referred to Faulkner, who attempted, he said, to include everything in one sentence. But Crane's verbal experimentation constricts upon language until finally meaning is subsumed in the reader's inability to locate a single, stable referent for the text. Grossman says, "The effect of the rhetoric of condensation is to assign more and more of the content of desire to fewer and fewer terms, until all that truly is is finally condensed upon a single word" (230). Whichever one wishes to identify as primary, the inadmissibility of homosexual desire that I have been tracing is inextricably linked, finally, to the inadmissibility of linguistic desire as well. Crane simply cannot say what he means, nor can he say what he means simply. As Grossman points out, "Obscurity of discourse in his poetry was for him a postponement and equivocation of the decision as to what relationships are permitted and therefore possible—an equivocation that we as readers enact when we dwell in the bewilderment of his style, and that we erase (but do not resolve) when we compel a 'meaning'" (223).

The bridge of "Atlantis" is, finally, what Grossman calls one of the "orphic machines" of shadowed wholeness in Crane, an anagram for the desiring homosexual body synthesized with its own desire and with its former elision from history, married to itself ("complighted") in "one vibrant breath made cry." "Atlantis" and "Voyages" refer to one another and to the same psychosocial moment in Crane's life of writing the homosexual (both take their final shape in sight of the transformative relationship to Emil). This part of *The Bridge* was written while Crane was composing "Voyages," and we see echoes of that text here

> And through that cordage, threading with its call
> One arc synoptic of all tides below—
> Their labyrinthine mouths of history
> Pouring reply as though all ships at sea
> Complighted in one vibrant breath made cry,—
> "Make thy love sure—to weave whose song we ply!"
> (*Poems*, 114)

The poem begins with a night stroll across the bridge, a poetic equivalent to the experience of ecstasy Crane reported to Waldo Frank in the letter of April 1924 identifying his lover as "the Word made Flesh." Despite the utter (later) failure to find a textual home for the transcendental sentiments of homosexuality in most of his epic, Crane began "Atlantis" with a clear echo of the "ecstatic dance" of his letter to Frank:

> Through the bound cable strands, the arching path
> Upward, veering with light, the flight of strings,—
> Taut miles of shuttling moonlight syncopate
> The whispered rush, telepathy of wires.
> Up the index of night, granite and steel—
> Transparent meshes—fleckless the gleaming staves—
> Sibylline voices flicker, waveringly stream
> As though a god were issue of the strings. . . .
>
> (*Poems*, 114)

—"As though" the Word had indeed been made Flesh. A fuller reading of "Atlantis" would reveal the urgency of this search for the "white, pervasive Paradigm" of "Love," the specific biographical urgency out of which "Atlantis," unlike the rest of *The Bridge*, was written. But if Crane most often sublimates homosexual to transcendental desire, in "Atlantis" the dream of a perfect civic and cultural structure does not forget the body; its final transformative vision originates in "the bright drench and fabric of our veins." In lines that are the only ones consistently to appear from its beginning in 1923 to its publication in 1930, the text marks its closure with this justification of modern, urban culture:

> iridescently upborne
> Through the bright drench and fabric of our veins;
> With white escarpments swinging into light,
> Sustained in tears the cities are endowed
> And justified . . .
>
> (*Poems*, 116).

If that justification seems in question, if the harmonic conclusion to *The Bridge* seems more asserted than earned, one of the blocks to that transparency must certainly be the impossible opacity, the utter unmarriageability of Crane's homosexual desire, the difficulty of which only became greater the further from 1923 (and from the New York ecstasies of 1924) he got. The "vision" Crane could not sustain in writing *The Bridge* was a vision of homosexuality as a centered, unifying experience capable of inspiring redemptive verse, where "orphic strings" would be "Like spears ensanguined of one tolling star" (*Poems*, 116). In that vision, "New octaves trestle the twin monoliths" (*Poems*, 114), and "White tempest nets file upward, upward ring / With silver terraces the humming spars, / The loft of vision, palladium helm of stars" (*Poems*, 115). This is a vision of phallic power that marks orgasm as the threshold of spiritual awareness and poetic authority (the seventh heaven of consciousness; a moment in ecstasy), and the bridge is, in this, the perfect phallus in both the Lacanian and the more colloquial senses: "steeled Cognizance;" "intrinsic Myth / Whose fell unshadow is death's utter wound" (*Poems*, 116). In this last phrase, the poem would have the bridge unwrite the wound of castration, making the Phallus (and the poet's access to it) whole again. This brings the poet into authority through the power of a magical language unmarked by absence or by the fallen materiality of the letter (this is the symbolic rather than the Symbolic). In a final appeal, the poet asks that the bridge buoy the head of Orpheus (beheaded, Orpheus is here also a sign of castration to be unwritten, to be turned into a sign of the authenticity of this verse and vision): "hold thy floating singer late!" until he can produce "One Song, One Bridge of Fire" (*Poems*, 116). In a reading that runs counter to much of the accepted wisdom about *The Bridge*, John Carlos Rowe finds that "Word, Myth, Bridge, Atlantis—these apparently transcendent ideals or supreme fictions are defined repeatedly as metaphors for the differential energy governing man's being in the seasonal timeliness of the world. . . . Crane's "primordial One" is the energy of differences, never a synthesis that would destroy those tensive and productive relations" (610–11). Homosexuality is the most fundamental of those differential energies in the text, especially in "Atlantis," the initiation that functions as conclusion.

Critics have usually read Crane's finale to *The Bridge* as his participation in a discourse peculiar to American modernity, what Leo Marx calls the "technological sublime." That discourse is identified as the conflation of continued technological progress (thought of as especially privileged within the American context of national destiny in spatial/natural conquest) with the notion of spiritual, cultural, and racial evolution toward a utopian destination that marks even the most pastoral and antitechnological appearances of the term "America." But Crane's intrigue with the technological innovations of the modern is more a debate with this American faith in technology than a simple repetition of its utopian claims. It may well be that "Seeing himself an atom in a shroud— / Man hears himself an engine in a cloud!" (*Poems*, 89), but as John Carlos Rowe has convincingly argued, the poem is not some simple celebration of Whitmanian enthusiasm over technology—rather, it "links the modern worship of sheer Power to the human yearning to overcome spatio-temporal bonds" ("The Super-historical Sense of *The Bridge*," 611). But the technological is not a simple threshold to paradise for Crane; while he writes that "The nasal whine of power whips a new universe . . ." (*Poems*, 90), and that it is necessary for poetry to "absorb the machine, i.e., *acclimatize* it as naturally and casually as trees, cattle, galleons, castles and all other human associations of the past" or else run the risk of "fail[ing] of its full contemporary function" (*Poems*, 261–62), he does not mean by this the mere poetic celebration of the technological:

> This process does not infer any program of lyrical pandering to the taste of those obsessed by the importance of machinery; nor does it essentially involve even the specific mention of a single mechanical contrivance. It demands, however, along with the traditional qualifications of the poet, an extraordinary capacity for surrender, at least temporarily, to the sensations of urban life. (*Poems*, 262)

This passage, taken from his brief 1930 essay, "Modern Poetry," exposes once again how for Crane all theory had to take account of the body and its life of sensation; even the machine "can not act creatively in our lives until, like the unconscious nervous responses of our bodies, its connotations emanate from within" (*Poems*, 262). This creativity is traced in the subject's relation to the Orphic machine of the bridge, which, like its signifier (the phallus), emanates from within him.

In seeing the technology of the modern machine primarily in symbolic relation to the human body, then, Crane's text presents a modern fable about engineering. But it presents that fable as concerned not only with the engineering of "means to shorter hours" but with the engineering of desire as well. The inclusive framework of *The Bridge* leads Crane to encounter any number of cultural questions (and we have here rather narrowly focused on only one), but over and over again this text—more urgently than many of his others—ponders the ways and means through which desire is constructed, empowered, and (alternatively) delegitimated. The reading offered here is only the first step in understanding how modernity, in its structures of intense differentiation, makes any final synthesis of those ways and means an arduous and perhaps impossible task. In *Prisms*, Theodor Adorno writes, "A successful work . . . is not one which resolves objective contradictions in a spurious harmony, but one which expresses the idea of harmony negatively, by embodying the contradictions, pure and uncompromised, in its innermost structure" (32). It is the virtue of *The Bridge*, I would claim, that its earnest attempt to construct harmony never completely resolves the conflict homosexuality names for American culture but inscribes it in its negativity, in the contradictions embodied pure and uncompromised in the innermost structure of its text.

Notes

CHAPTER ONE

1. It is in complete accord with poststructuralist assertions of the death of the author that I undertake here the study of one writer—not, however, in order to see him as the origin of his text; rather, in order to understand how various social forces implicate him in their working out.

2. Houston Baker's comments on the "integrationist poetics" that guided Afro-American writing earlier in this century are apposite here, for his critique centers on the claim that the democratic nature of American culture finds natural expression in the qualities of American literature. Baker finds that integrationist poetics rested upon two distinctions: a notion of a raceless, classless "AMERICA" that superseded any "limited" interest in *Afro*-America and to which all Americans might and need aspire; and formalist standards of literary value that were assumed universal and inherent in the style and structure of texts. Thus, Baker states, "faith in American pluralistic ideals" established a "single standard" for all literature (*Blues, Ideology,* 31), and American formalism appeared to be the highest expression of the political.

3. My use of the term "homosexual" as a noun more often than not connotes *not* an individual but a set of signs and practices in which individuals participate and by which they are inscribed. Thus, I am using "the homosexual" in much the same way that feminist scholars have found it productive to identify a category termed "the feminine." I do not intend it as a Platonic or essentialist term, for what "the homosexual" signifies is always multiple, culturally specific, and subject to historical change or conceptual alteration.

4. There is here the elided question of Dickinson's resistance to this position; her own privacy and the difficulty of her verse insulate her from mass appropriation in a way that Whitman's textual scope and poetic persona do not; her invisibility as a poet until this century complicates the issue of her "place" in any tradition. Nevertheless, it is important to see that if one wishes to indulge in such terms, she would also have to be accorded the honor of being America's premier poet.

5. I refer here to *The American Adam,* a text that held great sway in American Studies for a generation. Nina Baym, among others, has shown quite point-

edly how texts such as Lewis's enact what she terms a "melodrama of beset manhood," celebrating masculine experience and offering little or no position for female self-awareness or self-assertion. Lewis is also significant to my study in that he brought this same bias to the book he wrote on Crane (1965), the first full-length study of Crane by a "major" critic of American literature and one that inscribes Crane within a set of nationalist literary concerns, including such shibboleths of American myth criticism as the psychic and social alienation of the individual artist in American society, a Platonic or visionary quest for alternative experience, a celebration of the imagination's capacity to alter and improve reality. While Lewis's text on Crane is not damning in any way, it sets terms for his reading that would make a study such as mine irrelevant. For Lewis, the poet's value lies in his ability to address timeless themes, homosexuality not among them.

6. Whitman's experience of his sexuality was different, of course, from what we might transparently take homosexuality to be and mean. Michael Lynch has researched Whitman's indebtedness to phrenology for his concept of adhesiveness, and Lynch's work also documents the movement through which "homosexuality" achieved visibility (and therefore "meaning") in scientific discourse of the nineteenth century. There can be little doubt that there was male-male sexual desire and practice in Whitman's era, and while more archaeological research is needed to understand how such sexualities were configured, it seems useful, after this disclaimer, to identify Whitman's text as interested in homosexuality.

7. On the modernist fear of poetry's "feminizing" effects, one might (despite its infamous assault on Gilbert and Gubar) consult Frank Lentricchia's "Patriarchy Against Itself—The Young Manhood of Wallace Stevens," Sandra Gilbert and Susan Gubar's *No Man's Land*, and Ezra Pound's bizarre, literal equation of thought with spermatic activity (in an appendix to his translation of Remy de Gourmont's *Natural Philosophy of Love*).

8. Eric Cheyfitz's *The Trans-parent* is perhaps the best recent rereading of Emerson in light of poststructural notions of writing and difference—especially sexual difference. His first chapter quite powerfully analyzes the Oedipal contest of naming and textual production in Emerson, and later chapters detail how this contest moves beyond the personal to the social, political, and cultural levels. It remains for someone to investigate exactly how the decentered, fierce, and textual Emerson that Cheyfitz convincingly portrays became the pale center for more conservative, stable, and (actually) anti-Emersonian traditions.

9. Gay men and lesbians are not allowed to serve in the armed forces in America.

10. In Nazi Germany, of course, homosexuality was not merely suppressed; the elimination of homosexuals was an integral part of the program of genocide designed to ensure racial purity and national, heterosexual fecundity. It is there-

fore cruelly ironic that the homoerotic and lesbian iconography of a sizable Weimar gay subculture was appropriated into Nazi propaganda, providing it with images of male and female strength and beauty. (We see in American culture a similar visual appropriation from fifties gay body building in Sylvester Stallone's series of military adventurist heroes.) Among modern nations perhaps only Japan—and there only in a figure such as Mishima—have nationalism and homosexuality found comfort in one another; but Mishima is—in this respect at least—perhaps akin to Ginsberg in America, a figure who calls for spiritual renewal of a culture lost in materialistic vertigo. But if Ginsberg's celebration of homosexuality is not always easy to ally with his fondness for Whitmanian versions of America, neither is congruent with Mishima's social vision of Japan or with the historical convolutions of *his* homosexuality.

11. The term is Judith Fetterley's, from her introduction to *The Resisting Reader,* and signifies that process whereby even women readers and writers are defined within conventions designed to produce masculine identities and to articulate masculine interests. Thus, Dickinson's American-ness consists in her allegiance to or argument with Emersonian (or earlier, Calvinistic) vocabularies and not in her speculations on the domestic, marriage, or female identity and entrapment.

12. Bennett's essay addresses the issue of whether Marxist literary analysis can withstand a deconstructive critique; he suggests that Marxism has always positioned itself similarly to deconstruction—i.e., both see "truth" as a textual effect, as an ideological production. And he suggests that Marxism must rid itself of a naive notion of historical recovery and materialism that deconstruction has challenged in pointed ways. In this, his work is akin to a number of poststructuralist Marxist critics and theorists, most of whom derive their textual practice from Althusser.

13. It is interesting that both Eve Kosofsky Sedgwick and Fiedler are concerned with terror and the Gothic (Sedgwick writes of it not only in *Between Men* but also in her earlier study *The Coherence of Gothic Conventions* and in her essay on Henry James, "The Beast in the Closet"). For Sedgwick, the Gothic is predicated (in part) on the need to disallow homosexuality, on what she calls "homosexual panic." For Fiedler it is "sadist and melodramatic," "grotesque," and yet "sexless" (*Love and Death*, 29). What is most interesting in this light is that, if Sedgwick is correct, and the changes in patriarchal class structures in the nineteenth century call forth a new and seemingly ever more vitriolic homophobia, *and*, if Fiedler is correct, and America is one of the "great inventions of the bourgeois, Protestant mind at the moment when it stood, on the one hand, between Rationalism and Sentimentalism, and on the other, between the drive for economic power and the need for cultural autonomy" (32) then "America" and modern homophobia are indeed twins.

14. Two studies in particular codified the "tradition"—Hyatt Waggoner's

American Poets from the Puritans to the Present (1968), and Roy Harvey Pearce's *The Continuity of American Poetry* (1961). Not surprisingly, neither makes a space for homosexual inquiry, despite being written in the same cultural moment as Fiedler's *Love and Death*, and to some extent this results from a division of labor within literary study at that time that considered poetry less socially referential than fiction. Considered different formally, poetry and fiction called forth very different schemes for analysis and interpretation within a formalist era.

15. One can find a host of Puritanical biases buried in this statement; perhaps the one most germane to this study is the notion that allegiance to French Symbolism (that painted but empty whore of the nineteenth century) rather than American plain speech is to be deplored as inappropriate to the question of poetry in America. For Crane's work, such a notion is baffling—for he is, on the one hand, far more overtly concerned with America as a social, political entity than someone like Eliot. On the other hand, his work is far from the plain-speech tradition.

16. I mean "against" here in both its antithetical and figural senses. Crane, like Williams and others, was opposed to what he saw as the death instinct in Eliot; but he also saw Eliot gigantically, as the figure against whom any other writer of the age by necessity would judge his own work.

17. It is particularly interesting in the light of recent evidence suggesting that one of the biographical impulses behind Eliot's *The Waste Land* was the death of a male lover (see Miller) to ask why Eliot is so insistent upon the impersonality of his work. We have here, of course, a familiar modernist topos, seen as well in Mann's theory of contest between Apollonian and Dionysian energies in the artist or in Joyce's similar wrestling with discipline and *jouissance*. But Eliot is most insistent that it is discipline and tradition, the sacrifice of self and play, that are the hallmarks of the true artist, and one ought to investigate the meaning of this repression on a personal level and ask as well why this theory gained such acceptance as a cultural truth in Anglo-American letters. Eliot's avoidance of personality might well be linked to his general avoidance of psychoanalysis and its increasing currency and authority at this time. Undermining intention and meaning as well as exposing the sexual in ways Eliot might have found discomfiting, the repression of psychoanalytic discourse in his work is itself so remarkable as to be symptomatic.

18. Jane Gallop takes up a similar question in analyzing anthologies of feminist theory. She critiques what she sees as the Freudian narrative of the "inevitability" of adult female heterosexuality and the need to "transcend" the lesbian ("The Attraction of the Matrimonial Metaphor," a lecture given at Syracuse University, May 1989).

19. Eve Sedgwick, in an issue of *South Atlantic Quarterly* devoted to "Dis-

placing Homophobia," writes that "categories of gender . . . can have a structuring force for axes of cultural discrimination whose thematic subject isn't explicitly gendered at all. . . . [D]ichotomies in a given text—of culture as opposed to nature, for instance, public as opposed to private, mind as opposed to body, activity as opposed to passivity—are, under particular pressures of culture and history, likely places to look for implicit allegories of the relations of men to women" ("Across Gender, Across Sexuality: Willa Cather and Others," 55). A similar allegorical structure functions in regard to sexuality, and in particular to male homosexuality: indeed, the allegory is so strongly and openly coded as often to make homosexuality the "open secret" of a text.

20. Daniel Aaron's *Writers on the Left* traces this as well, and Alfred Kazin summarizes the positions in *On Native Ground* as follows:

> The Marxists, who never ceased to proclaim their devotion to literature and never proved it, steadily drove criticism into a corner of sociology, where it became either a political weapon or a sub-literary calculus concentrated on classes and social functions. The Formalists—many of them quasi-religious traditionalists and passionate devotees of a limited modern poetry—began, from a variety of motives, at the opposite extreme. To them literature became not merely a great moral and intellectual activity; it became the only activity. They reduced all human discourse to poetry, all poetry to the kind of poetry they cared to write and study, and like Talmudists reduced all critical discourse to the brilliant technical exegesis of a particular text. (402)

Matthiessen's text, Arac argues, foregoes such partisanship in the attempt to authorize a coherent national tradition (this in the face of growing international crisis) and *The American Renaissance* succeeds in bringing together a sociopolitical interest in the referentiality of literature with a Coleridgian theory of the symbol that is the legacy of formalism Matthiessen inherits.

21. Actually, he says this gave him a "hardon" (*Rat and the Devil*, 124), a specific detail that Arac euphemizes, thereby continuing the action of policing and repressing in the very act of claiming to correct it.

CHAPTER TWO

1. This is not, of course, a project I undertake alone; as the numbers of those working in gay studies grows ever larger, so too does the sophistication of theory with which its more urgent issues are addressed.

2. The following chapters make use of Crane's biography not in an attempt to present intentionalist or essentialist readings of his texts, but in order to see how homosexuality as a discourse was articulated in the nonliterary text of his life the better to see how it bent to the pressures of the literary. As Jonathan Culler has pointed out in another context, "The more a critical discourse at-

tempts to restore empirical authors to a place of honor, the more it opens the possibility of analyzing authors as victims of the forces they seek to control" ("Changes in the Study of the Lyric," 49).

3. Homosexual critique or gay studies would likewise challenge the naive notion of literary history upon which the curricula of many departments of English and American literature have been based. Byron's work, for instance, or Shakespeare's sonnets, Willa Cather's novels or Oscar Wilde's prison experience may be of as great or more interest for the discussion of Crane than are the works and lives of other American poets such as Emerson, Dickinson, Stevens, and Moore, or of other writers of the twenties such as Hemingway, Fitzgerald, and Faulkner.

4. See here Harold Beaver's "Homosexual Signs" and also texts such as Susan Sontag's essay "On Camp" or Eve Sedgwick's more recent work on kitsch, camp, and sentimentality. Beaver makes the undeniable and crucial point that homosexuals, denied any positive identity in Western cultures, are inscribed through their style: one "knows them" by their appearance, taste, etc.

5. I do not wish to imply in this chapter that homosexual desire or the social construction of homosexual lives is the same for all people in all times and places. As Crane himself wrote to Yvor Winters, homosexuality is "modified in the characteristics of the image by each age in each civilization" (*Poems*, 244). Thus, homosexuality in Crane's text should not be conflated with homosexuality in Whitman's, Wilde's, Genet's, or O'Hara's: each inhabits a different homosexual subjectivity the differences of which are sometimes insignificant and sometimes of stunning significance (O'Hara and Genet, for instance, could be far more openly homosexual than the others mentioned here). Nevertheless, the larger patterns of patriarchy in the history of Western culture suggest some continuity of homophobic ideology through the past century in Western culture, forcing all of these writers to experience related repressions and taboos. And it is perhaps only the disappearance of gay subcultures from the texts of written history that keeps us from knowing the more positive continuities in them that could well have existed across the past hundred and fifty years. Such speculation does not constitute a transhistorical approach to homosexuality nor does it assign essential or transcendental meanings to homosexual desire.

6. But here as well, in order to be accepted by the Eastern literary establishment, Crane had to position himself against other Midwestern writers in the Whitman vein who were considered too sentimental (writers such as Sandburg, Masters, Lindsay). He writes to Gorham Munson—an Ohio acquaintance—that the writer must "harden" himself: no effeminacy or sentimentality allowed (*Letters*, 31).

7. Joan Riviere's work on femininity and masquerade, where signs of deference and vulnerability are in fact a masking of the will to power, is particularly interesting in this context—not only for what it says about the history of psycho-

analytic readings of lesbianism (considered by Riviere more masculine, and less in thrall to masquerade) but also for the politics of drag, for what has become a male masquerade of femininity in masculine gay culture (or at least in its representations in recently visible texts such as *Torch Song Trilogy* and *Kiss of the Spider Woman*).

8. We can easily see the self/mirror figure in a number of texts of homosexual poets in America—Frank O'Hara's "In Memory of My Feelings," for instance, is consumed with the notion of identity transformation, as is "Meditations in an Emergency"; O'Hara's friend John Ashbery has numerous texts on the slippage of the self, perhaps most powerfully summarized in "Self-Portrait in a Convex Mirror"; Whitman's oeuvre is based on the problematics of identity, as is much of Crane's; and we find the trope in feminist theory's revision of the mirror stage and in Adrienne Rich's *Diving into the Wreck*: "The Mirror in Which Two Are Seen As One."

9. It is important here not to succumb to the following sentiments expressed by Allen Tate twenty years after Crane's death (that is, in 1952!), but it is crucial to see how such sentiments would have shaped the cultural articulations and disarticulations of Crane's homosexual desire:

> The "causes" of homosexuality are no doubt as various as the causes of other neuroses. But the effect on the lives of its victims seems to be uniform: they are convinced that they cannot be loved, and they become incapable of loving. This is not to say that they are incapable of strong affection; they are incapable of sustaining it in a sexual relationship. They may have affection *or* sex, but not both; or if both, both are diluted and remote. (*The Man of Letters*, 296)

This was written by one of Crane's most important literary acquaintances, the man who wrote the glowing introduction to his first book of poetry. Tate's pronouncements themselves are beyond comment at this particular moment, but we should recognize that Crane did at times espouse this view (as my discussion in chapter 3 will indicate); indeed, it seems to have been the particular burden of his generation to live their homosexuality between a conception of it as lust and a conception of it as a possibly affectionate union between two men: sex *or* platonic friendship was the choice. (This seems also to have been the choice offered lesbians in this era, about which one might read the following chapter or Carroll Smith-Rosenberg's final chapter in *Disorderly Conduct*.) The polarity is a nineteenth-century legacy, but the modernist could only attempt to navigate between these mutually exclusive and unsatisfactory categories. In Crane the bifurcation produced a schizophrenia or vertigo from which he could not recover.

10. A letter from the same period to Waldo Frank where Crane suggests that his epic "intellectually judged . . . seems more and more absurd" has become a

locus classicus in Crane criticism, however. The Spenglerian doom of this text, and its observation that "the bridge as a symbol today has no significance beyond an economical approach to shorter hours, quicker lunches, behaviorism and toothpicks" (*Letters*, 261), have been seized by critics interested in social-realist readings of *The Bridge*, but their interest in social realism has not extended to an interest in homosexuality as a real social structure or system.

11. This endless circulation of discourse receives its principal elaboration in Wilde, of course, whose "empty signs" and displaced meanings are employed precisely in order to validate nothing *except* their producer's position as the generator (but never the origin) of those signs.

12. This is not by any means to suggest that distinctions of class, race, and gender in the dominant culture are not reiterated and mirrored within homosexual subcultures, for they are. My point here is about cultural roots, and the fact that gay people must construct for themselves a new cultural system and not merely a modified one. What Whitman claims of the homosexual in *Calamus* seems still to be true; sooner or later "The whole past theory of your life and all conformity to the lives around you would have to be abandon'd" (*Leaves of Grass*, 116).

13. Although this is problematized somewhat by the white equation of blackness with certain forms of behavior, most African-American texts locate their moment of racialized trauma in a consciousness of difference as "anatomical" rather than "behavioral," a visible difference that is extended to behavior, to be sure, but not to actions considered within one's control (although the historical defiguration of the black body by black men and women in quest of whiter skin, straighter hair, etc., speaks to how powerful are the injunctions against the black body in white America, and to the fact that even that difference can come to be read as within one's power to control).

14. It is interesting that as of spring 1988, for instance, Amnesty International considered people imprisoned for their support of gay rights to be political prisoners but not people imprisoned for homosexual or lesbian acts.

15. For an interesting twist on this problem, see Frank O'Hara's "In Memory of My Feelings" and Marjorie Perloff's discussion of this poem in *Poet among Painters*. O'Hara revels in the fact that he is beset by identities, each of which is recognizable in the deployment of different signs.

16. Lee Edelman, although he does not make sexuality a specific part of his analysis, develops this idea at length in his study of Crane's rhetorical practices and the difference of his more typical tropes from those of the tradition that has misinterpreted him.

17. Certainly Crane's text may be read as indicative of desire rather than of a specifically homosexual or homoerotic desire. In addition to supplying an unacceptable universalist reading, however, such a critical maneuver masks the difference which is meaning in this case—that it is precisely the ways in which

the homosexual is not the universal that makes a suite of poems such as "Voyages" of interest as a homotextual event. It is the impossibility of making homosexual experience congruent with the conventions of heterosexual love poetry and with the expectations of a heterosexual audience that produces a frame of warning, loss, and disaster in which the homosexual takes place in "Voyages."

18. Castration had also been quite seriously argued as a humane "cure" for homosexuality, as the conclusion to Havelock Ellis's 1923 reprint of *Sexual Inversion* makes clear.

19. This would seem to be an acknowledgment that he is not able or prepared to read the poem more closely or fully; whether through fear or ignorance, the homosexual nature of the text eludes Lewis in his commentary, and indeed the poem does seem slight as a result.

20. It is not difficult to see why Lewis was attracted to Crane's poetry sufficiently strongly to prompt his writing of a critical book on Crane: Crane is, for him, a twentieth-century version of the myths of American literary art that provided the central focus for Lewis's earlier study, *The American Adam*. For Lewis, Crane's every nuance and desire is founded in what the critic figures as universal, mythic structures of poetic imagination and its expression.

21. Virtually no one argues against the homosexual referents in "Possessions"; when there is debate over the poem, it focuses on whether or not Crane could possibly have meant *only that*—much less condone it.

22. That they are both obscure is, of course, the case, and what Crane perhaps meant by "a more perfect lucidity" was precisely the condensation of numerous levels of discourse and reference within one linguistic structure.

23. Much of this remains unclear in a simple, linear, first reading of the text, but it is important here to remember how Crane's style already delegitimates the privileging of linear reading and also that no literary text—no text whatever its status in culture—is composed of a single discourse or produces a single meaning. Texts are the sites on which various voices, discourses, allegiances, knowledges, ideologies, perceptions, and misperceptions contest for cultural visibility and power. Readings that stress the Romantic epistemology of poems such as "Recitative" are not "wrong" readings; nor are readings that tease out the poem's homosexual figuration—both choose one of the discourses that shape and inform it. Once aware of the homosexual referents in this text, it is quite impossible not to imagine their importance to any understanding of the contest of voices it enacts and records.

24. In the recent debate over narcissism as a response to late capitalism we see a familiar moralistic vocabulary that always takes homosexuality as its object of scorn, but the debate is germane to understanding Crane's investment in a revaluation of narcissism. Russell Jacoby and Stanley Aronowitz rightly suggest that Christopher Lasch's well-known railing against the self-centered ego of late capitalism may actually be read as a screen for his desire to repress and/or con-

trol rebellion and libidinal play; his text presents a liberal nostalgia for a utopian nuclear family that has somehow miraculously escaped the demands and definitions of an advanced economy of exchange. This would seem to me to place valorized narcissism within a system in process away from that repressive regime. The more libertarian or Marcusean exhilaration over narcissistic energy seems, on the other hand, wholly naive in the face of the economy's stunning exploitation of "self" in the three decades since the publication of *Eros and Civilization*. Homosexuality may now simply demand its full complement of pursuits to happiness just as any other set of consumers may identify and fulfill other seemingly self-generated desires: homosexuals have become a market. This debate cannot be settled here, and it will be crucial in the coming years to see how AIDS solicits from the gay community a different notion of politics, enabling that community to reread (but not, one hopes, to rescind) its former calls for individual liberty. While Crane's text should not, it seems to me, be made to bear this burden, the issue is more than tangential to it.

25. The concluding chapter to Eve Sedgwick's *Between Men* offers us a view of Whitman as "*incarnating* a phallic erethism . . . rather than having a phallus, he enacted one." His text is not, therefore, merely a celebration of male phallicism but of "the deeper glamor . . . of being like a woman, since to have to enact rather than possess a phallus is (in this system) a feminine contradiction" (205).

26. Although not writing of homosexuality per se, Donald Pease comments on a similar slippage of self and other in Whitman's figuration of voice:

> In Whitman's poetry, "you" supplements "I" as the "latency" remaining unspoken in every utterance; thus neither "I" nor "you" alone can constitute the speaking voice. Only the profound relation *between* them can. When in good voice, Whitman's speaker alternately anticipates his listener's responses and changes places with the listener. . . . By alternately impersonating both sides of an implicit dialogue, then, Whitman's voice undergoes constant modulations, startling enough in their effects to be his voice's equivalent of the transformative power of traditional metaphor." ("Blake, Crane, Whitman and Modernism," 77)

As such, Whitman's text refuses the most hierarchical of reading practices—that of closed, Oedipal identity; and he cannot be read by a New Criticism devoted to reified individuated consciousness.

John Ashbery's well-known play with pronouns allies him to this practice as well, and in his text the practice turns much more serious than in Whitman. The following lines are the opening to "Worsening Situation," and we see in them a slippage from "he" to "one" to "I" and finally to "you." The burden of the passage, the terror and paralysis of nonidentification, is figured in the loss or castration of a "severed hand," the hand, as in Keats, that writes. The passage glosses the uncanniness of self—and the inability to escape the desire for fixity if only in the minimal, violent, and fetishistic identity a proper name can grant:

> Like a rainstorm, he said, the braided colors
> Wash over me and are no help. Or like one
> At a feast who eats not, for he cannot choose
> From among the smoking dishes. This severed hand
> Stands for life, and wander as it will,
> East or west, north or south, it is ever
> A stranger who walks beside me. O seasons,
> Booths, chaleurs, dark-hatted charlatans
> On the outskirts of some rural fete,
> The name you drop and never say is mine, mine!
> (*Self-Portrait*, 3).

More straightforwardly denotative passages in Ashbery's work point to his conception of identity as a destabilized field of being. The following is from the latter part of "Self-Portrait in a Convex Mirror":

> Is there anything
> To be serious about beyond this otherness
> That gets included in the most ordinary
> Forms of daily activity, changing everything
> Slightly and profoundly, and tearing the matter
> Of creation, any creation, not just artistic creation
> Out of our hands, to install it on some monstrous, near
> Peak, too close to ignore, too far
> For one to intervene? This otherness, this
> "Not-being-us" is all there is to look at
> In the mirror, though no one can say
> How it came to be this way. A ship
> Flying unknown colors has entered the harbor.
> (*Self-Portrait*, 81)

In Crane, this otherness, this "not-being-us," may be all there is to see in the mirror, but his faith in figurative language is stronger than Ashbery's, and he works to identify the unknown colors flying above the harbor, where the "bridge swings over salvage, beyond wharves" in "Recitative."

27. It is an index of just how difficult, abstract, and obscure is Crane's verse that he would build a poem around a turn that cannot be identified except as "one crucial sign," and the phrase invites a mystification or overreading. But the point here is to see how the mystery of the sign functions in Crane, and it would seem that the tears signify in this passage something like signification itself; they "yield attendance," a phrase that suggests "being with" and connotes thereby a social connection that the more expected word, "attention," would not. And

the attendance they yield is "to one crucial sign," the sign, perhaps, that marks, consumes, and *is* homosexual connection. As the lack of a specific referent perhaps suggests, the crucial thing about this sign is neither its particular shape nor its meaning but its very ability to attract an adjective—here, "crucial." The significance of that particular adjective is itself very interesting—if not crucial—for it is rich in possibility as a sign for and of the homosexual. The homosexual sign is "crucial" in that it is cruxlike, twisted, and double, and the word points simultaneously in two pragmatic directions: to effect (i.e., the sign is crucial in that it expresses social urgency, it marks one as connected to others) and to origin (i.e., the sign is the cross of the broken self in which begins the homosexual semiotic—hence, St. Sebastian as an icon). The homosexual sign, while empty of reference, is crucial because it is, like all signs, the crossing of self and other, the site on which the subject is constructed, the space in which transferential exchange occurs.

CHAPTER THREE

1. Benveniste wrote, of course, that "the basis of subjectivity is in the exercise of language" (*Problems in General Linguistics*, 226).

2. It is necessary, of course, not to conflate these various aesthetic projects. Objective correlative, in Eliot's classic definition of it, really defined an interior state of consciousness through an external display of objects; Imagism sought to present the object without appeal or attention to mediating consciousness; and if Stevens's more ambitious work claims to build itself "without external referent" (*Collected Poems*, 251), something seemingly at odds with both of the above, that phrase does not appear in his work until 1940—his work of the twenties ("Sea Surface Full of Clouds," for instance) is quite dependent upon the play between externally verifiable and internally perceived objects of consciousness. In any case, Crane's work is radically other than each of these aesthetics and has been judged lacking according to their principles.

3. It is not too much to suggest here that Tate has identified without being able to achieve a new critical task, one that moves beyond the close reading of individual poems into something like analysis of the textuality of a writer's work. Crane's work announces (in 1926) that something other than New Criticism will be needed to explain all of the products of the modernist imagination.

4. It is worth noting that in citing Crane and Whitman before him for their cultural and personal inadequacies Winters delivers himself of the following remark, one that is particularly striking given the context of unspoken homosexuality and Oedipal crisis that surrounds it: "The difference between Whitman (who is his own epic hero) and *pious Aeneas* is that the latter is not only obeying destiny, he is obeying his mother" ("The Progress of Hart Crane," 103).

5. It is more than likely that Freud's monograph on da Vinci reauthorized this reading of his life; it valorizes only sublimated homosexuality, finding that

the "origin" of da Vinci's curious power as an artist. Yet there is in it a telling contradiction: da Vinci's work would not have been successful, Freud's reading claims, if his homosexuality had not been sublimated and his relations with young men wholly void of sexual contact—*and yet* the very occasion of writing the monograph is the continuing assessment of da Vinci as an incomplete artist, as a figure of great genius whose work came to less than it should. It never occurs to Freud that this tragic aesthetic loss may be the symptom and cost of homosexual repression.

6. Weber's edition of the letters elides the words "balls" and "cunts" and so I have turned to Parkinson's more recent edition of the correspondence between Crane and Winters for this quotation.

7. And yet there is the insistent rhetoric of the masculine priority to aesthetics in a number of modernist texts: in an appendix he wrote for his translation of Remy de Gourmont's *The Natural Philosophy of Love*, Pound claimed that sperm was necessary to thought, that the brain is a repository of sperm and the dynamic of thought equivalent to male ejaculation. Similarly, André Gide, in *Corydon*, his apologia for homosexuality written around 1910 and reprinted in 1923, claims that excess biological coding or "overabundance of the procreative substance" in the male is different than in the female: "Yet whereas in the female this extra substance is immediately utilized for the race, what happens to it in the uncastrated male? It becomes material for variation . . . , which in almost all the so-called superior species makes the male into a creature of show, of song, of art, of sport, or of intelligence—a creature of play" (43–44). Such sentiments, which it is not at all clear that Crane shares, would nevertheless make the aesthetic realm, even when it is homosexual, "naturally" masculine.

8. See here the well-documented inducement of inspiration that led Crane to use alcohol, sex, music, and any other stimulant that could remove him from the demands of a historical body and present him instead with what seemed immediate experience and perception. Malcolm Cowley's anecdotes in *A Second Flowering* and Unterecker's detailing of the Tate-Brown-Cowley-Crane alliance in the mid-twenties provide sometimes sympathetic and sometimes lurid accounts of this. In sympathy as in sensationalism, however, Crane is ever the spectacle of failure and irrationality, subject to outbursts of jealousy or pique, an opinionated and self-alienating obsessive who rejected those who accepted him. If our interest here were in the history of friendship—and at some point in time, Emerson's trope and gay studies will come together to make that a compelling academic question—that is not our interest now, and Crane's quite obvious flaws in the bourgeois realm of friendship absolutely need to be read as part and parcel of his homosexual alienation from that institution. Cowley's account (mentioned above) is particularly suggestive about the ways in which the concerns of young married couples are often not the concerns of young homosexual men (although Cowley himself seems unaware that he has outlined this). In

order to understand how intertwined with bodily amnesia is Crane's process of writing, one should see his claim that sobriety is not an aid to composition (quoted in Cowley).

9. Although racial self-definition rather than sexual preference seems to have been the dominant "problem" for Countee Cullen, we see a similar pattern in the split allegiance of his work; he identifies with African-American experience but cannot imagine a black perspective universal enough for significant, "Keatsian" poetry: "Yet do I marvel at [God doing] this curious thing / To make a poet black and bid him sing" (*On These I Stand*, 3). Ultimately, like Crane, although he questions their validity at times, Cullen seems more often than not to have accepted universalist notions of the literary. (The comparison here is made even more interesting by Arnold Rampersad's recent biography of Langston Hughes, which reads the homosexual intrigues of black intellectual life and Harlem in the twenties a matter of course for some [such as Alain Locke] and a matter of consternation for others [such as Hughes]: Cullen himself seems to have vacillated between a homosexually identified and a heterosexually sanctioned existence.)

10. His first published poem ("C 33"), for instance, was in sympathy with the imprisoned Oscar Wilde, and several others of his early works depict sentimental male attachment ("Episode of Hands") or suggest a connection between homosexuality and poetry—"Episode of Hands," "Modern Craft," and even "Porphyro in Akron," with its closing line, "in this town, poetry's a / Bedroom occupation" (*Poems*, 146). A homosexual reading of "Porphyro in Akron" is granted further sanction by the fact that the poem was written after the dissolution of Crane's very first homosexual romance, what he thought might be "the romance of [his] life" (*Letters*, 31), with a man he referred to in letters as "Akron" because that was the man's home (Crane was living in Cleveland at this point). Crane claimed this man "the realization of one's dreams in flesh, form, laughter and intelligence," and this phrase suggests that "Porphyro in Akron"'s reworking of the dream-come-true in "The Eve of St. Agnes" places him (Crane) as a lover abandoned at the poem's close, his dream of a perfect complement unfulfilled. Critics have usually read the poem's closing image of poetry as a bedroom occupation as indicative of the failure of public appreciation for poetry in middle America, but it also suggests in the context of this biographical information that poetry is a lamentable substitute for other bedroom occupations. Other, more explicit texts will be analyzed in subsequent chapters.

11. In "On Some Motifs in Baudelaire" Benjamin asks "how lyric poetry can have as its basis an experience for which the shock experience [of modern alienations] has become the norm" (*Illuminations*, 162), and surely we must see Crane's interest in a lyric poetry built from the shock of homosexuality as an attempt to found a consciousness that can incorporate that experience.

12. Claiming same-sex sexuality "natural" (which we will see in Matthiessen's discourse below, as well), while appearing naive to an era that sees all subjectivity as constructed and none as "natural," seems to have been part of a strategic displacement of homophobia for early gay men and lesbians.

13. For an interesting intertext to this, see Unterecker's thoughts on the Platonic as "the best place to look for a description of what Crane was experiencing" in his relation with Opffer. Unterecker's reading of their homosexuality places it in the context of the *Phaedrus*, meaning that he can ignore its concrete manifestation in American culture—including the homophobia that made it such a contested mode of subjectivity. By Platonizing it, he can also claim (along with Opffer, interviewed forty years later) that "there was nothing dirty in it," as if all genital homosexuality were unclean and all nongenital homosexuality somehow not really homosexual (*Voyager*, 355).

14. The famous introduction to Proust's *Cities of the Plain* also offers evidence of this internalized self-hatred, characterizing homosexuals as the "race upon which a curse weighs and which must live amid falsehood and perjury, because it knows the world to regard as a punishable and a scandalous, as an inadmissable thing, its desire, that which constitutes for every human creature the greatest happiness in life" (13).

15. Thurman's text marks one of the first overt appearances of male and female same-sex possibilities in American fiction—and it is not surprising that that appearance should come out of the Harlem Renaissance, a spectacular cultural space of social and sexual experimentation whose appearance in an urban center would seem to follow D'Emilio and Freedman's theory that cities provided a site for the articulation of new same-sex social articulations.

16. We can also see this in Stein's savvy rewriting of *Q.E.D.*, a lesbian novel, as *Melanctha*, a "negro" one, a fact that suggests the intertext as well between the taboo of female sexuality in patriarchal culture and that culture's construction of its racial other as sexual.

17. It seems to me that this is how we should read Jeff Campbell's confusion in *Melanctha*; he cannot imagine an alternative between what he calls "just two kinds of ways of loving." "One kind of loving seems to me," he says, "is like one has a good quiet feeling in a family when one does his work, and is always living good and being regular, and then the other way of loving is just like having it like any animal that's low in the streets together" (370).

18. The role of alcohol as a cofactor in this is also, of course, well known if not terribly carefully understood. It would be useful to understand in a better way how alcohol has contributed to homosexual self-destruction—not only at present, but also in the past. Radclyffe Hall, for instance, anatomizes the phenomenon of self-hatred and alcoholism in her Paris chapters of *The Well of Loneliness*, and the story of Montgomery Clift, who has become something of

an icon in more recent gay culture, offers depressing and all too familiar parallels to Crane's "long suicide."

19. It should be added here that Crane did use an alias on some of these occasions. Susan Brown's *Robber Rocks* identifies one of these aliases as "Mike Drayton." But the use of an alias suggests more than an intense need to distance oneself from one's behavior. It is not surprising, for instance, in a subculture so given over to fervency that it developed euphemisms such as "in the life" and "church member" for its own activities. We might also interestingly note a similar act of naming in *Prick Up Your Ears*, where the practice of cruising solicits the use of an alias, and where "Joe" Orton comes to subsume and replace the previous "John" Orton, suggesting, finally, that the alias or "gay name" is a refusal of heterosexually defined social identities.

20. Guy Hocquenghem suggests that the rhetoric of transformation in Genet results from the ideological injunctions against homosexuality, making any single experience of it appear miraculous and powerfully transformative of self and reality.

21. Malcolm Cowley, in the video series *Voices and Visions*, recalls telling Crane that "Aztec" masculinity was much like that of ancient Greece—that it would perhaps be a better or more congenial place for him to spend a year than France (where Crane had recently been beaten and jailed and where he was generally socially outcast). While in Mexico, Crane wrote that "the nature of the Mexican Indian . . . isn't exactly 'sunny,' but he is more stirred by the moon, if you get what I mean, than any type I've ever known." And he finds these men acceptably masculine—i.e., bisexual: "The fluttering gait and the powder puff are unheard of here, but that doesn't matter in the least. Ambidexterity is all in the fullest masculine tradition" (*Letters*, 390). This, along with his sudden interest in Peggy Baird, suggests that it was not perhaps homosexual experience that Crane found oppressive by the time of his death, but homosexual identity as defined and understood by a literary community in the United States.

22. See the Israeli film *Drifting* and its examination of homosexuality through this metaphor.

23. That reading of homosexuality, which sees the male desire for anal pleasure as linked to the death drive, can be seen in explicit (if reductive) Freudian readings of Crane such as Wallace Fowlie's, and was no doubt active in Crane's imagination from Lawrence's reading of homosexuality as death in *Calamus* (in *Studies in Classic American Literature*, a text Crane seems to have been fairly familiar with).

24. Having made no mention of the often peculiar vocabulary Crane employs, I would like to suggest that we think of it, as in the word "irrefragibly," which seems so overwrought here, as part of the erotic charge of single words that Roland Barthes comments on in *The Pleasure of the Text*: "The word can

be erotic on two opposing conditions, both excessive: if it is extravagantly repeated, or on the contrary, if it is unexpected, succulent in its newness (in certain texts, words *glisten*, they are distracting, incongruous apparitions)" (42).

CHAPTER FOUR

1. George Chauncey, Jr., writes that "early in 1927 municipal authorities raided the theater where the American version of *The Captive*, a French play about lesbianism, was premiering," and also prevented *The Drag*, a play in which Mae West appeared, from opening on Broadway. "In an effort to protect 'immature' audiences from exposure to such 'corrupting influences,'" Chauncey writes, "the state legislature passed a law later that year which banned 'the subject of sexual degeneracy or sex perversion' from the stage" (34).

2. Robert Martin points this out in *The Homosexual Tradition*.

3. Naomi Schor has recently developed a theory of female textual practices that includes the wound as one figure of bodily fetishization that provide female readers resistance to male totalizing (*Reading in Detail*).

4. "Modern Craft" was written in 1918, and if we compare two other searches for a modern muse from the same period, Stevens's "Disillusionment of Ten O'Clock" (1915) and Williams's "The Young Housewife" (1917), we can see how glaring is Crane's discovery of representational lack in "Modern Craft." Stevens's poem suggests something awry in the modern world, and also begins with a sense of inadequate muses and inadequate representational strategies: it is easier for Stevens to depict what will not occur in this landscape than it is for him to say what will.

> The houses are haunted
> By white night gowns.
> None are green,
> Or purple with green rings,
> Or green with yellow rings,
> Or yellow with blue rings.
> . . . .
> People are not going
> To dream of baboons and periwinkles.
> Only, here and there, an old sailor,
> Drunk and asleep in his boots,
> Catches tigers
> In red weather.
>
> (*Collected Poems*, 16)

But as stunning as is the turn of the poem's close and its reversal of the terms that come before, Stevens's poem suggests only an old American cliché of domesticity avoided, paradise lost and then regained through the repossession of individual vision and the exotic within the self. "Modern Craft" examines the image that remains absent in "Disillusionment of Ten O'Clock" (the strange muse with "socks of lace / And beaded ceintures") precisely because Crane would make sexuality rather than its sublimation central to his text. It is not a mythic imagination ("Catch[ing] tigers / In red weather") that Crane glosses in his work but a historically situated subject who speaks a fractured, difficult text.

Williams, of course, refuses to consider the exotic or erotic except as it exists in the concrete and the mundane, and "The Young Housewife" traces one instance of Williams's encounter with his muse. Neither crafty convention nor ghostly presence, his muse is a young housewife who "moves about in negligee behind / the wooden walls of her husband's house":

> Then again she comes to the curb
> to call the ice-man, fish-man, and stands
> shy, uncorseted, tucking in
> stray ends of hair, and I compare her
> to a fallen leaf.
>
> The noiseless wheels of my car
> rush with a crackling sound over
> dried leaves as I bow and pass smiling.
> (*Collected Early Poems*, 136)

Williams's self-proclaimed comfort with female sexuality allows him to reverse a long tradition of stylized portraits of the muse and to find beauty, inspiration, etc., in a "real" rather than "idealized" woman. But we certainly cannot overlook the voyeuristic, even sadistic possibilities in this text—after authorizing his act of metaphor ("I compare her / to a fallen leaf") the young housewife is metaphorically crushed in the last stanza; regardless of the debatable tone of this ending, the movement here must be seen as evidence of patriarchy's and poetry's appropriation of the female body through gaze, description, and possession. Thus, Williams's poem is doubly conventional; for all its refusal of idealization, it quite assuredly depicts the muse in a manner that is conventional and unproblematic. And as in Williams, so in Amy Lowell's "Madonna of the Evening Flowers" (1919): when the modern poet goes in search of a muse, that muse is usually found:

> Suddenly I am lonely:
> Where are you?
> I go about searching.
>
> Then I see you,
> Standing under a spire of pale blue larkspur,
> With a basket of roses on your arm.
> (*Complete Poetical Works*, 210)

We might recognize the rejection of heterosexual poetic strategies in "Modern Craft" as a signal of aesthetic exhaustion, not unlike the strategies of Edna St. Vincent Millay, about whom Debra Fried writes, in tropes echoing those of Crane's poem, "By identifying the sonnet's scanty ground with an erotic grove of excess, turning the chastity belt of poetic form into a token of sexual indulgence, Millay invades the sanctuary of male poetic control" ("Andromeda Unbound," 17).

5. H. H. Smith's *Aaron Siskind: Photographer* describes the parallel between Crane and Stieglitz as the way in which objects in their respective texts are used not only to express inner states of emotion (as in Eliot) but also to suggest harmonies among them that allude to more transcendental laws or insights.

6. Pound's attraction to the ideogram, which would seem to be the point in modernism furthest from mimesis and closest to abstraction, is in fact based on the mimetic qualities of the ideogram and its ability to suggest relations in the real world without the mediating, antimimetic qualities of language. The ideogram becomes, in a purely linguistic sense, the "answer" to the search for a direct representation of the world. In another sense, it is without history in Western poetry and therefore also becomes a representation that has no mediating historical associations to block its transparency.

7. I draw here on Barbara Smith's helpful distinction between fictive and natural discourses in *On the Margins of Discourse*. Crane's work is not mimetic of any speech act or verbal behavior—i.e., it is neither a conversation poem, a confession, a hymn, or a meditation. If Crane's poetry is mimetic of anything, it is mimetic of poetry.

8. We cannot ignore, of course, the marvelous suspension of gender that occurs in Chaplin's films. If not gay, their main character often exhibits behaviors that make his gender identification ambiguous (he sews, he flutters his eyelashes, he blushes, is shy and practically defenseless); the list could go on, but it is clear, as James D. Baker pointed out to me, that a homosexual reading of the character is not impossible and may in fact have been part of its attraction to Crane and to generations of viewers. The Crane poem seems to have been a response to the Cleveland screening of *The Kid*.

9. There are other Ashbery poems that do not present any hint of a naive assertion of stable identity. But perhaps it is Ashbery's radical maneuver here to present homosexual cruising as a locus of stability in the face of his own canonical exploitation of decentered subjectivity. "The Ongoing Story" is an uncharacteristically Whitmanian moment in Ashbery, for the other typical objects of his parody are in evidence (Sydney Carton "mounting the guillotine," "a course / Called Background of the Great Ideas") but the moment of interaction between the two figures at the poem's close seems the only genuine experience in the poem.

10. It would be one thing—and an accurate one—to say that homosexuality

is denied its object of desire and hence its poetic correlatives; it is another—and suggests an altogether different notion of desire and its dissemination through cultural fields of knowledge—to suggest that homosexuality needs to be apprehended as allegory. I draw here on Paul De Man's comment on Benjamin, that "allegory names the rhetorical process by which the literary text moves from a phenomenal, world-oriented to a grammatical, language-oriented direction" ("Lyrical Voice in Contemporary Theory," 69). What we see in "Possessions" is the grammar of homosexuality and Crane's battle to align its paradigmatic and syntagmatic axes.

11. One can see why this is one of Bloom's privileged texts in the Crane corpus, for instance, in its intertextual examination of alterity, anteriority, self-reliance, and poetic authority. Bloom calls it a "perfect" poem of Orphic incarnation (*Agon*, 255).

12. What Coleridge might call the associational rather than imaginative relation between mental units.

13. R. W. B. Lewis suggests the thief is T. S. Eliot, and that the two figures here argue over poetry as living or dead. The poem's architecture of mythic reference would make such a reading too reductive, it seems. And since "Passage" traces the failure of Crane's quest for a pure poetry, it seems illogical to interpolate his debate with Eliot into the poem at this point.

14. Prohibition made alcohol, like homosexuality, not merely a "vice" but an illegality. The arbitrary and hypocritical nature of the taboos against both is something that a text such as "The Wine Menagerie" brings together.

15. This is congruent with Crane's practice, well documented by Unterecker and Cowley, of using alcohol to induce a state of forgetfulness in which he would apprehend the "proper" form of his poems. The tie to magic and incantation in Crane's practice of composition has been seen merely as irrational—either as a moral failure and intellectually curious thing (we hear Eliot at our backs in this) or as a true, mystical wonder and connection to visionary truths and energies. I would suggest that we think of it as the way Crane chose to free himself from the prohibitions against writing this study has been tracing throughout.

16. This poem has been read as a repetition of Crane's own indoctrinations into heterosexual predation by his mother and father (a reading of family romance congenial to the pathological scripting of homosexuality and to the pathological scripting of Crane). This may be one of its referents, but to see Crane as the urchin in the piece is perhaps to see only half of the story here.

17. The homosexual referents in the text were, of course, changed by Whitman to heterosexual ones, but manuscript evidence now incontrovertibly suggests the rightness of a homosexual reading of this poem—as with so many others where Whitman policed his eroticism to suit his expectation of his readers.

CHAPTER FIVE

1. Harold Bloom examines this trope in his book on Stevens, *The Poems of Our Climate* (this figure appears in the poem of that title); Bloom is arguably the most interesting critic on Stevens to date and certainly the most unavoidable discussant of the tropes of American poetry and culture in the past twenty years.

2. Interpretation of Crane as a religious poet ought itself to be interpreted. Brom Weber set the tone for these interpretations when he wrote in his 1948 biography, "In an age distinguished by the rapid decline of belief in a divine being and his agencies, Hart Crane stood apart as one who saw God . . . and who dedicated his major work to God's glory" (*Hart Crane*, 6). We should be aware in reading such a statement that part of Weber's devotion to Crane was expressed in the attempt to canonize his work, and ascribing a religious sensibility to the poet furthered that effort both by refuting claims of his ethical unacceptability and by making him similar to fashionably religious figures of the late forties such as Eliot and Auden. The religious reading was pursued by R. W. B. Lewis—"One can accurately say that from 1922 onward Crane never approached a subject in anything *but* a religious mood" (*The Poetry of Hart Crane*, 11)—although Lewis's sense of Crane's religiosity is difficult to separate from his interest in archetypal mythologies and naive American transcendentalism. This strain in Crane studies finds its belated apotheosis in Alfred Hanley's *Hart Crane's Holy Vision* (1981), where the poet is almost explicitly identified as a priest: "In most of Crane's poetry there is a constant attitude of worshipful reverence or longing before an ideal or idea—a supremacy. . . . So exalted, beneficent, desirable, and true is this perfection that the poet praises, thanks, supplicates, and propitiates it as its priest and victim, prophet and disciple, dedidated to the procurement of its favor, the proclamation of its goodness" (3). But this line of criticism clouds the fact that the position of the subject produced here is influenced as much by Aestheticism and Decadence (even when its subject is religion) as by St. Paul or Ouspensky. And such criticism almost automatically relegates sexuality either to invisibility or to a supporting role as analog of a higher, more legitimate spirituality from which it must be distinguished.

3. One of the most interesting recent readings of the relation between Crane and Eliot is John Irwin's "Figurations of the Writer's Death: Freud and Hart Crane" (in *Psychiatry and the Humanities, vol.* 4): "Setting out to confute Eliot's pessimistic rule, Crane found himself in danger of becoming an example of that rule." Crane was "faced . . . with both the need to free himself from Eliot's influence and the virtual impossibility of any direct repression of overt repudiation of Eliot" (255).

4. I mean "authenticity" here not in some naive sense of inspiration or radical newness but in the far more interesting sense implied in Harold Bloom's

theory of the anxiety of influence. "Authenticity" is meant here to point toward that desire—culturally grounded within a theory of the subject as autonomous—to produce a poetry that is un-indebted, that approaches "new" problems in "new" ways. This notion of originality accounts in part for Crane's insistent rhetoric of the New: he knew all too well how late, how already written he was—not only by Whitman, in the literary sense, but also by his homophobic culture as well; and yet, he shared with his culture's ideological construction of the poet the need to claim his own "perfect cry" of "constant harmony," to carry "the legend of his youth into the noon" of maturity. (Edelman offers a sustained reading of "Legend" [*Transmemberment of Song*, 56–72] from which these last quotations are taken; to his reading I would add only an injunction that one think of Eros in Crane's work as the materially difficult practice of male homosexuality and not simply through the paradigm of a universalized desire.)

5. This brings to mind "Emblems of Conduct," where overwhelming and genuine experience dims with time and is replaced (even in the figure of the hero) with "Dull lips commemorating spiritual gates" (*Poems*, 6); the poem suggests that all knowledge (history, oratory, science) is merely a late, historically diminished redaction of some genuine, originary moment that can never be recovered—or even initially recognized.

6. But Crane cannot quite resist the cultural pressures that would collapse the "new" and the renascent, making his project quite often nostalgic, as are virtually all modernist responses to alienation. In fact, time and again Crane stages the recognition of his fractured lateness (and the purely tropic quality of his textual virginity) as a surprise (in "Passage," "The Wine Menagerie"): almost every text drives *toward* a naive or earned wholeness ("Possessions," "Repose of Rivers"). When it is turned back from that desire—as it often is—death enters the text with a staunch insistence, as it does in the final section of "Faustus and Helen."

7. Allen Tate (in 1936, four years after Crane's death and seven into the Depression) asked an audience at the University of Virginia why "a middle-class capitalist from Pittsburgh" "desires an ante-bellum Georgian house near Lexington, Kentucky? . . . The middle-class capitalist does not believe in the dignity of the material basis of his life . . . and sees in the remains of the Old South a symbol of the homogeneous life." This echoes Crane's concern in the opening of the poem, and Tate is surely not alone in the thirties in seeing that modern industrial culture announced an ethical crisis of unprecedented proportions: "Man has never achieved a perfect unity of his moral nature and his economics; yet he has never failed quite so dismally in that greatest of all human tasks as he is failing now." But it is with no perceivable irony that Tate finds a model for a traditional society where morals and economics are not divided, where "the whole economic basis of life is closely bound up with moral behavior," in the ante-bellum South ("What is a Traditional Society?," 555–56). It is a truly

frightening and extraordinary thing to contemplate that a system of slavery offered Tate the highest in traditions of integration!

8. We can also, of course, read this relation in the other direction and suggest that the unconscious is itself one such economy. Jacques Lacan writes of the city as a figure for the subjectless movement of forces in the unconscious:

> I could see Baltimore through the window and it was a very interesting moment because it was not quite daylight and a neon sign indicated to me every minute the change of time, and naturally there was heavy traffic, and I remarked to myself that exactly all that I could see, except for some trees in the distance, was the result of thoughts, actively thinking thoughts, where the function played by the subjects was not completely obvious. . . . The best image to sum up the unconscious is Baltimore in the early morning. ("Of Structure as an Inmixing of an Otherness," 189)

The camp quality of that final sentence (and the tantalizingly phallic exception of the trees) we pass without further comment.

9. Edelman points out the erotic charge in these lines, and their relation to the "hiatus" of sky and purified "white cities" of section I, which produces "a vision of the relationship between Eros and Thanatos, between creation and destruction" (*Transmemberment of Song*, 117).

10. But "The Dance," which came to occupy a central section of *The Bridge* names the homosexual's relation to the fertility myths of sky and earth union as one of marginalization and martyrdom.

11. The rhetoric of circles, both as Emerson developed it and as it functions here, does not disallow the notion of exile or alienation traced earlier in the poem, but the circle is always all-inclusive, marking a distinct circumference, boundary, and center. It is the perfect figure for the dialectic of transcendence, the figure that enables the notions of centering and decentering that have functioned so prominently in my own language about subjectivity. And we should perhaps dwell for just a moment on the word "decorum," which suggests not only certain rites and behaviors but—more importantly—certain proprieties. Thus, it is a word that throws the counterweight of impropriety and immorality back on the "long-scattered score / Of broken intervals" in a world where one is "not for long to hold each desperate choice." It is the seal of transcendentalism and its sublimation of the homosexual body's knowledge of bliss.

CHAPTER SIX

1. It would be possible to explain this silence—and the subsequently more pessimistic poem that Crane achieved—merely by positing that, if one were living in a garret in Cleveland, Ohio, partly on parental good will and imagining oneself as a Midwestern spokesman like Sherwood Anderson or Gorham Munson, an optimistic program for the modern world would be imaginable in a

way that it would not be once one was living in New York and trying rather desperately to hold together an economic and emotional existence at odds with the dominant values of American culture. The poems that Crane produced in the years 1923–26 ("Voyages" and the dense, difficult lyrics examined in chapter 4) are texts that suggest he spent this time investigating the convoluted legacy of subjectivity that was his as a modern homosexual poet, a project that necessarily intervened in his completion of *The Bridge* as a hymn to the centered consciousness of modern culture. Although he never claimed that homosexuality was one of the overt thematic concerns of *The Bridge*, it dominated his thought about both the public and the private during these years when the text of *The Bridge* was continually forming and reforming in his mind, and it became one of the important (if censored) textual centers from which he constructed the complex weave of voices that was his epic. We know that one of the intentions of *The Bridge* was to provide a synthesis of America, to make a poem for the modern or machine age that would still valorize the humanist project, and its failure to achieve this is understandable if we remember that Crane's stake in the literary was seriously compromised, contradicted, and defeated by the competing homosexual subjectivity from which he was compelled to write. "Atlantis" and "Voyages" refer to one another and to the same psychosocial moment in Crane's life of writing the homosexual.

2. See Unterecker especially for the details of this fiasco of interpersonal incompatibility: how Crane, having found it impossible to work in New York, moved to Patterson with the relatively newly wed Allen and Caroline Tate only to quarrel horribly over domestic details. It too much heroizes Crane to recast this as the scenario of Blake's *Milton*, with Tate as Hayley and Crane as Blake, but perhaps no poet since Blake (or Swinburne) has been so ill served by friends as Crane. We need to remember how remote from the idyll of coupledom was Crane's own sexuality—how alienated he was, in fact, from the social structures through which Allen and Caroline Tate understood their lives in Patterson.

3. This may at first seem an untenable assertion—many still deny the homosexual text in *The Bridge*. But we can see that even first drafts of what became "Atlantis" were pointedly homoerotic in their figuration: Crane sent the following rather diffuse homoerotic stanza to his friends Charlotte and Richard Rychtarik on 21 July 1923 (italics added):

> The hand you carry to the rock knows lime
> And all the mineral wariness of earth . . .
> Yet, touch its cloudy buried throat where light
> Is branched like prayers unspoken that await
> *Your deepest thrusting agony* for answer: *strike*
> *Its breast precipitate, its lust-forbidden flanks,*
> *Sleek with your sweat's erosion,*—til we hear
> The sound of waters *bending and astride the sky:*

> Until, as though *an organ pressing doom*
> *Should set this nave of time atremble, we feel*
> *Through brimming clay and signalling upright,*
> Beneath us lift a porch, a living concourse
> *Whose alignment rears from equal out to equal*
> *Yielding mutual assumption on its arches*
> *Fused and veering to the measure of our arms.*
> (Weber, *Hart Crane*, 428).

We see from this, as we have noted before, that Crane's imagination of integration and transcendent union finds its most experiential analog for him in the union of homosexual bodies; if the figure of the bridge is another of what Allen Grossman calls the "orphic machines" of Crane's verse, images of shadowed wholeness in a world of fragmentation and dislocation, what passages such as this suggest is that the Orphic machine in Crane carries in it the trace of homosexual desire and is a poetic analog for the re-membered, centered, possessed and possessing homosexual body. And it is wholly in keeping with his more general swerve away from overt homosexual reference in his work after 1923 that subsequent drafts of "Atlantis" replace this erotic excess with the semiotic excess of style that leads (in the language of the final version) "Sight, sound and flesh . . . from time's realm" (*Poems*, 116).

4. To have said this, of course, is not to have said how or why the move to the Isle of Pines in 1926 enabled an epistemological or philosophical reunion with that construction of homosexual transcendence. But it is not coincidental that Crane managed a reinvigoration of his own authority only after breaking with the homophobic critics who had controlled and denied his access to any cultural centrality.

5. The poem's opening is well glossed by Waldo Frank's chapter on New York in *Our America*, from which the following passage is taken:

> New York is a resplendent city. Its high white towers are arrows of will: its streets are the plowings of passionate desire. A lofty, arrogant, lustful city, beaten through by an iron rhythm. But the men and women who have made this city and whose place it is, are lowly, are driven, are drab. Their feet shuffle, their voices are shrill, their eyes do not shine. They are different indeed from their superb creation. Life that should electrify their bodies, quicken them with high movement and high desire, is gone from them. And if you seek that life, look to the flashing steel and stone that stands above them, look to the fierce beat of their material affairs. America is the extraverted land. New York, its climax. Here, the outside world has taken to itself a soul—a towering, childish soul: and the millions of human sources are sucked void. (171).

6. In this, Crane is at odds with those artists and writers of the modern who celebrated motion both in the machine and in the text or painting. Lisa Stein-

man writes that "Cubists, Futurists, and Vorticists all emphasized movement in their work," and that "images such as Duchamp's superimposed and fragmented planes in *Nude Descending a Staircase* were probably related to scientific studies of motion done by photographers such as Muybridge" (*Made in America*, 36, 39). It is, therefore, one of the discourses of antimodernism that seems to found this opening moment of the poem.

7. See here Waldo Frank's condemnation of the "movies" in *Our America* (1919); with the exception of Chaplin's satire, which he reads as "the mere unconfessed desire of healthy men and women who are cowed by a ponderous Middle Class" (215), film represents for him the epitome of a spiritually and artistically bankrupt American culture.

8. John Irwin has written well of the anxieties of influence that ground the figure of the bedlamite and the speechless caravan in this first section, suggesting (in "Figurations of the Writer's Death") that William Cullen Bryant's "innumerable caravan" in "Thanatopsis" provides a screen image for Crane's more anxious relation to Eliot. Irwin does not, unfortunately, consider Whitman's role in "To Brooklyn Bridge," nor the role of Crane's sexuality in its composition. It would add to his analysis, I think, to ponder how Whitman—as homosexual authority—works as the counter to the figuration of his own death that occupies Crane in this text.

9. This is the shock of a title such as Jill Johnston's *Lesbian Nation* and the radical political potential of feminist texts such as Monique Wittig's *Les Guerrillères* or Charlotte Perkins Gilman's *Herland* (despite, in this context, the lack of reference to American culture in the former): so engrained in heterosexual assumptions is our thought about political anthropology that it is virtually impossible to imagine gay men or lesbians (or women) constituting anything like a nation.

10. This is not, of course, the usual way in which *The Bridge* is read. More normative recent readings have not differed very much from earlier ones in their terms of evaluation; we find in Crane criticism roughly four kinds of responses to the poem: that which sees *The Bridge* as a modernist essay on technology and alienation; that which interprets its significance according to the term "America;" that which centers its concern in the poet's imaginative abilities or genius, in his myth of his own biography as authority; and that which focuses on the language of the text, usually stressing the failure of some transcendental intention. As we produce a homosexual reading of the text, we will see how homosexuality appears not as a clear and uncontested presence in the poem but often in opposition or differential relation to one of these other urgencies. The inadequacy of such strategies, if one is interested in the question of homosexuality, lies in the fact that such thematic readings have the benefit of critical, cultural sanction and therefore the power to force the homosexual discourse of *The Bridge* underground, either by not seeing it or by seeing it as less

visible (and therefore less real and important) than something else. Because it is in the text alternately sublimated, repressed, or oppressed, homosexuality may be reduced to the status of a "minor theme" in the poem, illegitimate in the face of the more "real" because more "universal" themes mentioned above.

11. Edward Brunner briefly assesses the "puzzling" fact that Crane wrote to Kahn that this poem described the "conflict between the two races" (i.e., white and Indian)—puzzling because white people never appear in the text. Brunner tantalizingly suggests that "Crane may have had in mind not the effort to heal the conflict between the two races but rather—what may have been to him as difficult a task—the conflict between the two sexes (*Splendid Failure*, 160)—and, I would add, the conflict *they* had with the "third."

12. This follows even to the point of the epigraph's being (falsely) attributed to *The Republic* in volume 2 of *The Harper American Literature* (1987), inviting a reading of the utopian dimension of the text and a suppression of the erotics of it.

Bibliography

Abrams, M. H. "Structure of the Greater Romantic Lyric." In *Romanticism and Consciousness: Essays in Criticism*, edited by Harold Bloom, 201–29. (See Bloom.)

Adorno, Theodor. "Lyric Poetry and Society." *Telos* 20 (Spring 1974): 56–71.

———. *Prisms*. Cambridge: The MIT Press, 1981.

Althusser, Louis. "Ideology and Ideological State Apparatuses (Notes towards an Investigation)." In *Lenin and Philosophy*, 127–86. New York: Monthly Review Press, 1971.

Altman, Dennis. *The Homosexualization of America: The Americanization of the Homosexual*. New York: St. Martin's Press, 1982.

Anderson, Sherwood. *Winesburg, Ohio*. New York: Viking, 1960.

Arac, Jonathan. "F. O. Matthiessen: Authorizing an American Renaissance." In *The American Renaissance Reconsidered*, edited by W. B. Michaels and D. E. Pease, 90–112. (See Michaels.)

Arensberg, Mary, ed. *The American Sublime*. Albany: State University of New York Press, 1986.

Aronowitz, Stanley. "On Narcissism." *Telos* 44 (Summer 1980): 65–74.

Ashbery, John. *Self-Portrait in a Convex Mirror*. New York: Viking, 1975.

———. *A Wave*. New York: Viking, 1984.

Baker, Houston. *Blues, Ideology, and Afro-American Literature: A Vernacular Theory*. Chicago: University of Chicago Press, 1984.

———. *Modernism and the Harlem Renaissance*. Chicago: University of Chicago Press, 1987.

Bakhtin, M. M. *The Dialogic Imagination: Four Essays*. Austin: University of Texas Press, 1981.

Barnes, Djuna. *Nightwood*. New York: New Directions Press, 1936.

Barthes, Roland. "Change the Object Itself." In *Image—Music—Text*, 165–69.

———. "From Work to Text." In *Image—Music—Text*, 155–64.

———. *Image—Music—Text*. Translated by Stephen Heath. New York: Hill and Wang, 1977.

———. *The Pleasure of the Text*. Translated by Richard Miller. New York: Hill and Wang, 1975.

———. *Roland Barthes by Roland Barthes*. Translated by Richard Howard. New York: Hill and Wang, 1977.

Baudelaire, Charles. *Oeuvres Complètes de Charles Baudelaire*. 2 vols. Paris: Gallimard, 1975.

Baym, Nina. "Melodramas of Beset Manhood: How Theories of American Fiction Exclude Women Authors." *American Quarterly* 33 (Summer 1981): 123–39.

Beaver, Harold. "Homosexual Signs (In Memory of Roland Barthes)." *Critical Inquiry* 8 (Autumn 1981): 99–119.

Benjamin, Walter. *Illuminations*. Edited by Hannah Arendt. New York: Schocken Books, 1969.

Bennett, Tony. *Formalism and Marxism*. London: Methuen and Co., 1979.

———. "Texts in History: The Determinations of Readings and Their Texts." *Journal of the Mid-West Modern Language Association* 18 (Spring 1985): 1–16.

Benveniste, Emile. *Problems in General Linguistics*. Coral Gables, Fla.: University of Miami Press, 1971.

Bercovitch, Sacvan. *The American Jeremiad*. Madison: University of Wisconsin Press, 1978.

———. *The Puritan Origins of the American Self*. New Haven: Yale University Press, 1975.

Bernstein, Michael. *The Tale of the Tribe: Ezra Pound and the Modern Verse Epic*. Princeton: Princeton University Press, 1980.

Bersani, Leo. *Baudelaire and Freud*. Berkeley: University of California Press, 1977.

Blackmur, Richard P. *Language as Gesture*. New York: Harcourt, Brace and Company, 1952.

Blasing, Mutlu. *American Poetry: The Rhetoric of Its Forms*. New Haven: Yale University Press, 1987.

Bloom, Harold. *Agon: Towards a Theory of Revisionism*. New York: Oxford University Press, 1982.

———. "The Internalization of Quest Romance." In *Romanticism and Consciousness: Essays in Criticism*, 3–24.

———. *Poetry and Repression: Revisionism from Blake to Stevens*. New Haven: Yale University Press, 1976.

———. *The Ringers in the Tower*. Chicago: University of Chicago Press, 1971.

———, ed. *Romanticism and Consciousness: Essays in Criticism*. New York: Norton and Company, 1970.

———. *Wallace Stevens: The Poems of Our Climate*. Ithaca: Cornell University Press, 1977.

Bronski, Michael. *Culture Clash: The Making of Gay Sensibility*. Boston: South End Press, 1984.

Brown, Susan Jenkins. *Robber Rocks*. Middletown, Conn.: Wesleyan University Press, 1969.

Brunner, Edward. *Splendid Failure: Hart Crane and the Making of* The Bridge. Urbana: University of Illinois Press, 1985.

Butterfield, R. W. *The Broken Arc: A Study of Hart Crane*. Edinburgh: Oliver and Boyd, 1969.

Chauncey, George. "The Way We Were: Gay Male Society in the Jazz Age." *The Village Voice*. Vol. 31, no. 26. 1 July 1986.

Cheney, Russell. *Rat and the Devil: Journal Letters of F. O. Matthiessen and Russell Cheney*. Edited by Louis Hyde. (See Hyde.)

Cheyfitz, Eric. *The Trans-parent: Sexual Politics in the Language of Emerson*. Baltimore: Johns Hopkins University Press, 1981.

Clark, David, ed. *Critical Essays on Hart Crane*. Boston: G. K. Hall and Co., 1982.

Clarke, Bruce. "Wordsworth's Departed Swans: Sublimation and Sublimity in *Home at Grasmere*." *Studies in Romanticism* 19 (Fall 1980): 355–74.

Combs, Robert L. *Vision of the Voyage*. Memphis: Memphis State University Press, 1978.

Cowley, Malcolm. *Second Flowering: Works and Days of the Lost Generation*. New York: Viking, 1973.

Crane, Hart. *The Complete Poems and Selected Letters and Prose of Hart Crane*. Edited by Brom Weber. New York: Boni and Liveright, 1966.

———. *The Letters of Hart Crane, 1916–1932*. Edited by Brom Weber. Berkeley: University of California Press, 1965.

———. *White Buildings*. New York: Boni and Liveright, 1926.

Crew, Louie, ed. *The Gay Academic*. Palm Springs, Calif.: ETC Publications, 1978.

Crisp, Quentin. *The Naked Civil Servant*. New York: New American Library, 1968.

Crompton, Louis. *Byron and Greek Love: Homophobia in 19th-Century England*. Berkeley: University of California Press, 1985.

Cullen, Countee. *On These I Stand: An Anthology of the Best Poems of Countee Cullen*. New York: Harper and Brothers, 1947.

Culler, Jonathan. "Changes in the Study of the Lyric." In *Lyric Poetry: Beyond New Criticism*, edited by C. Hosek and P. Parker, 38–54. (See Hosek.)

de Gourmont, Remy. *The Natural Philosophy of Love*. Translated by Ezra Pound. London: M. Spearman, 1957.

De Man, Paul. *Blindness and Insight: Essays in the Rhetoric of Contemporary Criticism*. New York: Oxford University Press, 1971.

———. "Lyrical Voice in Contemporary Theory: Riffaterre and Jauss." In *Lyric Poetry: Beyond New Criticism*, edited by C. Hosek and P. Parker, 55–72. (See Hosek.)

D'Emilio, John, and Estelle B. Freedman. *Intimate Matters: A History of Sexuality in America*. New York: Harper and Row, 1988.

Doeren, Suzanne Clarke. "Hart Crane: Anamnesis and the Rhetoric of Memory." Doctoral dissertation, University of California, Irvine, 1980.

Dollimore, Jonathan. "Different Desires: Subjectivity and Transgression in Wilde and Gide." *Genders* 2 (Summer 1988): 24–41.

Doolittle, Hilda. *Trilogy*. New York: New Directions, 1973.

DuPlessis, Rachel Blau. "Romantic Thralldom in H.D." *Contemporary Literature* 20, 2 (Summer 1979): 178–203.

Eagleton, Terry. *Criticism and Ideology: A Study in Marxist Literary Theory*. London: Verso, 1978.

Edelman, Lee. *Transmemberment of Song: Hart Crane's Anatomies of Rhetoric and Desire*. Stanford, Calif.: Stanford University Press, 1987.

Eliot, T. S. "Tradition and the Individual Talent." *Selected Prose of T. S. Eliot*. Edited by Frank Kermode. New York: Harcourt, Brace, Jovanovitch and Farrar, Straus and Giroux, 1975.

Ellis, Havelock, and John Addington Symonds. *Sexual Inversion*. London: Wilson and Macmillan, 1897.

Emerson, Ralph Waldo. *The Complete Works of Ralph Waldo Emerson*. 11 vols. Edited by Edward Waldo Emerson. 1903–04. Boston: Houghton Mifflin Co.

Fetterley, Judith. *The Resisting Reader: A Feminist Approach to American Fiction*. Bloomington: Indiana University Press, 1978.

Fiedler, Leslie. *Love and Death in the American Novel*. New York: Stein and Day, 1960.

Fisher, Philip. *Hard Facts: Setting and Form in the American Novel*. New York: Oxford University Press, 1985.

Flynt, Josiah. "Homosexuality Among Tramps." In *Sexual Inversion*. Edited by H. Ellis and J. A. Symonds, 252–57. (See Ellis.)

Foucault, Michel. *The History of Sexuality*. Vol. 1, *An Introduction*. New York: Penguin, 1978.

Fowlie, Wallace. "The Juggler's Dance: A Note on Crane and Rimbaud." *Chimera* 2 (Autumn): 3–14.

Frank, Waldo. *Our America*. New York: Boni and Liveright, 1919.

Freud, Sigmund. *The Standard Edition of the Complete Psychological Works of Sigmund Freud*. 24 vols. London: Hogarth, 1957.

———. *Leonardo da Vinci and a Memory of his Childhood*. *The Standard Edition of the Complete Psychological Works of Sigmund Freud*, vol. 11, 57–137.

———. *Three Essays on the Theory of Sexuality*. New York: Basic Books, 1962.

Fried, Debra. "Andromeda Unbound: Gender and Genre in Millay's Sonnets." *Twentieth-Century Literature* 32 (Spring 1986): 1–23.

Friedman, Susan. "Who Buried H.D.? A Poet, Her Critics, and Her Place in 'The Literary Tradition.'" *College English* 36, 7 (March 1975): 801–14.

Fussell, Edwin. *Lucifer in Harness: American Meter, Metaphor, and Diction*. Princeton: Princeton University Press, 1973.

Gallop, Jane. *The Daughter's Seduction*. Ithaca: Cornell University Press, 1982.

Gelpi, Albert. *The Tenth Muse: The Psyche of the American Poet*. Cambridge: Harvard University Press, 1975.

Gide, André. *Corydon*. Translated by Richard Howard. New York: Farrar, Straus and Giroux, 1983.

Gilbert, Sandra, and Susan Gubar. *No Man's Land: The Place of the Woman Writer in the Twentieth Century*. Vol. 1, *The War of the Words*. New Haven: Yale University Press, 1988.

Giles, Paul. *Hart Crane: The Contexts of* The Bridge. Cambridge: Cambridge University Press, 1986.

Gounnod, Maurice. "Emerson and the Imperial Self: A European Critique." In *Emerson*, edited by David Levin, 107–28. (See Levin.)

Grossman, Allen. "Hart Crane and Poetry: A Consideration of Crane's Intense Poetics with Reference to 'The Return.'" In *Critical Essays on Hart Crane*, edited by David Clark, 221–54. (See Clark.)

Hall, Radclyffe. *The Well of Loneliness*. New York: Avon, 1981.

Hanley, Alfred. *Hart Crane's Holy Vision: "White Buildings."* Pittsburgh: Duquesne University Press, 1981.

Hartman, Geoffrey, ed. *Psychoanalysis and the Question of the Text*. Baltimore: Johns Hopkins University Press, 1978.

Hazo, Samuel. *Smithereen'd Apart: A Critique of Hart Crane*. Athens, Ohio: Ohio University Press, 1963.

Hertz, Neil. *The End of the Line: Essays on Psychoanalysis and the Sublime*. New York: Columbia University Press, 1985.

Hocquenghem, Guy. *Homosexual Desire*. Translated by Daniella Dangoor. London: Allison and Busby, 1978.

Hosek, Chaviva, and Patricia Parker, eds. *Lyric Poetry: Beyond New Criticism*. Ithaca: Cornell University Press, 1985.

Hughes, Langston. *The Weary Blues*. Ann Arbor: University Microfilms, 1968.

Hyde, Louis, ed. *Rat and the Devil: Journal Letters of F. O. Matthiessen and Russell Cheney*. Hamden, CT: Archon Books, 1978.

Irigaray, Luce. *This Sex Which Is Not One*. Ithaca: Cornell University Press, 1985.

Irwin, John. "Hart Crane's 'Logic of Metaphor.'" In *Critical Essays on Hart Crane*, edited by David Clark, 207–20. (See Clark.)

———. "Figurations of the Writer's Death: Freud and Hart Crane." In *Psychiatry and the Humanities*, vol. 4, edited by Joseph H. Smith, 217–60. (See Smith.)

Jacoby, Russell. "Narcissism and the Crisis of Capitalism." *Telos* 44 (Summer 1980): 58–65.

Jameson, Fredric. "Baudelaire as Modernist and Postmodernist: The Dissolution of the Referent and the Artificial 'Sublime.'" In *Lyric Poetry: Beyond New Criticism*, edited by C. Hosek and P. Parker, 247–63. (See Hosek.)

———. *Fables of Aggression: Wyndham Lewis, the Modernist as Fascist*. Berkeley: University of California Press, 1979.

———. *The Political Unconscious: Narrative as a Socially Symbolic Act*. Ithaca: Cornell University Press, 1981.

Kauffman, Linda, ed. *Gender and Theory: Dialogues on Feminist Criticism*. Oxford: Basil Blackwell, 1989.

Kazin, Alfred. *On Native Grounds: An Interpretation of Modern American Prose Literature*. New York: Harcourt, Brace and World, 1942.

Kolodny, Annette. *The Lay of the Land: Metaphor as Experience and History in American Life and Letters*. Chapel Hill: University of North Carolina Press, 1975.

Kristeva, Julia. "Stabat Mater." In *The Female Body in Western Culture*, edited by S. R. Suleiman, 99–118. (See Suleiman.)

Lacan, Jacques. *Ecrits: A Selection*. Translated by Alan Sheridan. New York: W. W. Norton, 1977.

———. *The Four Fundamental Concepts of Psycho-Analysis*. Edited by Jacques Alain-Miller, translated by Alan Sheridan. New York: W. W. Norton, 1978.

———. "Of Structure as an Inmixing of an Otherness Prerequisite to Any Subject Whatever." In *The Structuralist Controversy*, edited by R. Macksey and E. Donato. (See Macksey.)

Lawrence, D. H. *Studies in Classic American Literature*. London: Heinemann, 1964.

Lentricchia, Frank. "Patriarchy Against Itself—The Young Manhood of Wallace Stevens." *Critical Inquiry* 13, 4 (Summer 1987): 742–86.

Levin, David, ed. *Emerson, Prophecy, Metamorphosis, and Influence*. New York: Columbia University Press, 1975.

Lewis, R. W. B. *The American Adam: Innocence, Tragedy, and Tradition in the Nineteenth Century*. Chicago: University of Chicago Press, 1955.

———. *The Poetry of Hart Crane: A Critical Study*. Princeton: Princeton University Press, 1967.

Lorca, Federico Garcia. *Poet in New York*. Translated by Ben Belitt. New York: Grove Press, Inc., 1955.

Lowell, Amy. *The Complete Poetical Works of Amy Lowell*. Boston: Houghton Mifflin Co., 1955.

Lynch, Michael. "'Here is Adhesiveness': From Friendship to Homosexuality." *Victorian Studies* 29 (Autumn 1985): 67–96.

Lyotard, Jean-François. *The Post-Modern Condition: A Report on Knowledge*. Minneapolis: University of Minnesota Press, 1984.

Macherey, Pierre. *A Theory of Literary Production*. Translated by Geoffrey Wall. London: Routledge and Kegan Paul, 1978.

Macksey, R., and E. Donato, eds. *The Structuralist Controversy*. Baltimore: Johns Hopkins University Press, 1970.

Marcuse, Herbert. *Eros and Civilization: A Philosophical Inquiry into Freud*. Boston: Beacon Press, 1966.

Martin, Robert K. *The Homosexual Tradition in American Poetry*. Austin: University of Texas Press, 1979.

———. "Whitman's *Song of Myself*: Homosexual Dream and Vision." *Partisan Review* 42 (1975): 80–96.

Matthiessen, F. O. *Rat and the Devil: Journal Letters of F. O. Matthiessen and Russell Cheney*. Edited by Louis Hyde. (See Hyde.)

Michaels, Walter Benn, and Donald E. Pease, eds. *The American Renaissance Reconsidered*. Baltimore: Johns Hopkins University Press, 1985.

Miller, James E. *The American Quest for a Supreme Fiction: Whitman's Legacy in the Personal Epic*. Chicago: University of Chicago Press, 1979.

———. *T. S. Eliot's Personal Waste Land: Exorcism of the Demons*. University Park, Penn.: Pennsylvania State University Press, 1977.

Moon, Michael. "Disseminating Whitman." *South Atlantic Quarterly* 88 (Winter 1989): 247–56.

Munson, Gorham. "Hart Crane: Young Titan in the Sacred Wood." In *Critical Essays*, edited by David Clark, 43–51. (See Clark.)

Nelson, Cary. "The Psychology of Criticism, or What Can Be Said." In *Psychoanalysis and the Question of the Text*, edited by Geoffrey Hartman, 45–61. (See Hartman.)

O'Brien, Sharon. *Willa Cather: The Emerging Voice*. New York: Oxford University Press, 1987.

O'Hara, Frank. *The Complete Poems of Frank O'Hara*. Edited by Donald Allen. New York: Alfred Knopf, 1979.

Parkinson, Thomas Francis. *Hart Crane and Yvor Winters: Their Literary Correspondence*. Berkeley: University of California Press, 1978.

Paul, Sherman. *Hart's Bridge*. Urbana: University of Illinois Press, 1972.

PBS Television. "Hart Crane." *Voices and Visions*. WCNY, Syracuse, New York. 23 February 1988.

Pearce, Roy Harvey. *The Continuity of American Poetry*. Princeton: Princeton University Press, 1961.

———. "Whitman Justified: The Poet in 1855." *Critical Inquiry* 8 (Autumn 1981): 83–97.

Pease, Donald. "Blake, Crane, Whitman, and Modernism: A Poetics of Pure Possibility." *PMLA* 96 (January 1981): 64–85.

———. "*Moby Dick* and the Cold War." In *The American Renaissance Reconsidered*, edited by W. B. Michaels and D. E. Pease, 113–55. (See Michaels.)

———. "Sublime Politics." In *The American Sublime*, edited by Mary Arensberg, 21–49. (See Arensberg.)

Perloff, Marjorie. *Frank O'Hara: Poet among Painters*. New York: Brazilier, 1977.

———. *The Poetics of Indeterminacy: Rimbaud to Cage*. Princeton: Princeton University Press, 1981.

Proust, Marcel. *The Cities of the Plain*. Translated by C. K. Scott Moncrieff. New York: Random House, 1970.

Rajchman, John. "Lacan and the Ethics of Modernity." *Representations* 15 (Summer 1986): 42–56.

Rampersad, Arnold. *The Life of Langston Hughes*. Vol. 1; *I, Too, Sing America*. Oxford: Oxford University Press, 1986.

Riddel, Joseph. "Hart Crane's Poetics of Failure." *ELH* 33 (1966): 473–96.

Rimbaud, Arthur. *Oeuvres Complètes*. Paris: Gallimard, 1973.

Riviere, Joan. "Womanliness as Masquerade." In *Psychoanalysis and Female Sexuality*, edited by H. M. Ruitenbeek, 209–20. (See Ruitenbeek.)

Rowe, John Carlos. "The Super-historical Sense of *The Bridge*." *Genre* 11 (Winter 1978): 597–625.

Ruitenbeek, Hendrick M., ed. *Psychoanalysis and Female Sexuality*. New Haven: College and University Press, 1966.

Scarry, Elaine. *The Body in Pain: The Making and Unmaking of the World*. New York: Oxford University Press, 1985.

Sedgwick, Eve Kosofsky. "Across Gender, Across Sexuality: Willa Cather and Others." *South Atlantic Quarterly* 88 (Winter 1989): 53–72.

———. "The Beast in the Closet: James and the Writing of Homosexual Panic." In *Sex, Politics, and Science in the Nineteenth-Century Novel*, edited by R. B. Yeazell, 148–86. (See Yeazell.)

———. *Between Men: English Literature and Male Homosocial Desire*. New York: Columbia University Press, 1985.

———. *The Coherence of Gothic Conventions*. New York: Methuen, 1986.

Smith, Barbara Herrnstein. *On the Margins of Discourse: The Relation of Literature to Language*. Chicago: University of Chicago Press, 1978.

Smith, H. H. *Aaron Siskind: Photographer*. Rochester: George Eastman House, 1965.

Smith, Joseph H. *Psychiatry and the Humanities*. Vol. 4, *The Literary Freud: Mechanisms of Defense and the Poetic Will*. New Haven: Yale University Press, 1980.

Smith-Rosenberg, Carroll. *Disorderly Conduct: Visions of Gender in Victorian America*. New York: Knopf, 1985.

Sontag, Susan. "Notes on 'Camp.'" *Against Interpretation and Other Essays*. New York: Octagon Books, 1982.

Stein, Gertrude. *Melanctha*. In *Selected Writings of Gertrude Stein*, edited by Carl Van Vechten, 337–457. New York: Vintage, 1972.

———. *Q.E.D.* In *Fernhurst, Q.E.D., and Other Early Writings*, 51–133. New York: Liveright, 1971.

———. *Tender Buttons*. New York: Haskell House Publishers, 1970.

Steinman, Lisa. *Made in America: Science, Technology, and American Modernist Poets*. New Haven: Yale University Press, 1987.

Stevens, Wallace. *Collected Poems*. New York: Knopf, 1954.

Stimpson, Catharine R. "The Somagrams of Gertrude Stein." In *The Female Body in Western Culture*, edited by S. B. Suleiman, 30–43. (See Suleiman.)

Stockinger, Jacob. "Homotextuality: A Proposal." In *The Gay Academic*, edited by Louie Crew, 135–51. (See Crew.)

Suleiman, Susan Rubin, ed. *The Female Body in Western Culture: Contemporary Perspectives*. Cambridge: Harvard University Press, 1985.

Sundquist, Eric. "Bringing Home the Word: Magic, Lies, and Silence in Hart Crane." *ELH* 44: 376–99.

Tate, Allen. Introduction to Hart Crane's *White Buildings*, ix–xvi. (See Crane.)

———. *The Man of Letters in the Modern World, Selected Essays: 1928–1955*. New York: Meridian Books, 1955.

———. "What is a Traditional Society?" In *Essays of Four Decades*, 547–57. Chicago: Swallow Press, 1968.

Thoreau, Henry David. *Walden*. Edited by Wendell Glich. Princeton: Princeton University Press, 1971.

Thurman, Wallace. *The Blacker The Berry*. New York: Macaulay, 1929. (Reprinted. New York: Arno Press and the *New York Times*, 1969.)

Unterecker, John. *Voyager: A Life of Hart Crane*. New York: Farrar, Straus and Giroux, 1969.

Very, Jones. "Epic Poetry." In *Essays and Poems*, 1–37. Boston: Little and Brown, 1839.

Waggoner, Hyatt. *American Poets From the Puritans to the Present*. Boston: Houghton Mifflin, 1968.

Weber, Brom. *Hart Crane: A Biographical and Critical Study*. New York: The Bodley Press, 1948.

Weeks, Jeffrey. Preface to Guy Hocquenghem's *Homosexual Desire*, 9–33. (See Hocquenghem.)

———. *Sexuality and Its Discontents: Meanings, Myths and Modern Sexualities*. London: Routledge and Kegan Paul, 1985.

Weiskel, Thomas. *The Romantic Sublime: Studies in the Structure and Psychology of Transcendence*. Baltimore: Johns Hopkins University Press, 1976.

Whitman, Walt. *Democratic Vistas*. In *Prose Works 1892*. 2 vols. Edited by Floyd Stovall. Vol. 2, 361–426. New York: NYU Press, 1964.

———. *Leaves of Grass: Comprehensive Reader's Edition*. Edited by Harold W. Blodgett and Sculley Bradley. New York: NYU Press, 1965.

Williams, William Carlos. *Collected Early Poems*. New York: New Directions, 1951.

Wilson, Edmund. "The Muses Out of Work." In *Shores of Light: A Literary Chronicle of the Twenties and Thirties*. New York: Farrar, Straus and Young, Inc., 1952.

Winters, Yvor. *In Defense of Reason*. New York: The Swallow Press, 1947.

———. "The Progress of Hart Crane." In *Critical Essays*, edited by David Clark, 102–8. (See Clark.)

Woolf, Virginia. *A Room of One's Own*. London: Harcourt Brace Jovanovich, 1929.

Yaeger, Patricia. "Toward a Female Sublime" In *Gender and Theory*, edited by Linda Kauffman, 191–212. (See Kauffman.)

Yeazell, Ruth Bernard, ed. *Sex, Politics, and Science in the Nineteenth-Century Novel*. Baltimore: Johns Hopkins University Press, 1986.

Index